A Vineyard in
NORTH WALES?

It's Not Warm Enough!

The Story of the Origin of Red Wharf Bay Vineyard

Kevin Mawdesley

Grosvenor House
Publishing Limited

This book is published by
Grosvenor House Publishing Ltd
Link House
140 The Broadway, Tolworth, Surrey, KT6 7HT.
www.grosvenorhousepublishing.co.uk

A CIP record for this book
is available from the British Library

Paperback ISBN 978-1-80381-469-8
Hardback ISBN 978-1-80381-470-4
eBook ISBN 978-1-80381-471-1

This Book is Dedicated to All My Family and Friends
(it's probably the only book I'll ever write,
so I didn't want to miss anybody out) …

… but especially to Morag, Elinor and Lili.

Contents

Preface

I've been telling this story, in truncated form, to visitors to the vineyard for several years now and people seem to enjoy listening to it. I explain to them that the original 'vineyard' was planted on a whim in our field in Anglesey and that in those days I proved to be a pretty incompetent viticulturist, singularly ill-equipped for the task in hand. Indeed, now I know more about how it should be done, the scale of my incompetence astonishes me. A few years later I was made redundant from 'the day job' in IT. Whilst I continued working at that profession for a while, doing some consultancy work I manged to procure, in my heart I knew I'll never have (or want) another 'proper' job; one that involved turning up somewhere every day to work for someone. It felt very strange, part joy and part guilt, but that was where I found myself, so let's get on with something else.

I decided that, despite the strong evidence to the contrary, my viniculture experience would qualify me to successfully plant a vineyard in Andalucia and that this would be the 'something else' I would get on with. I persuaded myself that all my prior grape producing anguish would be resolved if I planted in a better climate and wouldn't it be so much easier to have a vineyard somewhere where there was a bit more sun and vines simply thrived: spawning sumptuous grapes that in turn morphed into delightful wine? Not to move to Spain though, that wasn't practical. I thought I could handle it remotely from North Wales and I would spend my retirement swanning out there whenever I felt like it, spending time pottering around in the sunshine, tending the land, meeting people and generally enjoying myself. Then eventually I would be coming back to the UK with bottles of this wonderful wine and turn up at the houses of friends saying, "this is from the vineyard in Spain", to general appreciation and envy. But that didn't work out either – though this time it wasn't my lack of skill that let me down (please read on, no spoilers here). Determined to continue in one way or another, I looked again at Anglesey, thought "What the heck" and that now I knew a bit more as to how to go about things I could make a go of a vineyard here. This is the story of how it all unfolded.

I think I should make it clear at this point that still by no means do I consider myself to be a viniculture expert. When I first planted vines, as I've said, I quickly displayed my total ineptitude for the undertaking. I am now better at teasing fruit out of the damn things but I don't claim to be any kind of leading authority. I just planted a few vines because I liked the idea of doing so and things simply developed from there – though they did sometimes get out of hand. The things I write about are what I think (or thought at the time) and the way I see things. I have a feeling that others with perhaps more knowledge and experience of vineyard management may see things differently to my way of thinking and may even be disparaging of my efforts and opinions (though over the time I've been involved in this business I've developed the theory that if you get ten vineyard owners/managers together in a room you are likely to get at least five different opinions on any particular subject). I repeat though, this is the way I see things – or did at the time – rightly or wrongly.

The final thing that I feel I should point out is that I'm doing this from memory, which in my case these days may not always be the best reflection of reality. Some of the events described here took place ten and even twenty years before I wrote about them. This is how I remember what happened and I'm sure that's really what happened, ... I think. I've already had one extensive 'discussion' with my wife which involved disagreements as to how one of the chapters unfolded. Of course, I'm right and she's wrong, ... I think.

Whatever, I hope you enjoy this book.

Acknowledgements

Many people have been very kind, generously giving their time, effort and the value of their experience to help me with this book or with the overall vineyard project, some both. I would like to sincerely thank you all and I hope you enjoy the end product, whether it be reading the book or drinking the wine. Much of this was written many years after the event and I've already alluded to the dangers of me relying on my own recall, so if there's anyone I've missed out I equally sincerely apologise.

Thanks especially to Lynne Eaves for her help and encouragement.

A big "Thank You" to Colin Bennet, Martin Vickers, Fintan O'Leary, Richard Norris, Colin and Judith Dudly and Rob and Nicola Merchant for their contributions to the book; and to Alexandra Sitwell for allowing me to publish my version of her families' story.

And also "Thank you" to the following for their help in one way or another: Ben, Clive and the staff at Halfpenny Green, Mike Eaves, Sarah and Richard Bell, The Wine Department of Plumpton College, Margaret Mitchel, Antonio Rizzo, Chris Lisney-Smith, Andrew Barnwell, Brian and Jo Evans, Donald Barr and the Walking Crew, Dave Rawlinson, Marco, Paul Jay, Dave Morgan, Hayden Jones, Derek Pritchard, Nefyn Williams, Margaret and Ron Savage, Paul Cross, Angharad de Bruin.

Introduction

I'm standing in an olive grove in Andalucia and I really would like this to be where I plant my vineyard. The setting is delightful. I'm on a river bank fringed with giant bulrushes, looking out to the limestone crags of La Capilla and La Sierra de Huma, imposing mountains about three miles away. At hand, as well as the olive trees, some of which are over a hundred years old, there are many orange trees with large, mature fruit; and also lemons, carobs and a few almonds and figs. There's constant chatter from many colourful and unfamiliar birds I can't name, but I know the raptors I can see circling closer to the mountains are vultures.

I had decided that I wanted to plant a vineyard in this area of Spain relatively recently. On a whim, several years back I'd planted a small number of vines behind our house in Anglesey. It hadn't gone particularly well but I became sufficiently enamoured by the concept to decide that I wanted to plant a proper vineyard. I was in my early sixties and deliberations as to what I would do in retirement had been playing around in my head. I had expected to continue with the day-job for another couple of years or so but redundancy had put paid to that. So I had been forced somewhat sooner than expected to decide how to spend, with luck as regards health, the hopefully extended period at the end of my more formal working life. I wasn't ready for full-time leisure but I was no longer going to do anything that involved just turning up at the same place every day to work for somebody else. I'd decided that I'd done enough of that. I started thinking of maybe a project, something a bit more than a hobby, that I could turn into a small business. And then I had the idea of turning the 'vineyard' in Anglesey into something that half matched up to the name. And then I thought, "Why not a vineyard in Spain?" Wouldn't it be so much easier and much more fun to plant a

1

vineyard somewhere where there's a lot more sun? Somewhere where grapes, well, just grew big and juicy and ripened easily, instead of having to be dedicatedly teased into maturity in the chillier fields of North Wales. And then it became one of those ideas that just takes over. So here I was, looking for somewhere to make it happen.

I'm on land belonging to Paqui, the partner of friend Dave, whom I've known more or less since I started coming to this part of the world about twelve years ago. The land is Paqui's family land. On another part of it there is a low stone-built ruin of three small rooms, the house where Paqui was raised before the family built and moved to the larger house at the top of the plot, the house that she and Dave are now slowly refurbishing.

The land is in the village of Bermeja, a barriado or suburb of the small town of Alora, about 7 km away. Alora is about 40 Km north west of Malaga, which in the UK is mostly known as the airport you pass through on your way to the sun, sand and Irish pub holiday hotspots of the Costa del Sol. But it's much more than that: both the city itself, which teems with vibrancy and tradition, and the vast inland hinterland of mountains, lakes, forests, white walled towns and Spanish life which combine to give this region its wonderful character.

In total Paqui's land is about 3 hectares, about five rugby pitches in proper units of measurement. It's divided into two parcels separated by land belonging to a neighbour. They have decided to sell off some of the land to make the agricultural side of their life simpler. The larger plot is round the house and they want to sell about half of that. But this includes the ruin, which means there is de facto planning permission to build a house, currently more or less banned in the countryside in Andalucia in the wake of all the planning scandals that have come to light from the construction boom years. Given the wonderful setting this makes it quite a valuable plot and way over my budget.

I'm standing in the second parcel, which they also want to sell. It's about 6,000 m², a good size for what I want and, most importantly, it has water, both from the river and a well. The well must be close to the water table and thus reliable, because of proximity to the river. Other advantages are that it's a good price, it's adjacent to the road – a decent highway with easy access to Alora – and I think it would be a reasonable plot to farm. I started off with many other desirable criteria for the land I wanted but I've come to realise that I'll be lucky to find somewhere that provides just these few essentials, so everything else I'll have to take as is and work round. In truth, even this plot is maybe a bit steep and I'd have to grub up the olive trees, even the hundred year old ones, and I'm not sure about wanting to do that. Bermejo has a few shops and café/bars, making working here a lot pleasanter than being somewhere in the remoter countryside in the middle of nowhere, which has been the case with many of the plots I've seen. Also, with Paqui and Dave as new neighbours I would have the goodwill of somebody whose family have lived in the village for several generations, which I think would be a huge bonus. And what's more, they would keep an eye on things for me when I'm not there and I'm pretty sure they would let me store equipment and the like on their land until I'd got myself organised.

However, I can't buy this land and I'm just going to tell them that. It's true that it's adjacent to the road but only at the top corner of the plot and even that is below a steep bank above which tower the backs of large roadside houses. Paqui's family have never needed separate access to the road from this bit of the land, so have never worried about it. But if I can't make my own track to the road I'd always be hostage to the neighbours and/or whoever buys the other parcel, which obviously is not viable. Paqui has been to the council and they have said that they will allow me to build an access to connect to the road at the corner point where I'm standing but, even though it would only be a 25 metre track, it's incredibly steep and I can see it would be a major bit of construction that could easily finish up as a money pit. And it would be cheek by jowl to the foundations of the houses that are towering over me. What if I cause problems there? It doesn't rain often here but when it does it can be truly monsoonal. If I clear all the nicely tangled vegetation and its intricate root systems below the houses, unless I spend a fortune on concrete, there's a good chance of at least some erosion and I'll just be leaving myself open to be blamed for any structural movement, no matter how small, perhaps deservedly. I've now been here for half an hour, failing to envisage how I might make it work because of the access issue (and, I have to also say, wondering that maybe I'm being a bit blasé about working this slope and thinking that I would hate to be the one that chopped down the hundred year old olive trees). Now I'm going to tell them that I've decided that I can't go ahead with it.

I'm going to buy their olive oil though. Paqui is divorced, one consequence of which was that for a number of years the land was left to itself and now needs quite a bit of work to restore. As well as refurbishing the house she and Dave are getting the land and trees they want to keep back into shape. They've recently restarted harvesting the olives and now they have olive oil to sell. If I'm arranging wine shipments back to the UK, why can't I include a few cases of olive oil as well, to sell at wine tastings, maybe sell to restaurants? A limited edition, first press, extra virgin olive oil from an old family estate, hand harvested from a few selected hundred year old trees, specially packed with owner's (real) signature on the label, how wonderful is that? I'll ask Paqui if I can put a picture of her on the bottle as well.

CHAPTER 1

Arbitrary Fortune

Maybe you have a picture of a vineyard in your head? Perhaps in France you would imagine it surrounding a chateau, or in Tuscany it would be next to an old farmhouse, or maybe it would be behind a rambling Corjito in Rioja? There would be a large old stone-built house bounded at the sides and back by tall, green pines. It would maybe be positioned at the head of a valley of rolling fields, covered with vines as far as you can see, stretching out in perfect green lines. There's a cluster of old stone buildings with terracotta tiled rooves near the house. One is a tasting area for guests and you go inside and the walls are lined from floor to ceiling with racks crammed with bottles. "The estate was planted by the grandfather of my grandfather," you are told. "We produce 100,000 bottles of delicious wine every year and everything is perfect in this vinery paradise." Well, my vineyard in Anglesey is nothing like that.

Red Wharf Bay Vineyard is a micro vineyard (let's say in the spirit of micro-breweries) of just four hundred vines, though by the time you read this there should be many more. It's situated fifteen hundred miles from where it was originally planned to be in a fairly remote corner of the British Isles that, when I arrived in 2001, I hadn't seen for forty years and, even if I had ever thought about it, wouldn't have expected to see again. Where I still look around and gratefully think, "How did I get to call this place 'home' (see below)?" The vineyard is behind a house we obviously couldn't afford and in a field we didn't want. It was planted on a whim and totally mismanaged for many years. It feels like a series of random and arbitrary events have happened over the years and now there's a vineyard. It's doing alright, though.

I'm originally from Lancashire but in my early twenties drifted down to London. The day-job was in IT, in those days mostly working for banks. By my mid-thirties I was sick to the teeth of having to commute for two and a half hours a day to spend a working life in a room with a window overlooking another room with a window. I was at the time successful, travelling to New York and Zurich on the bank's behest, very well paid and if I didn't do something about it, I'd be sixty and wondering where my life had gone (a familiar theme to this type of story but not the point of this one). I changed jobs and it felt much the same, so at the age of 36, by this time a marriage and divorce also behind me, I threw it all in and took a Geography degree. Three years later I graduated and this thankfully led to a job.

Back in a bank working in IT. To get through the degree course I'd spent all my savings and more and needed to replenish the coffers. At least the new job was at a bank in Dorset, not London, and I moved there. Mercifully some things had changed. One of my university tutors was part of a large, ongoing research project in Nepal, trying to prove that land use change and soil erosion were nothing like as bad as many people then believed. She was looking for volunteers to work for the project in the field during the summer my year group graduated and so, before I started the new bank job, I spent six weeks in Nepal living in the most basic of huts, a day's walk over a 7000 foot mountain pass from the nearest road or supplies; splashing around in mud and water buffalo shit in the monsoon (often at night), eating rice and vegetables, picking off the leeches and collecting data for the project. I loved it. When it was over I went back to the bank job but for the next couple of years was able to take sufficient leave to go back to Nepal regularly to work with the project. After three years (my finances a bit more stable) they were able to fund a full-time job for me in the field in Nepal. I was to collect data from eight different sites spread over several hundred square miles centred around Pokhara, in the west of the country. I used to like to tell people my job was to wander around foothills of the Himalayas measuring things.

This came to an end. Land use change and soil erosion were duly proved not to be as bad as many people had believed. To do the measuring of the things I had to measure I had to build crude but effective erosion plots. These were basically an area that was bounded by tin sheets so that rainwater couldn't run in or out, with a series of oil drums cemented in at the bottom of the enclosed space beneath some piping, to capture all the rainwater that fell in the plot. You measure rainfall with a rain gauge and relate this to the amount of soil that's been eroded from the plot and finished up in the drums as a consequence of the rainwater run-off. If you do this in enough places, on enough different land use types, in enough storms of different strength, in enough different soils, you can get a pretty decent picture of what's going on. I won't bore you with tales of how difficult it was to construct and cement in all these erosion plots in the heat and humidity of Nepal in the first place but, as responsible researchers leaving the land in the same state we found it, at the end of the project I had to take them out again and I wasn't looking forward to it. So, I was grateful for the arrival of Morag McDonald, a Scot (the name sort of gives it away) who was at the time living on Anglesey near her job at Bangor University. She wanted to take over the erosion plots for a research project of her own and I was more than happy to agree and not have to dig them out. As a collaboration it went rather well and a while later we were both delighted to find that she was pregnant. But in the UK I lived in Dorset and she in Anglesey – not the best of situations from which to start a family. Moreover, by the time this happened I had just come to the end of a contract in the day-job, so she lived in Anglesey and had gainful employment and I lived in Dorset and didn't. The onus was very definitely on me to move, arbitrary fortune.

CHAPTER 2

Looking for land

Paqui's land wasn't the first plot I'd looked at, I'd been searching for several months up until that point. I should tell you that the idea of planting a vineyard in Andalucia wasn't an escapist, up sticks, fantasy. We weren't going to go and live in Spain permanently or anything like that. For many years as a family we had been going to Alora two or three times a year, so I had good knowledge of the area, many friends and acquaintances there and I thought I knew my way around. The retirement plan had evolved to the splendid idea that I would take off to Spain regularly and spend time pottering around in the sunshine tending the vines, also meeting friends, cycling and generally enjoying myself. Then eventually I would come back to the UK with shipments of this wonderful wine which I would serve to friends, "This is from our vineyard in Spain," to general approval and envy. I wasn't thinking of the rolling hillsides afore mentioned, filled with my vines for as far as the eye could see. No, just to plant a thousand or so of them and to make a modest amount of wine, though commercially, not just as a hobby. There would be a fair bit of hard work involved on the land, but not too much, I thought. And I'd do most of it myself of course. Why not? I like gardening.

My intention was to spend maybe a couple of weeks out in Spain in March each year, at the beginning of the growing season and then a couple of weeks when the harvest was due in August. In between I'd go out for maybe a week a month, doing what needed to be done. I was hoping that I would be able to buy a plot near somebody I knew so that they could keep an eye on it for me when I was back in the UK, as would have been the case with Paqui's land. And maybe employ somebody local to keep down the weeds when I wasn't there. And that, unbelievably, when I started this little adventure, was the extent of my planning. Go to Andalucia, buy land, plant vines, flounce over when I felt like it to do a bit of gardening and eventually bring back wine. What could go wrong? I'm assuming (there's a little clue in the title of the book) you've already guessed that how this eventually turns out was not as the original plan.

I should also say at this point that this is not a book about people who are desperate to change their lives and give up everything to start some daring new adventure, and the subsequent hard work and tribulations endured before they sit basking in the success of their endeavours, drinking wine and watching glorious sunsets (though there has been a good deal of hard work, many tribulations and I have drunk a bit of wine, at sunset and other times, along the way). On the contrary, as I've already mentioned, I'd done the bit where you throw everything in and start again in my thirties. These days we sat on a fairly comfortable middle-class perch and at my age it struck me that was pretty important to keep hold of what you have. Maybe you can (should?) take risks when you're younger but if you lose whatever wealth you've managed to accumulate at the point in your life that you are thinking of retiring, then there's not much chance of building it back up again, is there? No, I did this because I wanted to do it, though I admit it got out of hand sometimes. I wanted a project for my retirement that was more than just pottering around and came to really like the idea of running a vineyard as a small business. And now it's a story I want to tell because I think there's a story there and I like telling stories, because I enjoyed it (am enjoying it) and because I think it's a good story. But, of course, you have to be the judge of that.

I should further make it clear that by no means do I consider myself to be a viniculture expert. When I first planted vines, as I explain as we go along, I quickly displayed my total ineptitude for the task in hand. I know a bit more about it now but I don't claim to be any kind of leading authority. I just planted a few vines because I liked the idea of doing so and things simply developed from there (arbitrary fortune). The things I write about are what I think (or thought at the time) and the way I see things. I have a feeling that others with perhaps more knowledge and experience of vineyard management may see things differently and may even be disparaging of my efforts and opinions (though over time I have noted that if you get ten vineyard owners/managers together in a room you are likely to get at least five views on any particular subject). One thing that I have learned is that mostly, in the context of your own vineyard, you have to work it out for yourself.

When I first unveiled the vineyard idea friends were enthusiastic and much discussion was provoked as to how to I should go about the project. Two or three proved to be pretty knowledgeable (more so than I, I couldn't help thinking for the first but not the last time) and I learned more than I expected as we sat drinking the stuff this is all about. Everybody knows something about vineyards and wine production. 'Everybody' knows that good wine comes from vines planted in bad soil (part myth, part true, it depends what kind of bad soil) and we talked about me finding a nice rocky plot half way up a mountain (there are plenty of mountains around Alora). Another theory was of water depravation in the early growing years. If you deprive the vines of water near the surface they have to put down deeper roots to find it, so they dig into 'more interesting' minerals that are eventually reflected in the flavour the wine. This theory stayed with me for a while.

I knew one of the estate agents in Alora, Margaret Mitchell of Alora Properties; and soon got to know another, Paul of Andalusian Homes. Both were great, couldn't have been more helpful and if ever you decide you want to buy property in this part of the would I suggest you contact one or both of them. Once again I'm back in Spain and Margaret is showing me plots of land that might be viable for the venture (so part one of the retirement plan is working, I'm swanning off to Spain every month or so, meeting people, doing a bit of 'work' – or at least research, cycling and enjoying myself). She usually deals with houses and it's good of her (and also Paul) to spend so much time with me. How much commission can they make if the sale is only going to be a scrap of land for maybe 20,000 euros? I don't want to waste her time but this is our third afternoon of excursions into the countryside and none of the plots I've seen so far have felt right. We're in another dry olive grove on another dry hillside and I'm trying to evaluate the possibilities. The trees in front of me are quite young and quite spaced out and shouldn't be too much trouble to grub up (I thought). Grub them up, plant the vines, flounce over to look after them every so often, let them grow for a few years, harvest the grapes, make wine, flounce back to the UK with a few hundred bottles to general appreciation and envy. There was a lock-up to keep tools in, that was a bonus. We were about five kilometres from Alora but I if could leave my equipment in the lock-up I could cycle here (I don't want the expense of car hire every trip). Olive trees need very little water but whilst the water depravation theory had stayed with me, I wanted to hedge my bets and it would be good if there was some irrigation. On this plot there was a bore hole drilled deep into the hillside that acts as a well. By deep I mean several hundred feet. Would it be reliable? If it's not the vines will just have to work harder and find more interesting minerals, as per the water deprivation theory. But it's not going to happen as it's another plot that doesn't feel right.

Later I'm out cycling and a route I often take involves crossing the dam of a reservoir. The water's low, it has been for a couple of years now. A few more miles pass and I have a thought. I've been reading a lot about vine management in the last few weeks and I've picked up a bit more knowledge. The water deprivation theory is all well and good but in southern Spain water will surely always be an issue. I've recently read that vines need a minimum of 400–450mm water in the growing season, how much rain is there in this area in summer (I guess the answer is not very much)? In Anglesey there's plenty of rain and it's not something to which I've ever given any thought as regards the vines I planted there; water is just not a problem on Anglesey, sunshine is the limiting factor! I finish my bike ride and then go to the local internet café and spend five minutes on Google. Average rainfall in Alora is about 100mm between April and September, usually a total of about 15mm in June, July and August. This is southern Spain, we have climate change and whatever that will bring, it doesn't rain much anyway and the only desert in Europe is only a few hundred miles to the east, to say nothing of the Sahara a similar distance to the south. In this region the vines are always going to be naturally water deprived and the plot I buy needs copious and guaranteed water. It's taken three months and three trips for me to work that out.

CHAPTER 3

Anglesey Life

Anglesey is a wonderful place but it is a bit, well, out of the way. An island (though with road bridges to the mainland) off the north west coast of Wales, it's about the most inconvenient place there is to get to anywhere, unless you fancy a trip to Dublin. I remember a joke about travelling in a remote area and asking a local for directions. "Well, you wouldn't start from here" being the reply. That's what it can feel like living on Anglesey. In the early months of our relationship, as you can imagine, I'd visited Morag quite a few times, from Dorset a tedious six hours each way in the car. As the time came to move there permanently I started to feel the wrench of leaving my south coast sanctuary and wondered what I had let myself in for. What it would be like to live in this remote outpost where I had now realised half the people spoke a different language, quite a shock in the UK. I knew that there was a Welsh Language, I just didn't appreciate how many people spoke it as their first language.

I needn't have worried and settled in happily. If I had loved the dramatic landscape of the Purbeck Hills, the Jurassic Coast and The English Channel; I now had The Irish Sea, the ferocious Menai Straits and the mountains of Snowdonia beyond and, as a bonus, the rich culture that goes with the language. Anglesey in general is a pleasant rural area peppered with numerous rugged villages and historic towns, and isn't it lovely to live in a pleasant rural area? But Anglesey is so much more than that. It's not just that the spectacular backdrop of Snowdonia is lying in wait around almost every corner or at the crest of every rise. You also have wide sandy beaches and dramatic seascapes; banks of sand dunes; rocky crags and stony coves round the north and west of the island; many forests full of buzzards and red squirrels (not always a harmonious combination);

and the culture always shining through at the Eisteddfods and reflected in the dozens and dozens of Celtic ruins. If I thought the Purbeck Hills dramatic, The Menai Straits are something else as the mountains slope down to the shore and the Telford and Stevenson bridges impose their majesty. On the spring tides the tide race is so fierce that you will find white water kayakers trying to negotiate the two metre drop of water backed up under the Telford bridge. Nelson said that if you could sail the Menai Straits you could sail anywhere in the world and he insisted that every ship of the line had to have navigated through the Menai Straits under full sail; he wouldn't go into battle with a captain who hadn't managed that. What wasn't there to love in this Celtic heaven? Well, I'd give Holyhead town centre a miss on a Friday night.

I moved into Morag's house near Red Wharf Bay in the spring of 2001 and Elinor joined us that August. Morag had bought the house a few years previously, a tastefully converted cowshed (outbuildings to the somewhat more spacious conversion of the farmhouse next door) up a lane a few hundred yards from the bay. It was very comfortable, two bedrooms with large, immaculate gardens in a beautiful part of the island. The bay and its surrounds are an Area of Outstanding Natural Beauty (and if you ever get the chance to stand in the middle of the beach and looked around you would not dispute the categorisation). It was the perfect country cottage for a professional person living on her own. Trouble was she was no longer on her own, the population of the house having tripled in a few months. We began to think of finding something a bit bigger, especially as there were thoughts of a further increase to said population. So, we started looking around but there was no great urgency.

It quickly became apparent that one of the advantages of moving from one of the property hotspots of the South East to an island off the coast of North Wales was that you got an awful lot more house for your money up here. My banking career had allowed me to get myself on the property ladder early and through all the financial roller coaster of my adult life I've clung on to the bricks and mortar, usually by renting out any habitable spare space. My first property was in Barnes, in south west London (sounds impressive but not many people know there's a seedy side); then Weybridge, Cobham and finally (before Anglesey) Langton

Matravers in Dorset. All relatively expensive property areas and though never living in anything like a mansion, the proceeds of the house I would sell there would go a fair way in Anglesey. Between us there would be no problem funding a decent three-bedroom house in a place that you would enjoy living and look forward to coming home to each evening. We worked out a budget and started looking.

Red Wharf Bay is a pretty big expanse of sand, about three miles across and a mile and a half deep, all tidal. It's so big and flat that during the war there were serious worries that the Germans might land planes and try to make Anglesey a bridgehead for the invasion of the UK. Stakes were hammered in all over the beach to hamper such plans, many of which are still in place today. Prior to that, Edward and Mrs Simpson used to take advantage of the remote 'landing strip' and were flown in to spend secret trysts at a secluded hotel close to the shore. It's also famous for being the place that Maurice Wilks originally sketched out the design for the Land Rover, the 70th anniversary of which was marked in 2017 and, if you want to look, can be seen on YouTube. Apart from that, except for the occasional visitor driving on to the beach and getting their car stuck in the sand as the tide comes in, it's been pretty uneventful corner of the world.

The geography and the road system combine to make the trip by road from Benllech at the western extremity of the bay to Llanddona Beach at the east end a journey of some nine miles. The road skirts through the villages that surround the bay, the topography keeping it a mile or more away from the high water line. This means that there are countless side roads and paths branching off the main road and ending in a cul-de-sac at the bay. Morag's house was on one of these, running from the village of Pentraeth ('Beach Head' in Welsh) down to the shore. There are several similar, roughly parallel, tracks and roads which on foot can be linked to make pleasant routes for walking, running, etc. I was walking down one of these one day when I came across a new 'For Sale' sign at the end of a drive. I stopped to look, started to get excited then quickly realised that I could do little other than dream.

I had the feel of the local house market sufficiently to know this place would be way out of our reach. The house didn't look that big from the front but sneaking round the side of the clearly empty property I could see that it was fairly substantial, probably four bedrooms and everything that goes with that, maybe three bathrooms, spacious living areas, etc. etc. A house that size would be way over our budget. And even if the size itself hadn't taken it out of our price bracket its situation surely would. It was truly stunning. Up on a hill a few hundred metres from the bay which just opened up in front of you. It was on the side of a shallow valley through which flowed a small river. A field dropped away from the house, sweeping down the valley to a salt marsh full of reeds in subtle shades of green, brown and purple, and to the river. To the left there were a few small cottages dotted about, and a view around the west side of the sand to another small village. At the end of the salt marsh a small stone bridge marked the edge of the bay and then, the tide was out at the time, your gaze took in this vast expanse of sand all the way down to the sea, a mile or so further. Wow! The light, the space, the feeling that you could wake up to this every day. Maybe we could, you never know.

I carried on walking, thoughts consumed by what I had just seen. We were being pretty prudent with our finances when we worked out the budget (enough financial ups and downs in our respective lives and we now had a responsibility like never before, so making sure we stayed on our comfortable perch was a priority). But maybe if we stretched the budget a little? No, who am I kidding, a bit of budget stretching wasn't going to be enough to buy that house. Maybe if we took the risk of a really big mortgage; no, who I am kidding, we're not in a position to do that? By the time I arrived home I'd given up on the idea. We can all look at big houses and dream and this was a dream, totally unfeasible. Of course, I'm going to have a look on the estate agent's website, show it to Morag, "wouldn't that have been great?"

So I look, and not only is it affordable for us, it's not even a stretch. It's easily within the prudent budget we set ourselves. What's going on here? Or more importantly, what's wrong with it, there had to be something wrong with it? Subsidence? Is the roof falling in? Sitting Tenant? Gruesome murder of the previous occupants (maybe I could live with that one)? Is it fit to move in with a three month old child? We talked to the estate agent. The person selling it is the son of a local builder. He bought it as a refurbishment project a few years previously. He's done a lot of work but hasn't finished it and he wants to take his money out for another project he has in mind. Okay, let's go and have a look.

We arrive at the house. Again the view takes all my attention, I'm looking at the bay, not the house (I don't care what's wrong with it, let's buy it!). This time the tide is in and there's no sand to be seen, just blue water all the way up to the little stone bridge, through which it flows and half submerges the salt marsh. It's completely different, the sea was a mile and a half away last time I was here and now it's only a few hundred yards from the doorstep. It must change like this all the time.

We go inside and we find that it's less than conventional. The front room is composed of the whole of the cottage that was originally on the site. It's probably more than 200 years old (I've traced it back to the Ordnance Survey of 1851 and it was there then), the walls are three feet thick, there's a fireplace at each end, so presumably for most of the time it's been in existence there have been two very small rooms and maybe a bit of space beneath the roof as the only living area. One fireplace is large and recessed with a curved wooden beam above, presumably original; the other is small, more functional. It's delightful. We then go down some steps into an extension that was added in the seventies and, in complete contrast to the room we have just been in, it reflected the style of that era. A small kitchen and minute bathroom in a layout that would contravene building regulations if built from scratch today. We then move into the part of the house the builder has added. It's best described by saying that he's just built over the two sections of house that we had just been in and extended the previous structure to the west and to the south to make the fairly large property it had become. We continue down a corridor that leads to a dining room and a downstairs bedroom. Both nice big rooms.

We go back into the front room and up the stairs to the upper floor, all added by the current owner. Upstairs there are three bedrooms but nothing else (or so I thought). There's no bathroom, toilet, handbasin or any such service that you might expect on the upper floor of a normal house. We go into the first bedroom, a sort of mezzanine structure above the front room where the roof of the original cottage would have been. It's a small room, a decent enough fourth bedroom, but you can't help but notice that the window is bricked in. I look at the estate agent and she shrugs her shoulders. I start to think about the layout of the building as a whole and it's as though everything possible has been done inside the house to ignore the view of the bay, as would have been provided by the bricked in window. It's as though the house has been planned by somebody trying to shut out the sight of the sea; as you might try to shut out the sight of a factory spewing obnoxious substances or to block a giant TV mast, should you be unlucky enough to live next to either, rather than focus on the amazing view on the doorstep. Maybe the builder had an unimaginative architect but I suspect there's more to it than that. I remember one house we had looked at, also on a hillside overlooking the bay. The owner had done some renovation but as here it was focused away from the bay. The main room had large picture windows looking up at the hillside but only a small 'cubby' window overlooking the bay. I asked him why it was arranged so and he told me that it was at the insistence of the council planning department. I don't know when things moved on but it seems that in times past you were not allowed to do anything that changed any view from the bay. Maybe that was the reason behind the conservative development of the house we were looking at.

We continued the viewing into the other two bedrooms, both well finished and decent sizes. We go into the first, it's on the corner of the house and could have been built with a window overlooking the bay but no, the window was put in a different wall with a pleasant enough view of the countryside and a squint down to the sea. The last one, the biggest bedroom, was spacious and attractive and no doubt the one we would take as our own (getting ahead of yourself, Kevin). However, as I turn around to leave the room I notice a three-quarter door in the wall, raised about a foot from the floor. I open the door and step in to further full sized room, which again had no window to the outside world. It's dark but I can see the outline on the chimney and 'shoulders' of the original cottage on one wall. You could open this up and put in a shower, toilet, wardrobes, dressing space, etc. but it's just been left as a dark mess.

We go back downstairs and out of the back door. There's a base been laid for a conservatory and the dwarf wall on which the glass panels would sit has been built. Again, totally in keeping with the ethos of the house it looks away from the bay toward the garden, the sea view being completely hidden round the corner of the house. The garden is a good size, or would be if most of it wasn't taken up by car space. The layout of the plot meant that if you wanted a garage the drive had to come around two sides of the house, where a space had been left and a turning circle laid (needed because backing out round two sides of the house would have been a challenge). However, the combination of this and the drive took so much of the space that very little garden remained, and what was left was dominated by a large, breeze block, dog kennel standing about two metres tall. A gardener he wasn't.

Overall, I thought it was about as perfect as it could be if we were going to get a house like that at the price advertised. Lest it seem that I'm being disparaging about the builder, not at all. I thought that he had had done a really good job. Everything (to my untrained eye) seemed well built, well finished and well fitted out. It was just designed a very oddly, maybe partly due to external constraints, and he just hadn't completed the job. Maybe he just got fed up after a few years working on it (I know that feeling). Or maybe he'd seen another opportunity that really fired him and he didn't want to miss, but needed the money to fund. I didn't know and we didn't care. We wanted to buy it.

We were about to go back inside and the estate agent said, "Of course, it comes with the field."

"That's interesting," I remember thinking before the reality struck that actually it was another on the list of problems we would have to sort if we moved into this house, "What the hell do we need a field for?" I mentioned that there's a large field sloping down towards the bay. To the south-west of the house towards the river, abutting the garden, there was also a small field of about one acre, surrounded by a hedge. It must have been on the estate agent's particulars but it hadn't registered with me, I was just interested in the house and the view. We turned around and stood looking at it, what would we do with that? Fields don't look after themselves and I was pretty sure it would be hard work. One acre is small for a field but it's quite a big space as the adjunct to a house. It took me back for a moment, houses in Surrey and Dorset in the price range I've ever looked in don't come with a field. I remember thinking, "Well, this is Anglesey, land is cheap and lots of houses in the country here probably come with a field." It was just another on the list of issues, maybe we could sell it off? I now know that it's quite unusual. After I had lived here for a while I worked with people who kept horses who had just moved to the island and had great difficulty finding a house with sufficient land for a paddock. On the 1851 Ordinance Survey map the acre plot is also already designated to the original little cottage. The rest of the valley belongs to local landowners who have been on Anglesey for generations, literally hundreds of years. Why do they own the rest of the valley but there in the middle of it is this little cottage with its little plot of land? There must be a reason, has somebody been bought off? Oh, I want to know the story!

Anyway, whatever, we didn't want it but it was just another problem. We would sort that out when the time came. What mattered was that the house was perfect. Well not perfect, sure it's got issues but it's got everything we want (and needed to look after a three-month-old baby) and all the problems were things that didn't really matter to us. We could take it on then slowly do what we thought was needed. We put in an offer which was accepted. Further on in the buying process I heard that the builder had said he couldn't believe that somebody would pay that much for that house. We thought that we couldn't believe somebody would let that house go for that price. So, everybody happy with the arrangement and isn't that how it should be?

I look back at the time we've been here and we've now added quite a lot, consulting a now more enlightened planning department at every step. We started off with basics, putting windows where they were needed (and knocking down the dog kennel). The space next to our bedroom was converted, the conservatory built (in the same place but bigger than originally planned, so that you can see the bay). Much of the car space was changed back to garden and a home office put where the garage was supposed to be (the cars can stay at the side of the house, who puts cars in a garage these days, garages are for piling junk in). Bigger kitchen, bigger bathroom, a Juliet balcony on the bedroom (somewhere else where we can see the sea, yippee!) a porch and a second conservatory, full on to the bay.

We moved in at the end of March 2002, full of the excitement of a new house and a new(ish) baby. We'd also decided to get married in June that year, so there was plenty to keep us busy. We had thought that having a child together was about as much of a commitment as you could make to each other, and hadn't bothered one way or another about something as mundane as getting married. Though when Morag was a few months pregnant I thought it would make things more complete if we did (and it was a good excuse for a proper party) and so one bright and sunny afternoon on Llanddwyn Island, a little outcrop of land off Newborough Beach, whose Welsh name translates as Lover's Island, I asked and was accepted. By the time we would have been able to organise a wedding and all that entailed Morag would have been nearly due and probably not up for enjoying it to the full, so we decided to put it off for a year. So by the time we moved in, as well as both working full time we had a new house to sort out, a baby to look after and a wedding to plan. Days were full.

Sometime mid-May, after we had been in the house for a couple of months, I was standing at the back of the house drinking coffee and looking at the view, which I often did and still do now, almost two decades on. I glanced over the field and was hit by the realisation that the grass was growing, as it has a tendency to so do. Hmmm, what am I going to do about that. I can't just get the lawnmower out (but fifteen years later...). I talked to a local farmer who agreed to keep the field in shape if we let him have the hay. This worked out fine for seven or eight years, until he retired. By then we had friends with horses and they paddocked them with us for a few months each year. The field isn't quite big enough to support a horse all year but two or three coming 'for a holiday' kept our grass down and fed the horses for nothing for a while.

And it turned out that the field was actually quite useful. I've always liked 'outside projects' but in all the houses I've lived in, and in the houses most people live in, the outside area is a finite space. If you decide that you are going to build, say, a pond you lose some of the space you have, usually a bit of lawn or something. If you want a shed, you lose a bit more of the lawn. But here no, we realised one day when planning a play area for the children (Elinor was joined by Lili in March 2003). A swing? Seesaw? Slide, Trampoline? Climbing rope? Zipwire? Let's just put them on the edge of the field. Pond? Vegetable patch? Let's just put them in that corner near the hedge, plenty of space.

There was one rather unsightly part that was a bit of a problem. The field started with a steep bank suddenly dropping about two metres at an angle of about 45 degrees, then levelling off. This was only two metres from the back door, so pretty prominent, but we just left it, much to Morag's annoyance, to grow wild. It fairly quickly became overgrown but was pretty much unusable, not without a lot of effort and imagination anyway. If it was cleared one year it's all just going to grow back and have to be cleared again the next. Better just to call it 'the wild garden' and leave it to its own devices, I thought. Good for biodiversity! Morag thought differently and once a year or so would indignantly strim it, but it was a very low-key bone of contention, though relevant as we move on.

Another facet of my arrival on Anglesey was that I needed a job, or at least to earn some money. When I first pitched up the thing that most filled our thoughts, wonder mixed with a tad of anxiety, was of course, impending first-time parenthood. The second thing I had to be anxious about was how I would earn a living. You will not be surprised to hear that Anglesey is not by any means one of the financial capitals of the world, so my previous fallback of finding a merchant bank that needed somebody with knowledge of foreign exchange systems to work in their IT department for a while wasn't going to work here. At the time (don't know whether or not it's still true) Anglesey had the lowest GDP per capita of all the counties in the UK. Jobs were scarce and many in the public sector (collectively by far the biggest employer) were proscribed to non-Welsh speakers. All the IT work I had done since university, even at the bank in Dorset, was as a freelance contractor so I decided to set myself up in similar fashion as a small IT company (i.e. one employee, a freelance contractor with a company name). And I would specialise in? Well, what do you need? I provided a bit of training, a few miscellaneous jobs for small companies, set up a few websites, helped a company with a grant application, other bits and pieces. It earned some money and Morag was working full-time at the university, so things were okay.

Morag's department was at that time The Centre for the Environment and Natural Resources. One day I was talking to one of her colleagues who was interested in my time in Nepal. She had some field data that she wanted 'sorting out' and was happy that

I had the skills to do this. Collecting data of some description is the point of most environment related field research and 'sorting out' data at the end of the data collection phase of a project is the bane of many a researcher's life. I say 'many' because some are very well organised, but 'many' are not. I started to see a gap in the market for somebody who had a lot of IT experience and also knowledge of the research process.

So, I carved out a niche and it brought in enough money to be worthwhile. We were settling here and life was progressing comfortably. It wasn't all plain sailing and there had been a couple of times when we thought of upping sticks and moving back to England. Morag had led quite an itinerant academic life, with long spells in Canada and Jamaica. Indeed, she told me that when she arrived in North Wales she'd decided to give it five years and when I turned up she'd already been here four and a half. Roots were not yet put down too deep. There was a point after we'd been together a few years, when her career seemed to have stalled (and you couldn't really call what I was doing a career, could you?) that we seriously wondered about leaving. One idea was to go back to Dorset and Morag made some noises about re-training as a solicitor. This came to a head when Elinor started primary school. Primary schools on Anglesey are bi-lingual and in our local school one week was taught in English and the next in Welsh – full immersion. Most of the teachers were first language Welsh and so that was the predominant language of the school. Whilst we enjoyed being surrounded by the rich Welsh culture, our children were obviously from an English speaking household and they were both slightly dyslexic. Isn't it going to be a bit of an ask for them to be taught in a language they didn't understand? We thought we would give it a year and if it didn't seem to be going well, we would have leave, at the very least for the sake of the children. However, it went fine, both are now impressively bi-lingual and eventually Morag's career much improved.

You might wonder where this story is going? This is supposed to be a book about planting a vineyard and words like 'plant' 'vine' and 'grape' have not appeared anywhere in this chapter. That's because nothing could have been further from our thoughts. However, you are now at least aware of the arbitrary fortune that brought me to Anglesey, there's no way what eventually happens could have transpired in Dorset as I wouldn't have had access to or wouldn't have been able to afford the land. Also you are aware of the similar providence that brought us to the house where the vineyard was eventually planted, even though we didn't particularly want the field. But if the field hadn't been there, there wouldn't now be a vineyard. As you will see, when the vineyard idea hatched it became possible because we had a bit of land, I certainly wouldn't have gone out and bought land to plant on. Arbitrary fortune.

The Wider Picture I:
Climate Change

Whilst there were vineyards in the UK in Roman times and sporadically since then, it's only in the last few decades that the phenomenon of home grown UK wine production has become widespread. Many heroic pioneers of the current industry planted, with varying degrees of success, in the second half of the twentieth century but the establishment of a vineyard sector on a wide scale here is only possible because of one thing: climate change. And even that has been greatly assisted by the development of more suitable vine varieties. But mostly it's climate change.

Let's be clear, just because climate change is going to help my grapes grow in North Wales, I am a long way from seeing the gradual warming of the world as good thing. Rather, it seems to me that it's a looming disaster. The likely consequences are well documented: sea level rise leading to catastrophic coastal flooding; widespread areas experiencing severe drought and famine; mass migrations of people; species extinction; increased numbers of forest fires; more severe weather events and much more, little of it good. If warming continues unabated it's likely to have calamitous economic and social consequences and may even be an existential threat. And no matter what we do to try to prevent it happening we are not going to be able to stop it in its tracks. The time lags in climatic systems are such that even if we reformed our behaviour on a worldwide scale overnight and totally mended our ways (unlikely), world temperatures would continue to rise for many years, probably decades. The science is all about slowing it down and capping the damage, nobody thinks we can turn it off like a tap. The one great saving grace is that it's happening relatively slowly, so there will be time to mitigate the coming disasters and adapt both socially and economically (though this is also one of the biggest problems as it allows politicians and power brokers to just kick it into the long grass). My planting of a vineyard is not going to save or harm the world, I just planted it for the fun of it, but at least I'm adapting to changing circumstances. I tell my children I'm a visionary, that in a few decades time when the wines of Wales are famous throughout the world I'll be remembered as the far-sighted founder of the famous Red Wharf Bay Vineyard, the oldest vineyard in the Anglesey 'appellation'. People will come from all over the world to visit the wineries here on the island and especially to view the vine filled slopes of Red Wharf Bay, at the centre of it all. My children don't take me seriously (and neither do I).

A very short technical bit to help plainly illustrate how climate change will transform UK wine production. There is a common tool used in vineyards in the UK (and elsewhere) that allows us, amongst other things, to clearly track climate change: the calculation of something called Growing Degree Days (GDD). This provides a scale, known as The Winkler Scale after A. J. Winkler, one of its creators at The University of California way back in 1944. He and fellow academic Maynard Amerine were trying to link wine quality to climate, based on the idea that the most important factor in the ripening of grapes is temperature. California has a more diverse climate than most people realise, varying from hot desert to alpine tundra and Winkler and Amerine divided the state into five temperature regions, basing their research conclusions on the characteristics of each of these. Categorisation of vines had not been previously undertaken in this manner and in a comparatively short time the scale came to be widely adopted and the vine growing world came to be roughly divided into the five categorisations they proposed. Consequently, you can now place your vineyard in its wine climate region, starting with the places that only just scrape onto the scale (Anglesey!!!), moving through France, Italy, Spain, etc. until you hit the really (literally!) sun scorched areas of the world such as the central valley of California itself and, especially, inland Australia.

Despite it sounding like it could be very technical, one of the reasons it has been so widely adopted is its basic simplicity. To calculate your GDD you take the maximum and minimum temperature at the vineyard on any particular day and then calculate the mid-point of that temperature range. For example, if maximum temperature is 26°C and minimum is 16°C then the mid-point is obviously 21. You then subtract ten from that number (because vines are dormant below 10°C) and the resultant figure is the GDD for that day, in this example, 11. You measure GDD every day and simply add up the GDDs for every day of the growing season (April to October) and that's the GDD for the vineyard for that year (and that's the technical bit over, quite easy really) and you can even download an app to do it for you.

As the manager of a vineyard, what the GDD total then gives me is a figure that is a rough and ready comparison of my vineyard 'climate' this year to that of previous years. It also allows me to compare my vineyard 'climate' to that of other vineyards in the UK and even to crudely compare my vine growing environment to the vine growing environment of different countries. It's far from perfect but if my yield this year is down on last year maybe I will understand that a little better if I realise that my GDD figure this year was down by 100 (or maybe it was some other reason, this is not an exact science). When I look in envy at the yields in southern England compared to my own perhaps I can gain comfort and comprehend things better when I look at our comparative GDDs; and when I consider planting a vineyard in Andalucia I can so do with the expectation that yields should be at least double those even in southern England because the GDD in southern Spain is so far up the scale.

Many technical papers have correctly identified weaknesses in GDD comparisons; its focus solely on temperature to the detriment of other climatic factors such as rainfall, humidity and sunshine hours; duration of temperature (peaks may be for only minutes but low temperatures may persist for hours) and microclimatic conditions are but a few. It is a methodology that's easy to criticise and many do; and linking the Winkler scale to wine quality is pretty subjective as well, don't you think? For a start, what constitutes a good bottle of wine? In my view, if you are drinking a glass and enjoying it then it's from a good bottle of wine. It might be a bottle of red you liked the look of and paid £7 for in the supermarket; it might be a bottle you have paid £20 or £30 for somewhere more upmarket. If you are enjoying the £7 bottle it seems to me that you have just saved yourself at least thirteen quid. And if you train your palate to like the £20 plus bottles you've costing yourself a lot of dosh as you strive to satisfy your enhanced appreciation and set yourself on the path of paying ever more money. I'll return to this theme later.

Despite its deficiencies the great advantage of the GDD scale is that, as explained, it's simple to calculate. So, for the record, these were the climate regions and corresponding wine quality into which the Winkler system then divided the wine world. Region I, with less than about 1350 GDD, produced 'excellent whites and good reds' and included Chablis, Loire, Hawkes Bay and Champagne (and Anglesey); Region II produced 'the finest reds' from around GDD 1500 and included Bordeaux and Burgundy; Region III could only manage 'very good reds' at approximately 1800 GDD, even though it included Rioja, The Yarra Valley and Umbria; in Region IV, GDD 2100 or so, the wines of Stellenbosch, The Napa Valley and Barossa somewhat patronisingly fell into the grouping of 'acceptable table wine quality at best'; and in Region V, where GDD is greater than 2200, the wines of The Hunter Valley, The Swan River, Madeira and Jerez were written off as suitable only for 'bulk' production. Tastes and wine fashion have changed since the scale was devised but even accounting for that, GDD as a barometer of what is a good bottle of wine, nah! I'm not running with that. But GDD as a measure of climate change is very revealing.

Plumpton College in Sussex, a former Agricultural College now part of the University of Brighton, has been tracking GDD in southern England for over thirty years. Until about 1990 they would expect somewhere between 850 and 900 GDD in any season. From that time until 2015 the GDD they have calculated has risen to the extent that they now expect 1100 GDD per growing season. This is climate, so it's about long term trends and measurements on their graph jump about a bit but the long term pattern of climate change could not be clearer.

Thirty or forty years ago when the idea of climate change was first being muted I, like many, was a bit sceptical. Sure, at that point there had been an increase in global temperatures but there could be many explanations for that, not least the fluctuating climate cycles that have always occurred. In the nineteen eighties, when climate change was first mentioned, there was a lot of talk along the lines that Britain would come to have a climate like the south of France. There was also talk about the problems of sea level rise, projection maps were produced that showed the UK minus East Anglia and other large swathes. I remember thinking that if this was going to be as serious as they suggested and we needed to do something to stop it, it was being presented rather poorly. That if we were going to get a climate like the South of France most people would say, "Sod East Anglia." However, over time the accumulation of evidence has become irrefutable and slowly I came to accept climate change was occurring, that it was almost certainly manmade and that it was serious (and that I shouldn't be so blasé about East Anglia). However, it wasn't until I saw the graph from Plumpton College, of the change in Growing Degree Days in southern England, representing minute and precisely measured data collected over a sustained period, showing an indisputable trend and such a dramatic increase, that I realised how stark the 'phenomenon' of climate change had become. That's the moment it really struck me for the first time that climate change wasn't just a 'general idea', some imprecise concept in the background to which the solutions were pretty nebulous, but was something very serious that sooner rather than later the world had to get to grips with.

Thirty years ago the average GDD in Champagne was 1100, after two decades of the twenty first century that is now the GDD that Plumpton expects. So Plumpton now has the same GDD as Champagne had thirty years ago. If you like, the climate of Europe has moved 200 miles north in 30 years. This has huge implications for the wine industry, and I'll get on to some of these shortly.

CHAPTER 4

Black Puddings

About a month after my 'revelation' that the need for guaranteed water on the land I was hoping to buy was more important than anything else I'm back in southern Spain doing more 'research' and still looking for a suitable plot. I think I've shown that I'm starting this project from a fairly low knowledge base and whilst ideally my required assault on the inevitable steep learning curve would be full on with crampons and ropes; my brain seems to be taking a more gentle, circuitous route round the foothills of the mountain of understanding I need to take on board.

One of the things I start to think about on this trip is how I would actually manage the 'arm's length' model I've been intending to execute. Remember, I'm planning to come out for a week or so roughly every month during the growing season; plus a couple of weeks in the spring and in the late summer when there's a bit more to do. I didn't see why this wouldn't work, I'm only thinking of about 1000 vines after all. I know that as the grapes form and mature each year there's an amount you have to do to keep on top of things but for such a small number of vines I think you can compact most of the jobs into a week a month, so long as you have somebody on the ground to keep the vines watered (very important, you know) and keep the weeds down. However, so far I had mostly only given thought to buying the land and then the planting and growing of the vines, I've given hardly any thought as to how I would make the wine. This may seem to you a bit over relaxed and remiss of me but in my defence, given that I had first to find the land, go through the process of buying it, then plant, then wait three or four years before the vines produced a grape harvest fit for wine making; I reckoned that I had at least four years to crack the production problem. When

I had given it brief consideration I surmised that during these intervening years the main things I needed to do were a) to learn how to make wine from grapes, b) to buy quite a bit of equipment, and c) to find somewhere to run the operation. I thought these were surmountable but I was beginning to wonder if the actual work involved in making the wine (or at least keeping an eye on how the process was going) would require more frequent attention than the one week a month I was planning to be there.

I'm having a break from 'research', drinking with friends Brian and Jo in a bar in Alora. They are originally from Blackpool, where Brian built up a chain of butcher's shops. Eventually and whilst still quite young he decided the stress wasn't worth it, sold up and they moved to Alora. After a while here he decided he needed or wanted a job, which he didn't seem to have much problem achieving. I have no way of assessing such things but you have to imagine that he's a pretty competent butcher and he was certainly a hard worker. He didn't have much trouble finding employment and was at the time working for a company importing meat into Spain from the UK, to cater for demand from the British ex-pat population, mainly down on the coast on the Costa del Sol. You would wonder how much of a market there was for this, I mean, a Spanish cow has the same number of legs and other bits as a British cow. But it turns out the market is quite substantial as it seems that a Spanish butcher will cut the meat in a different manner to a British butcher and ex-pats want the cuts they are familiar with. Processed meats are also very different in the two countries. Sausages are an obvious example but there are many other concoctions of minced, stewed and fried cow and particularly pig that are very different in Spain to what we are used to in the UK.

Out of the blue Brian asks me a question, and I think it's one of the best questions I've ever been asked.

"Kevin, how much do you think it costs to transport a tonne of black pudding from Bury to Malaga?" I look at him and wonder if I heard him right, and then try to think of something to say.

"Go on, have a guess. It's what I had to arrange this afternoon," he prompts. Apparently, the black puddings of Bury are highly prized, and even though I'm originally from only about twenty-five miles away from there, I didn't know that. I tried to get my head round the idea of a tonne of black pudding all in one place, and then the thought of it moving seamlessly from Bury to Malaga. I mean, it would have to be refrigerated, packed and picked up, plus all the paperwork. They can't fly it out (can they?) so it's coming all the way by road, ferry or channel tunnel. How many black puddings are there in a tonne? Maybe one thousand? No, that would make them a kilo each and that's a big black pudding. So maybe five thousand? If you are transporting that many in one go then a thousand quid for transport only means and extra 20p on the price of each black pudding. If you were an ex-pat on the Costa de Sol missing your home produce you would pay an extra 20p to have a black pudding brought all the way from Bury, wouldn't you?

I hadn't really got a clue but it's not going to be cheap, is it? I went for £1,000. I thought probably more but you knew he was only asking the question to catch me out and the answer would be unexpected, astronomically high or cheaper than you would imagine. So I went for cheaper. Even two thousand quid would still only add 40p per pudding to the price, still viable. Since that evening I've asked many people this question, I mean, who wouldn't engage? Answers have ranged from £500 to £5,000 and they're all way too high. It's a hundred and fifty quid. A hundred and fifty quid, come on! That's less than bringing out a couple of bikes on EasyJet, and it's got to be refrigerated, paperwork, driven fifteen hundred miles, boat across the channel; surely it can't be?

But it is, I've phoned up a shipping company to check. Lorries go from the UK to Spain picking up and dropping off pallets of all kinds of stuff here and there, refrigerated ones for food stuffs. They then go back to the UK with whatever people need to take back, the refrigerated ones taking mainly fruit and vegetables from Andalucia, the off-season stuff you see in the UK supermarkets in the winter, again picking up and dropping of stuff all over the place. It's a logistical nightmare and very competitive but there are hundreds of lorries going each way every week (let's keep Brexit out of this conversation). But wait, if there are refrigerated lorries taking fruit and veg from southern Spain to the UK, they could transport grapes as well, couldn't they? A tonne of grapes will make about 900 75cl bottles of wine. At £150 that adds only about 6p a bottle to production costs. Wouldn't it make sense just to ship the grapes back to Anglesey each year and make the wine there? Sorted!

The Wider Picture II:
Migratory Wine Regions

Twenty years of so in the future the climate of Champagne may well not be conducive to the production of Champagne; and other wine regions will probably be having problems as well. I've said that measuring and comparing Growing Degree Days for Champagne and for southern England suggests that the climate of Europe has moved 200 miles north in thirty years. This change of climate is now driving the improving fortunes of vineyards in the UK and that is probably also the case in other cooler climate wine regions but the converse of this is that it's causing problems elsewhere.

The situation in Champagne is particularly notable because of the region's prominence in the wine world. The trouble with warming in this region is that the grape varieties grown to produce Champagne, principally Pinot Noir, Pinot Meunier and Chardonnay, don't like very hot summers and the quality of the vintage suffers. If there is long term warming the quality of the of the wine will go into long term decline. To date it's thought that the increase in temperature has been good for Champagne producers; quicker ripening, generally improving sugar levels whilst curtailing frost damage and lowering acidity. But it's becoming a case of too much of a good thing. Too much sun causes these grape varieties to ripen too quickly and to produce too much sugar, thus more alcohol, both of which change the characteristics of the resultant wine to the perceived detriment of quality. Also, as average temperatures continue to increase, extreme weather events become more common. In recent years several producers in the region have reported losses because long hot spells have caused the grapes to burn and shrivel, thus rendering them useless for wine production. Longer periods of drought will cause obvious issues. It is being speculated that the 'benefits' of warming have peaked in the Champagne region and conditions have started to deteriorate.

Global warming can't be stopped in its tracks. It will take many years of action (assuming sufficient political will is garnered) and the lags in the climatic system will ensure continued warming even if the underlying causes are brought under control quickly. So the trend for warmer summers in Champagne is only going to continue, at least in the short to medium term. The champagne growers have known this for some time and are deploying measures to mitigate the change, developing new varieties of vines to attempt to produce the desired grape qualities in a warmer climate and introducing new methods of cultivation. However, the will to change the way things are done, have always been done, is hampered by the ultra-strict rules in place to protect the champagne brand. Some producers are more conservative than others when it comes to amending these. Many people know that sparkling wine can only be called Champagne if the grapes were grown in that very specific geographical area. There are also restrictions as to vineyard practices, the methods of cultivation and the total production in any one year. Altering traditional methods and practices is a slow process, and even if you manage this there is only so much that you can do. If the climate changes to the extent that the produce you want to grow will no longer flourish, sooner or later you will have to accept that and grow something else or grow somewhere else.

Some of the major Champagne houses are taking quite drastic measures, hedging their bets and buying land in the chalklands of the South Downs and other areas of southern England. As temperatures increase there are many areas in southern England (and Wales) where the land and increasingly the climate will be perfect for producing sparkling wine. This is already being seen in the number of awards sparkling wines from English and Welsh vineyards are winning in blind tasting competitions. More and more, English and Welsh wines are coming to the fore. If twenty years of so in the future the climate of Champagne really is not conducive to the production of Champagne it will be very interesting to see how the Champagne goalposts are manoeuvred in the coming decades. Champagne is, after all, one of the most recognisable appellations and thus one of the most valuable brands on the planet. If the product starts to deteriorate year on year, the producers are certain to move to protect their brand and market. Maybe the South Downs will be geographically designated French for the purposes of the Champagne appellation? That would have been an interesting part of the Brexit negotiations.

Stating that the climate of Europe has moved north by two hundred miles in thirty years based on one set of data from southern England is a valid illustration of climatic trends but as science it's a bit simplistic. Changes may (or may not) be dramatic but they will not be uniform. Climate is very complex and the climate of any one area is an intricate combination of many factors. Start changing a few of those factors and who knows what the consequences will be. I've come across references to vineyards being considered as the canary in the coal mine in this regard. Small changes in climate can drive big changes in vineyard circumstances as vines are particularly sensitive to a change in their environment. If you think about it, any particular wine region tends to produce the style of wines it does because that's what works in the climate of that region. You are not going to try to produce Riesling in southern Europe or Shiraz in Wales, are you? But if the grape varieties grown in any one region are a reflection of the climate of that region and that climate permanently changes then the vineyards in that region are in a bit of a bind, aren't they?

When trying to decide what to plant in southern Spain I became aware that that many grape varieties were not suitable for cultivation in the hot climate there, some expectedly so but others were a surprise. Tempranillo is probably the most famous of all Spanish grapes because of its use in Rioja, and was an obvious candidate for me to consider if I was planting a vineyard in Spain. But Rioja is in northern Spain, I found out that Tempranillo won't flourish in the south. Simply, the winters don't get cold enough to allow the plant to go dormant, as it should over the cooler months. The vine gets 'confused' and can't work out when it's spring and the growing cycle is disrupted. As temperatures increase throughout Europe this phenomenon can only spread northwards and many varieties may no longer be suited to the climate of their traditional location. In the same way that southern England might become the best place to produce 'Champagne' it might well be that, say, the Bordeaux region becomes best suited to be growing Tempranillo and thus the best place to produce 'Rioja'; we might find that the permitted traditional grapes of the Bordeaux appellations, Cabernet Sauvignon, Cabernet

Franc, Malbec, Merlot and others, grow better in the Loire valley; and the white wines of the Loire valley might work best if produced in, well, let's say Champagne. That's going to shake things up a bit, isn't it?

So the issues for the wine industry thrown up by global Global warming are going to be complex but it's likely that the UK wine industry will be one of the few beneficiaries. As it becomes warmer growing conditions will become less marginal here and UK vineyards are likely to prosper as the climate 'improves', with both traditional vines and new varieties benefiting from the changed environment. The UK also has a more subtle advantage in that it is, to a large extent, a blank canvas. More and more vineyards are being planted and many established vineyards are expanding (more of this later). But this expansion is almost always into new ground, land being converted from other uses to vine cultivation for the first time. If you are doing that you make your choice as to which variety you plant based on many facets but prominent amongst your considerations are going to be which style of wine will sell and which type of vine will flourish in your climate and environment. As regards the type of vine, when planting on your blank canvas you have the great advantage of understanding the likely impact of climate change and choose your varieties accordingly. Established vineyards in Europe don't have this luxury.

Imagine owning a vineyard that's been in your family for generations. A chateaux in France, a Tuscan farmhouse, a rambling Corjito in Rioja? A large, old, stone built house at the head of a valley of rolling fields, covered with vines as far as you can see. "The estate was planted by the grandfather of my grandfather and we produce 100,000 bottles of delicious wine every year." The wine has always been produced according to the rules of the local appellation and the appellation, or DOC, or DOP, has a worldwide reputation. However, as we look into the future, maybe over the next decade or so your vintages vary from year to year and at some point you realise it's been quite a few years since you have had what you would consider to be a good vintage. Indeed, the trend appears to be one of a slow deterioration. It's the same for your peers in the region and people are beginning to realise that the climate seems to have been permanently transformed. At what point do you decide to grub up the vines that were planted by the grandfather of your grandfather and plant new ones that are more suited to the changed climate? At what point do you stop producing the type of wines that has made your vineyard famous, that you have been producing for generations and start produce a different style of wine? Imagine having to contemplate these things and sooner or later realising that you are going to have to do it. Or maybe you drastically change the rules of your world renowned appellation (or DOC, or DOP), or do whatever else you need to do; or even abandon your brand (sell it to the region a few hundred miles to the north?) and start trying to build a new market for your new style of wine? It's not going to be easy, is it?

And whilst contemplating this migratory dilemma, I did wonder what I was planning to get myself into. Alora is twenty five miles north west of Malaga. I've stated already that it's not that far from the only true desert in Europe and you don't have to spend much time perusing a map to work out that it's only two hundred miles north of the Sahara, a worrying thought when you consider the scale of climatic migration that already seems to be occurring and that 'the climate of Europe has moved 200 miles north in 30 years'. In the fifteen years I've been going there regularly, several of those years have had very low rain fall. I've said that the reservoirs were noticeable lower compared to when I first visited. Is it such an improbably scenario that desert or semi-desert climatic conditions become more widespread in Andalucia? After my realisation that the most important criterium for the plot of land I was looking for was that it needed guaranteed water I did also start to ask myself whether or not this was absolutely the wrong region to plan to plant a new vineyard. Should I give up on the idea completely (No)? Should I go somewhere further north in Spain (not practical)? Eventually I just took the ostrich approach, dismissing the thought and deciding to just carry on anyway. What the heck, the Mediterranean forms a pretty massive climatic barrier and I didn't think much would happen quickly. Surely I would be okay for at least a decade or two? Looking back, I had absolutely no basis on which to come to this conclusion. I think I was just emotionally in too deeply to back out over something as imprecise as a worry as to what the climate might be like, say, in twenty years' time. Just make sure the plot I choose has guaranteed water, eh.

CHAPTER 5

The First Vines and The First Wine

In 2009, doing the day-job, I had a short contract to produce a website for Barnwell Parker Geoscience Ltd, run by Andrew Barnwell and Sara Parker from their home in the Conwy Valley. You don't know what you started, Andrew! I was to work in the office next to their house and the first day I was there Andrew was showing me around and at one point asked if I would like to see their vines. Of course, I say, "Yes."

I'm not sure what I expected, a few vines in a greenhouse? But instead we step outside and there was a small vineyard, maybe fifty vines. A vineyard in North Wales, it's not warm enough! I thought, then said. But clearly I'm wrong. They looked pretty healthy with a good crop maturing. I was genuinely amazed, it was so improbable. Then later on in the day he gave me some wine to try and Wow! This is very pleasant and drinkable. As I've already hinted, my attitude towards wine tasting is not that sophisticated. If you have a glass of wine in your hand and you are enjoying it, then it's from a good bottle of wine. However, this was perfectly drinkable (and pleasant) wine grown on outdoor vines in North Wales. Truly it was a revelation. I remember remarking how difficult I thought it was to make your own wine, beer or whatever. Or it's easy to make it, it's just difficult to make something you can imagine looking forward to sitting down and drinking. Like many people, I and friends had tried making wine and beer from kits or miscellaneous fruit when I was younger (and the green tomato wine a friend brought to a party of my youth deserves a chapter all to itself, but not in this book). Sometimes it worked out okayish. I remember making one brew that got you pissed on a pint, but mostly I remember all the 'not quite pleasant' tasting drinks where something had gone a bit wrong. Life moves on and you start to earn a bit more money and subconsciously start to think, "to hell with this, I'll get it from the supermarket." The brewing equipment gathers dust somewhere and gets thrown out next time you move house. But here I was drinking very pleasant wine made in North Wales from grapes grown in North Wales. Remarkable!

And driving home the idea had grown to the extent that I'm already thinking, "This could be fun, I'm going to give it a go." I've alluded to the vegetable patch. We had the usual stuff growing there, potatoes, beans, peas, etc., it could just be an extension of that. But when I got home I realised that if we planted vines with the vegetables there would be no room left for said vegetables and that and I'd need a little bit more space. So what about our usual tactic of grabbing some more of the field? At the time there were horses in residence and I clearly couldn't just plant them there as the horses would just eat them. And the fence had just been moved and it seemed a lot of faff to do so again for something that was, after all, just a bit of a whim. And I didn't really envisage needing that much space anyway. Okay, planting would be too much for the vegetable patch but, thinking of the size of Andrew's planting, not much more was needed. So where? And then I looked at the contentious bank near the back door I told you about, the overgrown 'wild garden'. What about there? It was already 'in the garden', so no extra fencing needed. It was about the size I was envisaging and isn't the side of a bank the traditional kind of place to plant vines (I thought)? Morag would be happy that I was finally sorting out the jungle and I was fired up by the thought of another project. Wouldn't it be wonderful to plant some vines there, look after them for a couple of years and then eventually produce grapes to make our own wine, to have wine from grapes grown on your own land! And maybe there were even some thoughts in there of being able to take a couple of bottles to a dinner party and say, even if my tongue would be firmly in my cheek, "This is from the estate." I could clear the bank and dig in little terraces so that I could stand up to tend them, put in the vines and watch them grow. Surely it couldn't be any more difficult than growing beans? It would be quite a lot of effort at first but whilst clearing an overgrown bank just because it's a bit untidy is a tedious and unpleasant job; clearing an overgrown bank to plant vines to produce grapes to make wine from your own land to take to a dinner party and say, "This is from the estate," would be tremendous fun! And so it began; but that's all it was, planting a few vines on a whim to make a few bottles of wine so that we could show up at a dinner party with wine from 'the estate'. There were certainly no grand concepts or ambitions.

I quickly found out that, predictably, the best time to plant vines is late spring, so plenty of time to clear the bank, which I did in stages over the winter. As I looked into it further a pleasant surprise was that I discovered that, whilst when you buy vines from a garden centre you probably have to pay £12 or £15 a plant, if you buy them from a commercial grower they only cost £2 to £3 each. However, you have to buy them in batches of 25. I have no idea why and I've still not found anybody who can tell me why, but that's the industry standard and it seems it has been forever. It doesn't matter if you want to plant 100, 1110 or 10,009, they come in batches of 25. I found this out when I Googled something like 'buying vines from commercial growers' and, from the several that appeared, I selected one in Somerset because I liked the look of the amateur, out-of-date feel of their website (I figured that a cheap looking website probably meant that it was a very small business, maybe somebodies' side-line, and thus they would be more conducive to dealing with somebody like me doing things on a less than grand scale). But when I phoned them sometime in March 2010 I was dismayed to find that, whilst you plant in the spring you need to order the vines the previous autumn, so that the grower has a six-month lead time to source and prepare the vines to fulfil the order. However, having been told about the 'standard batch size', when I said that I only wanted twenty five, as it was such a small order the very patient gentleman I was talking to thought it would be okay. He then asked.

"What variety was I thinking of planting." Variety? Hadn't given it a thought, I was just asking what was possible. I then said that I guessed white wine would have a better chance of working out than red in the UK climate.

"No," he said. "What variety of grape?"

"Oh! Dunno, what did he recommend?"

"Whereabout in the country was I?"

"Anglesey."

"That's quite far north, I have 25 Solaris on SO4 rootstock that should go okay up there." Solaris? What kind of vine is that? And why is he talking about rootstock? Surely Solaris vines have Solaris roots? But what the heck.

"Yes, that's great," I said.

"Let me know exactly when you are ready to plant and I'll send them up in good time," he responded without further comment (but I wonder what he was thinking?).

A month later I had finished preparing the bank and when they arrived planting was just a few hours work. Then I just had to wait to see what happened. And well, they grew. I didn't actually think of this as something as grand as a vineyard at the time, just a few vines planted on a whim to have some fun, to produce grapes to make wine from your own land to take to a dinner party and say, "This is from the estate." But most of them are still there and they are the original vines of what has now become Red Wharf Bay Vineyard.

I bought a book about growing vines in the UK and, as far as I could see, they progressed as expected in the first growing season. Twenty-five vines only took up part of the bank so, enthusiasm growing along with the vines, that autumn I ordered another fifty Solaris vines on SO4 rootstock for planting the following spring (hey, I'm a professional, I know which vines to order and the right time of year to do it!). Again, they duly arrived and were planted, maybe squeezed in a bit closer than the book suggested in order to fit in all fifty in the available space, but what did that matter? The author of the book suggested the vines should be planted a minimum of 4 feet apart in rows that were also a minimum of four feet apart. However, there was only one short paragraph in the whole book dedicated to this, so he didn't seem to attach much importance to it and I wasn't going to be purist about perfect spacing and then have to throw away those left over. So let's just bunch 'em up a bit and get 'em all in.

Looking back, I hadn't a clue what I was doing and my lack of knowledge and experience was eventually starkly confirmed. It has to be true to say that, if you decide to plant a vineyard (even if only a few dozen vines) when having no previous experience of viniculture, you make your biggest decisions when you know least. The big three decisions are what are you going to plant; where are you going to plant and how are you going to plant. Because, let's face it, once they are planted you are rather committed. It will be at least three years before you take your first harvest of grapes and another six or eight years before the vine reaches full maturity. If at some point during this time you start to think that maybe you wished you had planted them elsewhere, that maybe you wished you had planted a different variety, that maybe you wished you had spaced them or had orientated the rows differently, frankly it's a bit late. The roots by then are sufficiently deep so that if you tried to transplant them you would just kill them. Assuming that you don't want to grub them up and start again, all you can do is try to improve your tending regime to make the best of a bad job or plant some more in a more appropriate place and in a manner that allows for better nurture (both of which eventually happened here).

Let's start with what I got right. Solaris vines on SO4 rootstock are very appropriate for Anglesey, so thank you to Derek Pritchard of Winegrowers Supplies in Somerset for that sound advice (the website still looks much the same but if you are thinking of doing something similar there's loads of information there and Derek is friendly and very helpful). Solaris is a hybrid vine adapted to thrive in cooler climates (see the later chapter about vine varietals suitable for the UK). It's early ripening, which gives it a better chance in a growing season such as we have here, it's also very vigorous, disease resistant, high yielding and 'reliable in a cool climate'. I subsequently also found out that it has 'very strong growth requiring a lot of summer leaf work', which is relevant to what comes next. And another thing I found out; you may be surprised to hear that Solaris vines don't have Solaris roots. I was amazed to find out that almost all of the vines in Europe, maybe 98%, are grafted onto the rootstock of vine varieties native to America. All those famous varieties that produce the traditional fine wines of France; Bordeaux, St. Emillion, Champagne, etc. from all those grand Chateaux and wine estates; all that white wine from the Loire valley; all the Rioja from Spain and Douro from Portugal; all that lovely Italian Barolo, German Riesling and all the rest from the many and varied countries and wine regions of Europe. All the vines grafted onto American rootstock. This is common knowledge to all in the wine industry but, as I've now told the story many times, I would guess no more that 10% of people outside the vineyard/wine trade are aware of this. I certainly wasn't.

It is the doing of an aphid type insect called Phylloxera that came to light as long ago as the 1860's. Phylloxera is a bug of less than one millimetre long that attacks the roots of vines. Once contaminated the vine, virtually without fail, will slowly stunt and die. It was introduced into Europe along with many plants (and diseases) imported by the great Victorian plant collectors of the nineteenth century. It spreads easily from plant to plant, but also on the wind, farm equipment and by people who come into contact with it. When first introduced it spread slowly but remorselessly and eventually most of Europe and North Africa were affected, including half of all the vineyards in France. There seemed no practical way to contain it and many wine regions never recovered, overwhelming for the economy of poor rural farming communities where this was the main or only crop. It took until the 1880's for researchers to discover that American vine varieties were resistant to the bug and that the only way to prevent the infection of European vines, if the traditional vine varieties were to be preserved and continued, was to graft these on to the American rootstock. And that's what happens to this day all over Europe. All those traditional vines in the major wine regions of France, Spain, Italy and elsewhere, all growing through American roots. SO4 rootstock adapts to the majority of soils, encourages early development and maturity and is the 'definitive' rootstock in UK vineyards. So, Solaris vines on SO4 rootstock is a good choice for Anglesey and at least I did something right.

How about the second of the big decisions, where I was going to plant, site selection? If you were looking to plant a vineyard commercially you would spend considerable time and effort finding the right site. You might look at climate (or how it might change), soil, wind exposure, topography and the surrounding flora, there's more about this later. A fairly widespread thought is that vineyards should be on a south or south west facing slope, so the vines make the most of the evening sun, in the warmer half of the day. However, I'm not so sure that this is so important – great if you can but there are many other variables (you put ten vineyard owners/managers in a room and you are likely to get at least five views about any aspect of the business).

It is actually pretty easy to grow vines in the UK. The problem you have is not of getting them to thrive, to produce strong shoots and foliage and even grapes. The problem you have is getting the grapes to ripen sufficiently to produce decent (or drinkable) wine. For this you need sunshine and temperature and, in a still marginal wine region such as the UK (and certainly the more northern areas), to steal a Tesco slogan, "Every little helps." So if you can plant on a slope with a south or south west aspect, all well and good. But to me it doesn't really matter if the land is flat or even gently sloping 'the wrong way'. If the vines get enough warmth and sunshine they will be okay. Several years later, when I eventually planted the rest of the vineyard here in the field in Red Wharf Bay, I did so on a gentle north east facing slope, in theory probably the worst aspect. But in Anglesey we have a micro-climate, influenced by the sea and the mountains and in our case by the bowl shape of the valley in which we live. Furthermore, we are in the north and west of Wales and so in the summer we get longer days than most areas in England and all of Wales. From the start of May until mid August the sun will rise before 5.30 am and set after 9 pm and on a sunny day the vines in the main part of the field will get twelve, maybe even thirteen or fourteen hours of sunshine.

However, the problem with those first vines planted on the bank was that the aspect was to the north-west and the slope was quite steep, and it was also shaded by the house and even by the trees on the other side of the house. Although the rest of the field does get long hours of sunshine each (sunny) day, the bank doesn't. Indeed, it's about one thirty in the afternoon before the sun gets around to provide the vines with direct exposure. I needed to get as much sunshine on the grapes as I possibly could get them to ripen and I've gone and planted the vines in about the shadiest bit of land we have (...if after a few years you decide it would have been better if you had planted them in a different place, frankly it's a bit late).

So I got the 'What' right and the 'Where' wrong, let's move on to the third big decision, the 'How?'. By this I mean the preparation of the site and layout of the vines. It is considered a good idea to plough a site before the vines are planted because it chops up all the grass and weeds that would act as competition (though this can be contentious). Even if I'd have known this it would have been impossible on a steep bank. But, because it was a steep bank I had cut small terraces, each about a eighteen inches wide; alternatively, one to plant the vines on and one for me to stand on to tend them. This cut up the ground quite a lot and was pretty much the equivalent of ploughing, so perhaps another half tick to me. Many will say that the rows of vines should be aligned north-south, so that they cook evenly on each side as the sun moves across the sky. I'm not sure this matters much and there are other theories. The terraces I had dug out were perpendicular to the slope (how else could they be) and so aligned south west to north east, not perfect but I don't think this in its self is a big issue (if they hadn't been in the shade). It was the plant spacing that accentuated the problems I was making for myself.

I mentioned that I had squeezed the vines up a bit as I was planting them, to fit them all in. This didn't seem to be an issue in the first couple of years when what is above the ground gets pruned very severely to encourage root growth, but after that (…if after a few years you decide it would have been better if you had planted them in a different place, frankly it's a bit late). In those first years you just want the plant to get stronger. When you first plant the vine it will send out shoots all over the place. You don't want that, it's wasting too much energy. You select the strongest, straightest shoot and cut off all the others. You want the plant to just put roots down and concentrate on sending one shoot upwards. Any further extra shoots it tries to grow you cut off as soon as you see them, so it's quite a scrawny plant in that first year. When the plants are dormant during the first winter you boldly take your secateurs and cut the one shoot you have left growing back to where it started. That took some doing – I've watched them all growing for the best part of a year and now I'm just going to cut all the growth off? I can't do it, I'll kill the plant! But you do it and what you have then looks the same as a year ago but you have a stronger plant with a stronger root system.

Second year goes exactly the same as the first: select the strongest, straightest shoot and cut off all the others. That second year your one remaining shoot will grow sturdier and taller than the previous year and this will eventually become the stem of the mature vine. But for the moment it's still pretty scrawny. During these first two years the plant may even try to produce grapes. Not allowed. Again, you can't have it frivolously wasting energy and you strip any grapes off. During the winter at the end of the second year you again cut the single shoot back but not as much as in the first year. Hopefully the stem will have grown to something like two metres. Cut it down to about 120 cm, take off any buds in the lower 50 cm or so and bend the top half of the remainder along the bottom wire of the trellising system you constructed earlier. You are then left with a cleaned stem and a cane with four or five buds on it, fastened down to a wire and ready to spurt heavenwards next year. The following spring the buds will burst and produce new canes with foliage and, you hope, from around sometime in May/June, flowers and then a few bunches of grapes. It was at this point, as they became more vigorous in the third year, that it became obvious that, being planted so close together to squeeze them all in, they were going to shade each other out. So I need as much sunshine on the grapes as possible to ripen them and I've planted the vines in about the shadiest bit of land we have, spaced in a manner that's going to augment the shade. (…if after a few years you decide it would have been better if you had planted them in a different place, frankly it's a bit late).

Another big mistake, once we got beyond the second year, was the way I went about the pruning. I was nowhere near robust enough and they finished up looking more like rose bushes than grapevines. As a vine is maturing each year it will become more vigorous and thus has the capacity to produce more foliage, especially a vine like Solaris that 'has very strong growth requiring a lot of summer leaf work'. It's always a battle between me and the vine. The vine doesn't want to produce grapes, it just wants to grow. If you leave it to its own devices it will mostly produce canes and foliage rather than grapes. Only when it's stressed will it start to produce, in any quantity, the grapes I want it to produce. At that point it's programmed to 'think', "Help, I might die, I'd better spawn some seeds for the next generation" and grapes proliferate. Left on its own the plant is happy to produce more and more foliage throughout the growing season and you need to keep on top of it.

Additionally, you need to go about it in the correct manner. Vines should be pruned into a very thin hedge, maybe a metre and a half tall. This has two advantages, firstly the grape bunches are always on the outside and so get the full benefit of the sun. Secondly, as you will always get plant diseases in vineyards and in the UK mildews are common, a thin hedge allows the sun (or the wind) to get in and dry the leaves, thus helping to prevent the mildew. Despite Solaris needing 'a lot of summer leaf work' I didn't have the nerve to be severe enough and left much too much foliage on because I thought I would damage or even kill the plants – but this meant that whatever the grape bunches the vine could be bothered producing were mostly shaded out by the leaves. I need as much sunshine on the grapes as possible to ripen them and I've planted the vines in about the shadiest bit of land we have spaced in a manner that's going to augment the shade, and I then prune them in a way to create even more shade. You can sum up my attempts during these early years as, whilst I should have been doing whatever I could to get the sun onto the grapes to ripen them, I was inadvertently doing everything I could to keep them in the shade.

One final thing about this bank, it's full of hogweed. Thankfully it wasn't giant hogweed, the sap of which can produce a very nasty burn. No just ordinary, run of the mill hogweed. Ordinary, run of the mill hogweed is 'just' a skin irritant but that's something else I didn't know. If the sap gets onto your skin, particularly on a sunny day, there is likely to be a reaction and for the next week or so you will have a mildly irritating rash that you keep wanting to rub. I'd obliterated the weeds when I built the terraces before the start of the growing season and before the hogweed was active, and I've previously given myself a half tick for 'almost ploughing'. But the weeds had been established on that bank for decades and were deep rooted, so despite my efforts they eventually came back as strong as ever. I wanted to keep the grass down, together with anything else trying to grow near the vines, so that there's no competition for nutrients, etc. As the weeds started to grow back I realised that I'd have to keep strimming regularly to keep them down (ironic payback for all the years I hadn't bothered and let the 'wild garden' grow rampant?). In the summer I'm more or less always in shorts and short-sleeved shirt when I'm working outside and, thus attired, I set about the weeds one afternoon. The next morning I found out what ordinary, run of the mill hogweed does, waking up scratching everywhere that had been exposed and realising what had happened. However, the weeds have to be kept down and the bank requires regular strimming. It's hard work and it's usually warm. I have to dress up like a bee keeper when I do it, long trousers, long sleeved shirt, hat, goggles, gloves. The rows are planted too close together and I keep banging into the posts and getting the strimmer caught on the wires. The terraces are narrow and slippery if damp and I've yet to find a strimmer that feeds out the thread without getting constantly jammed. I hate it. If I sometimes left it too long and allowed too much competition than was healthy for the development of the vines, I plead that I'm only human.

So overall I've not done very well, though that wasn't evident for the first couple of years. Indeed, as far as I could see the first two years went as they should and at the start of the third year the original twenty-five vines were looking fit and well, tied down on the trellis wires and already producing that season's canes and foliage, waiting for me to mismanage the pruning. The second tranche of fifty, one year behind, had had their first year's growth amputated but were growing again as required. Despite my mismanagement, in that third year grapes appeared on the original vines and, with a decent summer as regards weather, they even kindly ripened. Eventually, I decided they were ready for harvest and I set about this, a task that didn't take long. Growing the grapes is, of course, only the first half of the process. You then have to pull off the somewhat tricky skill of turning your raw grape juice into wine, preferably the drinkable kind. Solaris produces white wine, much easier to make than red wine (no, I didn't know the two processes were different then either). Basically, with white wine you squash the grapes, ferment the juice and, hey presto, x months later you bottle it and you have your wine. Okay, I'm vastly simplifying a very skilled process but broadly, those are the main steps. Anyway, I had my harvest in and first we had to extract the juice from the grapes and, not having any equipment, and we were doing this for fun anyway, we decide to tread them in the age-old traditional fashion. I bought a brand-new plastic dustbin, disinfected then washed everything and was washing my feet in preparation when in walks Elinor. She's now eleven, by the way.

"What you doin', dad?"

"I'm washing my feet so that they will be nice and clean when I stand in that bin and squash those grapes so that we will have grape juice."

"Can I have a go, dad?"

I can't see why not, but she's in her school clothes and I say okay, but you'll have to take your tights and skirt off and wash your feet really well. This she does, in she gets, and she has great fun doing a good job. I take a picture to show Morag later. We look at it that evening. A happy child who just happens to be tramping grapes in her knickers. Child labour exploitation or even worse?

When we'd produced the juice I strained it off, then we needed a vessel to ferment it in. It needed to be air tight, just the right size so that there was no free air in the top of the container and something that I could stopper with a bung. The bung would have an airlock fitted through it, so that the carbon dioxide gas produced by the fermentation process could escape without letting fresh air in. A demijohn was too big because it would leave free air in the top (that's maybe a clue to the size of the harvest) and I managed to rig something up with an empty lemonade bottle (another clue). It worked, and six months later we bottled our first batch of wine, all two bottles of it. However, it was two bottles from the grapes in our field and a few weeks later we did indeed go to a dinner party with wine, "from the vineyard." It was alright, not brilliant but drinkable, about 10.5% alcohol by volume, quite respectable and people didn't have a sip and surreptitiously drain it into the nearest plant pot. We found a do-it-yourself wine labelling system and made it look quite presentable, and if we put the year it was bottled on the label as the vintage, rather than the year in which it was harvested as should have been, it was all part of the learning process. AND IT WAS WINE FROM OUR FIELD!!

Two bottles wasn't very much wine but it was a start and I wasn't despondent. The vines were looking healthy and production should increase in the years following. By the next harvest the second wave of fifty more vines should also produce some grapes and the original twenty-five should be stronger and so provide a better yield. For the next four, five, six or more years the vines should get stronger year by year and, weather and other hazards permitting, should produce steadily increasing harvests of grapes. Things would improve. Also, by this time I had found a couple more vineyards in North Wales and tasted their very pleasant and drinkable wine, which was encouraging because it meant that Andrew's wine wasn't some fluke of a micro-climate in his garden and meant that wine production in North Wales seemed perfectly feasible.

However, the following year the combination of a poor summer and my vine management skills kept production down to the same two bottle level as the previous year. And the year after that, despite all seventy-five vines now looking strong and healthy (foliage all over the place) production wasn't looking any better. Indeed, when I did the harvest that year I could see that there wasn't even enough grapes that had actually ripened to produce even two bottles (I'm an old hand, I can calculate a two bottle harvest with just a glance). This is the fifth year, the family is getting justifiably sceptic and I don't want to totally lose face. Everybody is out when I do the harvest so, after assessing the miserly bounty, I sneak off to the local supermarket and buy some extra grapes and bung them in the mix. When the family get home I hold up the now familiar lemonade bottle contraption.

"Look, two bottles again this year!"

The Wider Picture III:
The Expansion of Vineyards in the UK

When I first started to arrange vineyard tours in 2018 I used to explain to the attendees how the UK vineyard sector was expanding and tell people that in the spring of that year there had been more than one million new vines planted in the UK. I would then say that was a huge number for this country and I would then follow up with, "...and there will be another million planted next spring." Move forward a year and the equivalent figure for 2019 turned out to be over three million. Put together these two years represent about a forty percent increase of the acreage under vines in the UK. In two years! We can be fairly confident of these figures because if you plant more than 0.1 of a hectare of vines, by law you have to tell Defra, so these are the returns reported to Defra and likely to be accurate. The number of vineyards in the UK has correspondingly increased and now stands at over 800, a figure I think most people will find surprising. It tends to be common knowledge that there are vineyards in the UK, but more than 800 (and some in Scotland!)? It's irrefutable that this expansion is being facilitated mostly by climate change but the speed at which it is happening is astonishing.

Everybody seems to believe that the Romans first planted vineyards in Britain. Urban myth or truth? Almost certainly truth but the extent and level of success achieved are perhaps questionable. They certainly enjoyed drinking the stuff, as is evidenced by the amount of wine paraphernalia that is uncovered by archaeological excavations concentrating on that time period. Whether they drank home produced wine or imported most of it is more contentious. Certainly, you can imagine that if they had imported their wine drinking habits and were importing wine to satisfy them then at some point they would have attempted to produce their own grapes, if only to improve the supply line and make life easier. Whether those first vineyards flourished or were eventually defeated by the climate is difficult to ascertain. I've read suggestions that mostly the home grown grapes of that period were thought to be used to produce drinks fortified with other liquors or mainly for mead like beverages.

Throughout the following centuries there is sporadic evidence of vineyards being established in Britain, vineyards attached to monasteries is a common theme. But there is little evidence of vineyards becoming widespread and well established in our climate. A high point was after the Norman Conquest, the Doomsday book records several dozen vineyards in Britain, which coincided with a brief period of climatic warming. But after that time the climate reverted to type and the home wine industry more or less petered out. True, there might have been other reasons over the centuries for the decline, the Black Death, the Dissolution of the Monasteries, growing ease of importing wine from France and Spain. I'm not trying to give you a history lesson (though if you are interested there is very well researched account of the history of UK vineyards from Roman times onwards on the WineGB website). My point is that throughout our history whenever people have been valiantly inclined to try to establish vineyards in this country they have eventually failed and that's usually been because of the climate. As we get closer to modern day times there are more examples.

As the British Empire expanded and opportunities for trade amplified this country became more prosperous. A class of 'super-rich' entrepreneurs and merchants was established and they demonstrated their wealth by building superb houses and developing large and impressive country estates. Some got the idea in their heads to also plant a vineyard. I can relate to that! I mean, it had to be about the fun of it, didn't it? Maybe, like me, a bit of vanity? They weren't short of a bob or two. If they wanted to drink wine they could have all they wanted by just sending a footman to the local wine merchants, or even a boat across to France. Maybe, like me, they wanted to go to dinner round at their mates and take wine from their vineyard, to general appreciation and envy? They were people with plenty of money to allow them to indulge their fantasies and they had no problem initially planting and establishing their vineyards. But when it comes to the rub the pesky grapes don't ripen properly in some, most or all of the years. The vineyards at Painshill

Park in Cobham, Surrey and that of Lord Bute in Castel Coch in South Wales are often mentioned in this context. Maybe it was not just climate, but climate was always a problem and if you have other problems (like being fed up of throwing money at a venture that is producing only sporadic results) it often tips the balance. Some managed to continue for decades but all eventually failed ...until relatively recently.

After the second world war there was a revival in UK vineyard fortunes, albeit a slow one. Two of the original and most famous vineyards established in that period were those planted in Hambledon and Beaulieu in the fifties and it would be fair to say that they came into the previous category of landowners with the financial wherewithal to indulge their ambitious passion. But then in the nineteen sixties and seventies a different trend started to be established. People from all kinds of diverse backgrounds started planting vineyards, for all kinds of reasons: for fun, for commercial gain, for a lifestyle change. You can imagine Tom and Barbara in The Good Life so doing (I remember a plot line about some very alcoholic elderflower wine). And you have to reason that somewhere in the thinking of all of these pioneers is the underlying notion of, "Wouldn't it be fun to own a vineyard?"

And then something remarkable happened that had rarely (if ever) occurred in the previous two millennia: some of the vineyards started to flourish. Not all, some fell by the wayside: wrong site, wrong vine variety, wrong methods, change of heart, life. But many, with new methods, new vine varieties, new knowledge and above all a slowly improving climate, began to succeed and by the end of the nineteen seventies there was a small, struggling and often ridiculed British wine industry.

Throughout the eighties and nineties we see more new entrants, more land planted, wine production rising but more importantly more successes and a steadily enhanced reputation for British wine. By 2005 there were about three hundred and fifty vineyards in the UK but then things really started to take off, not just an increase from that number to today's eight hundred plus but also a quadrupling of vine acreage and a fivefold increase in the number of bottles produced. And not only is the wine industry expansion gaining momentum but this is going hand in hand with increasing quality and an increased worldwide reputation for British wines. I've explained previously that I believe climate change to be a looming disaster on the global scale but for the British wine industry it's been more of a godsend.

It's one thing to think about this in the abstract, what does it really mean down on the ground in the vineyards? Here are two examples of what I'm talking about, the first a delightful story perfectly illustrating much of the above. Renishaw Hall in northeast Derbyshire, a stone's throw from Sheffield, has been the family seat of the Sitwells for almost four hundred years. The most famous of the family was Dame Edith Sitwell, renown novelist and poet, who the family happily describe as grandly eccentric. You might think that the eccentric genes popped up again in 1972 when the then head of the family Sir Reresby Sitwell, with great aplomb, decided to plant what was then officially recognised as the most northerly vineyard in the world. Wonderful! It seems to me it's one thing to plant vineyards in the UK in the second and third decades of the twenty first century, as global warming provides a climate more conducive to making UK vineyards viable. It's another thing entirely to have planted as far north as Derbyshire in the early seventies. A true a pioneer of this industry – and I can't help but imagining him having just woken up one morning and thinking, "wouldn't it be fun to have a vineyard here in Derbyshire," and then just getting on with it. However, I've said before that it's easy to grow vines here in the UK but often the problem is getting the grapes to ripen.

Move on a few years to when the vines mature and I'm afraid that was what happened here. The Renishaw Hall vineyard produced wine but, they are the first to admit, it was of dubious quality (which is a nice way of saying, "awful"). Sir Reresby did indeed enjoy producing it for friends at dinner parties and much of it was served to house guests. But current owner, daughter Alexandra Sitwell who inherited the estate on her father's death in 2009, remembers standing behind him as he offered it to his fellow diners, indicating that they shouldn't touch it. Sir Reresby stoically insisted that it was fine with a drop of gin in it.

But they persisted. Over the decades, new methods, different varieties, new knowledge and, above all, a slowly improving climate and if we fast forward to today the picture is completely different.

Renishaw Hall Vineyard is flourishing, producing and selling about ten thousand bottles a year. And not just producing wine but producing medal-winning still and sparkling wine, winning awards in blind tastings, being compared favourably to famous Champagne houses. Ten thousand bottles a year, award winning wines, being compared favourably to famous Champagne houses, in northeast Derbyshire. Wow, compare that to forty odd years ago! Alexandra Sitwell says that her father would have been delighted and felt vindicated (Hear! Hear!). And it provides the perfect illustration of what wasn't possible in the nineteen seventies but is now.

The second story also illustrates what it now possible. Halfpenny Green Wine Estate (which also appears later in the story) is in rolling countryside a few miles south west of Wolverhampton which, like Sheffield, is not usually associated with vineyards and of which any industry mentioned is unlikely to be associated with wine. The estate at Halfpenny Green Wine is truly impressive. It was started by Martin Vickers, who in 1983 planted a half acre vineyard in a field in Staffordshire. The estate into which it eventually blossomed is now overseen by him, son Clive and his stepson Ben. Again, it's one thing to plant vineyards in the UK in the second and third decades of the twenty first century as the climate change provides a more favourable environment. It's another thing entirely to have planted so far north at that time, in this case in the early eighties in Staffordshire. Another true pioneer. Halfpenny Green these days boasts seven vineyards spread over thirty acres. The complex is a cross between an upmarket garden centre and a stylish country restaurant, with shops, delicatessen and tasting area. There are also a dozen or so independent craft shops and for good measure, a petting zoo and a fishing lake. Just as remarkable is the winery. They've invested more than a million pounds in the wine making operation and now produce more than fifty thousand own label bottles a year, winning many regional national and international awards in the process; together with making wine to order for fifty or so other vineyards. And that's all been done in the last forty years or so, starting with half an acre (much the same as I've planted here on Anglesey!).

I asked Martin what motivated him to set out on this, on the face of it, rather daunting venture.

"I just wanted to try," he said. Halfpenny Green was a farm in those days. Martin explained that he had always had an interest in wine in general and living and working on a farm he started making country wines from hedgerow fruit, usually sloes, blackberries and damsons.

"This went well up to a point but I began to realise that only wine grapes contain everything you need for wine, all other fruits require things like water, sugar and yeasts." So why not try the real thing? In 1983 a corner of one of the arable fields on the farm became available, south west facing and free draining. He took advice (freely given) from another pioneer, Tom Day from Three Choirs in Gloucestershire and planted 300 vines. Nothing more than a serious hobby really – but it worked out. At that point I'm guessing that his farmer's head combined with the enjoyment of the hobby and they decided to plant a few more vines and (despite the name, not doing things by halves) at some point the vision to create a vineyard on a par with continental estates formed. By 1991 (not doing things by halves) a further twenty two acres had been planted. And it carried on working. And now we have Halfpenny Green Wine Estate, a vineyard that can more than stand its own with any continental site.

Vineyards flourishing in Staffordshire, northeast Derbyshire, Anglesey (and even Scotland). What is the wine world coming to? And this is a microcosm, a couple of examples I've picked, one because it so much reflects what I've been talking about and the other because of, as you shall see, personal experience. There are dozens more, pioneers that now have wine estates that match those in any of the major wine growing regions. Three Choirs was mentioned above; Camel Valley in Cornwall; Ridgeview in Sussex; Denbies in Surrey; to mention but a few. And there are now also literally hundreds of smaller but very successful vineyards, all adding to the rich tapestry of the wine industry in the UK.

Planting a vineyard has a centuries old magical fascination that has never lost its sparkle and I offer my heartfelt appreciation to all who throughout the years have tried. Many might have failed but as you have seen, less so in more recent times, and I know that if it hadn't been for all those wonderful pioneers I wouldn't be enjoying my own modest adventure. But a cautionary last word from winemaker Kieron Atkinson, who since 2012 has overseen the success of Renishaw Hall.

"It's a real homegrown success story. It's a story of an industry that's now producing wines that are top quality and can compete with wines from around the world. In 40 years time, it will be warm enough to grow full-bodied red wine here, like cabernet sauvignon and merlot. As a winemaker, that's exciting. As a human, it's scary."

CHAPTER 6

A House in Spain

We own half of a small townhouse in Alora (if you remember from the Introduction, the town near where Paqui's land is situated), which is how come we manage to be there so often, how we know so many people there and why I was confident I could manage planting and maintaining a vineyard there whilst still living in the UK. We bought the house together with another couple in 2005 and whilst it's not been as straightforward you might expect, I've never once regretted it. I'm not bragging or griping, it's brought us a great deal of pleasure and the problems of owning even half of a small second home in Spain won't elicit or deserve much sympathy. Alora and the house there are simply part of the story.

Early in 2004 Morag suggested that we go on holiday that summer. I was a bit bemused and didn't really know what she was getting at, we went on holiday every year, usually twice. Often we would go back to Dorset, which I still loved and where I still had many friends; sometimes we went to Scotland to stay with her brother; or mid-Wales, where my sister and family had a caravan. We'd also been to a few other places in the UK and even went to Ireland on honeymoon (from Anglesey, an easy boat hop over the Irish Sea).

"What do you mean? We always go on holiday," I said.

"No," she said, "I mean on a proper holiday. Get on a plane and go to the Mediterranean or something." Well, there's a novel idea!

"Why not, I suppose." We'd just never considered it as a family thing before. I hadn't been on a plane since the last time I went to Nepal five years earlier and at which point, after the best part of a decade travelling between there and the UK, I guess

I was subconsciously 'travelled out'. It's not that I was against the idea, more that in the last five years there had been two new babies, living in a new part of the country, a new house, a wedding and a new career (well, new way of earning a living).

Life had been a bit full on and such a thing as 'a holiday in the sun' had never crossed my mind and, I guess, not crossed Morag's either. She had previously lived four years in Canada and seven in Jamaica. In Canada for her a break from work was to go skiing or kayaking in The Rockies. In Jamaica her holidays consisted of jaunts such as diving trips to Cuba. At the time that I had met her she had research projects under way in Nepal, Ghana and Costa Rica (perfect academic career, all travel and research and no students and teaching to worry about!). For the first years we were together she was travelling between Bangor and these three places, trying to cut trips down the shortest time possible so that she wasn't away from the children for too long (and thus finally having to engage with students and teaching). We'd been travelling, done that. New house, babies, stability; it was great. Who needed to go anywhere? But nonetheless yes, what an idea. This year let's get on a plane and go for a holiday to somewhere warm and sunny.

And so we did, we got on a plane and went to Spain. Neither of us much fancied the idea of a beach holiday so we chose to rent the annex of an old farmhouse in the countryside close to the small town of Santa Pau, in Girona, northern Spain. We did lots of very ordinary things that tourists with young families do; visiting places, sightseeing, walking (children in backpacks), eating and drinking. It was brilliant and we loved it, why hadn't we thought of this before? We definitely have to do this again.

Shortly after we returned I 'won' £1,100 on the premium bonds. At the last bank that had employed me, the one in Dorset, the department I worked in had a premium bond syndicate and when I left I dutifully kept paying in my monthly ten quid. Eventually they decided to disband the syndicate and when they got in touch I was pleased to find that my share was £1,100. I should say that about £1050 of that was the money I'd been paying in over the years, we didn't actually win many prizes but whatever, it was a nice surprise. Morag's birthday is in November so I thought after our holiday in Spain a great birthday present that year would be to use some of the 'winnings' to pay for another holiday, a week of winter sun somewhere. I looked around and Tenerife in January seemed perfect. The island is warm enough in January, university term didn't start until the middle of the month, Elinor wasn't yet at school so we could avoid school holidays, which meant the rental was really cheap; as were flights and even, as Lili was not yet two, she went for nothing (those were the days). So we went, did much the same sort of things as we had done in Santa Pau, and Tenerife was brilliant as well.

Towards the end of this second holiday we were walking round one of the more tourist centric coastal towns and I looked into the window of an estate agent. Just curious as to what was there, a fairly normal trait of the property-owning class.

"Gosh, they're not cheap are they?" I said, "but wouldn't it be great to own a property somewhere near the Mediterranean, to be able to visit whenever we wanted?" I was conscious of my change in attitude. This time last year the thought of going on to a hot country for a holiday could not have been further from my mind. Two holidays in Spain and I've gone from not being on plane for five years to wanting a house abroad and hopping on the plane every few months. Morag agreed that it would be nice but pointed out some of the many impracticalities, not least the cost and that she had an employer that generally liked her to be in attendance Monday to Friday, even if my work was a bit more haphazard. And there was the small matter of two children that needed looking after and soon schooling. Also, it's not that everything in the estate agent's window was way above what we could afford, most of the properties there were so far above what we could ever imagine affording that it was a pipedream, a lottery winning fantasy. Nice idea though, we agreed.

However, I may have gone on about it a bit over the next few days, probably at times when we were drinking wine. Somehow a ten year plan emerged and we agreed that okay, we now liked going on holiday abroad so let's try and do that once a year (such élan) and over the next ten years go to as many different places as possible. Then after ten years we'll choose the place we liked best and we'll try to buy a house there, if by some miracle we could afford it by then. At least it was a plan, even if the goal was a little distant. From Morag's point of view, she was perhaps getting fed up of me talking about it so much and this kicked it into the longest of grass to shut me up for a bit. Five months later our offer for the house in Alora was accepted.

I was happy that we had 'a plan' but when we returned to the UK I more or less forgot about the idea for a while. Well, a few weeks anyway. Then I started searching online for places we might like to go on holiday the following summer and we decided we liked the idea of southern Spain. Even though by then Lili was two and we had to pay for her flight, flights to Malaga were still pretty cheap outside school holidays, as was accommodation somewhere inland, which again we liked the idea of rather than the more crowded coast. I looked through the various holiday rental websites and came up with a list to show Morag. Then, of course, I couldn't resist looking at the estate agent's websites in the corresponding places. And that turned out to be a bit of a revelation. Bloody Hell! Property is unbelievably cheap in inland Andalucia. I was looking in an area broadly centred on Orgiva, where Chris Stewart's book Driving Over Lemons is famously set; in Granada Province and about two hours drive to the east of Malaga. And I was looking at two and three bedroomed houses and flats in the surrounding villages, some in the town of Orgiva itself, for less than euro 100,000; some only euro 50,000. And these were times when the pound bought you euro 1.40. So you could buy a house for around £35,000! It's not that we had £35,000 hanging around but then I thought that if we got a small mortgage it might be possible. As I write this I've checked the estate agents websites again and house prices in that region are much the same today as they were then, though you get a lot fewer euros for your pound these days. If you like the sound of this and think you might be interested just Google 'Estate Agents, Orgiva'.

Back then, when I first looked, all this all seemed incredible. For comparison I looked at prices on the coast in the areas the British usually buy property in southern Spain and the prices there were just as astronomical as in Tenerife. Why such a difference, I wondered? All these years later I still don't really know. Economists will tell you that price of anything comes down to the balance between supply and demand and if the prices were high on the coast then, in a large and mature market like housing, there must be the demand. If the prices are so cheap inland it must be because there is (much) less demand. People must place little worth on owning property in the small towns and villages? Why? To me they are delightful. However, I wasn't worried about philosophising about the economics of the property market in Spain. I was exultant. Morag! Come and have a look at this......

I then decided that I wanted to go out for a few days to have a proper look.

"But we decided last month that this was a ten year project...". Well, I know but I hadn't seen the price of these properties then, had I? Maybe it's possible that we could do it now, wouldn't that be great? Work wasn't very demanding at that time. I was again doing mostly freelance work and had a couple of contracts I was working on at home, due to be completed by Easter, still a couple of months away. There was no reason I couldn't take four or five days off over a weekend. At the end of February or early March flights were cheap; car hire was cheap; cheap hotels were cheap. I reckoned I could spend five days out there looking at property at a cost of about £150. And, oh boy, wouldn't that be fun! So I started to trawl through estate agents websites and picked a list of possibilities around Orgiva and Huescar, a small town about an hour's drive further to the east. I got in touch with the agents, made appointments for the first week in March, booked the flights and hotels in each town. Then early one morning at the end of February I was on a plane from Liverpool to Malaga. Brilliant!

The next bit I couldn't have started to imagine. It was an uneventful flight (as, thankfully, most are) and I disembarked and went through customs without incident. I picked up the hire car, no problem, a lot more straightforward then than the hassle you get at Malaga car hire desks these days. I nervously navigated the Malaga motorway system and found the right road to the east, again no real problem. It was a bit colder than I anticipated, I expected 15, maybe 20 degrees. On the plane the captain had said 10 degrees and it felt like it, I was glad I had a spare jumper. I remember driving along the motorway away from Malaga, once I was sure I was on the right road, feeling pretty pleased with myself, not bothering much about the dark clouds ahead – a bit unfortunate if it rained but sunny tomorrow with a bit of luck.

I carried on driving and, bloody hell, it's snowing! It doesn't snow in southern Spain. Yes, in the mountains of the Sierra Nevada but not at sea level. And this isn't a bit of a snow flurry, suddenly it's snowing really hard and traffic is crawling along. I can't stop (and what? Sit there on the hard shoulder!) so I carry on being as careful as I can. Soon, the road is like the M62 over the Pennines in the blizzard we were once caught in. All the traffic is in the inside lane in a long slow line and there's a thick covering of snow in the outside lane. Please, everybody be sensible and nobody make any mistakes and crash. This carried on for about half an hour but thankfully after five miles or so we're back in sunshine and the roads are clear again. I found out later that I was one of the last through that section of motorway before it was closed for the night (and then where would I have gone?). However, I was able to carry on, there was a bit more snow later but nothing like as bad as that first storm and I eventually got to Huescar and found my hotel, relieved to end a journey I wouldn't want to repeat in a hurry.

Later that night a twenty-four-hour blizzard started (in southern Spain!). I woke up the next morning and it's snowing again, really heavy snow and the strong wind is blowing it horizontal. It snows all day and the town is cut off. I should point out that Huescar isn't some hill village on the side of a mountain with steep roads in and out. It's a mid-sized town in the middle of a wide valley with flat roads spiralling out in all directions. The snow is just so all-encompassing that all surrounding roads are impassable, blocked by deep drifts. I'm supposed to be on my first day driving around the sunny countryside of southern Spain looking at houses and I can barely get to the end of the street. I do go to the end of the street and walk fifty metres past the last house. I turn around and the snow is so thick that I can't see the house I've just passed. In my younger days I did some winter walking in The Cairngorms and I've been in whiteouts where you are just submerged in snow and mist and cloud. You can't distinguish anything, it's just white – and this is the same. On the television that night there are pictures of frozen water fountains in Madrid, minus seven degrees there. I couldn't then speak any Spanish at all but over the course of the next few days when I met British people they told me it was the first time it had snowed, or it was the worst storm for 50 / 75 / 100 years (depending on who you spoke to – I now know quite a few ex-pats in Spain and, though almost all are very pleasant people, many have a tendency to exaggerate or pick the most sensationalist line). Because of the maritime climate in Anglesey it hardly ever snows on the island. In the twenty years I've lived there, much to the children's chagrin, in Pentraeth we have only had enough snow to make a snowman three times. My first day in southern Spain and you could build bloody igloos if you wanted.

Fortunately, the snow didn't hang around for days like it does in the UK and, once the tap is turned off and the sun comes out, it melts and life returns to normal pretty quickly. On my second morning in Huescar there was still snow about but the temperature was rising and it was fast melting. I managed to get in touch with the estate agent I should have met the previous day (he assumed I wasn't coming and had turned his phone off) and we managed to meet and we were able to go and have a look at a few houses, though but not as many as I had hoped as he wasn't expecting me. Whilst it was good to finally get to look at some houses there was nothing that I could see us committing to. I soon realised that, of course, if you are looking at houses that are the cheapest on the market there's always going to be something wrong with them. Maybe I should have thought of this earlier? In the end the Huescar leg of this trip was pretty disappointing and didn't get me any further forward with this project, probably not surprising given the chaos caused by the weather.

The next day I moved on to Orgiva and things perked up. Orgiva is a bustling market town, provincial capital of the Alpujarra region, close to the Sierra Nevada mountains. There were lots of bars, restaurants and pavement cafes and it was large enough to have all the facilities you might need; small enough to walk everywhere. It felt like the kind of small Spanish town I had imagined. In contrast to the previous two days, all the arrangements went smoothly and I was able to view about a dozen properties in the two days I was there. But they were again a disappointment and the feeling I'd had in Huescar that maybe I had pitched this badly resurfaced. I was probably expecting too much anyway. Yes, there were houses at the prices I had seen on the websites but they could be very small (poky, not cosy); 'bedrooms' could be in corridors;

houses could be squeezed up side streets with no outdoor space; apartments in decrepit buildings, town houses that needed work or needed a lot of work; on main roads or in the middle of nowhere, etc., etc. What did I expect at those prices?

Interest sparked a little when I was shown around a cave house near Guadix, famous for such dwellings. These are houses literally hewn into the rock. In the right landscape you buy land near an escarpment and literally quarry out the space you need into the cliff face, in days gone by with a pickaxe, these days with a JCB with specialist kit. You can make them as big as you like, just dig into the solid rock, it's not going to collapse. Then you simply build internal walls and cover the hole at the front with a brick house façade. I thought these had wonderful character, many northern Europeans do. But in Spain they are considered sub-standard housing, traditionally build by poor people who were despairing of finding somewhere to live and were desperate enough to try digging a hole into a cliff. Many non-Spanish people bought them (turning the back of the cave into a small private cinema was then very trendy) but the estate agent explained that you had to pay cash. In Spain they were thought so poorly of that none of the financial organisations would accept them for a mortgage, and it was becoming increasingly obvious that if by any chance we did manage to do this, it would have to be with a mortgage of some form. I went back to the UK for a re-think.

I still believed we were on to something and could make this work but the figures now seemed tantalizingly out of reach. Whilst it had been a revelation to find a desirable region where property was relatively cheap, it was clear that we would have to spend more money than had seemed the case before I went to look, and more than we could reasonably cobble together even if some of it was provided by the kind of mortgage we could afford. I then had the idea that maybe we could buy a house jointly with somebody else. If it was somewhere to go for only a month or two a year, surely we could arrange a schedule to avoid each other or, even better, go together, assuming we would only go into partnership for something of this magnitude with somebody else if we thought we liked them enough to go on holiday with them anyway. I send an email to a few friends, but it seemed a bit of a longshot. However, Antony and Ania quickly replied. They had been thinking about buying a property abroad, weren't sure what to do about it, didn't have time to research it. If I'd done the groundwork they were definitely interested. Wonderful, game back on!

I had known Antony and Ania for about twenty five years and was very comfortable with the idea of going into a venture like this with them (and it seemed, they with us). We talked, I told them what I'd been up to and we hatched another plan. We decided that we would look for possible places on the internet and then go out in June to look at them. After a bit more research we thought that we would go back to the area around Orgiva and also have a look at Competa, a picturesque mountain town of which we had all heard. Then we spent a couple of hours trawling through websites of various towns, looking for inspiration for a third place to visit, and eventually coming across Alora, whose only difference from the other twenty or thirty places we'd just viewed was that it had a small castle. Weary of the search and for the want of any other obvious candidates, we put it on the list. At least it would provide the contrast of an 'ordinary' town to the more well known towns of Orgiva and Competa that we were getting quite excited about.

So June found the group of us once more in Orgeva looking at properties there and in the celebrated surrounding smaller communities, Lanjaron, Bubion and Trevelez. However, it was once again a disappointment. Even with the increased spending power of now being two couples, none of the properties we looked at in Orgiva seemed right. And, though the surrounding villages were lovely to visit, they were a fair distance into the mountains, fine for walking but a heck of a trek from the airports and to go and do some proper food shopping. And the local economy seemed based mostly on attracting tourists to buy things in the daytime and it would likely be pretty quiet at night. We (definitely) weren't looking for the Costa del Sol type disco night life but somewhere with maybe a restaurant or two; a few bars and places where you would meet the people you would hopefully get to know; a few shops and services, maybe the occasional local fiesta or pageant?

However, we had great hopes for Competa. It was a reasonably sized town, about 4000 inhabitants, not too big and not too small. We had seen from maps that there were maybe half a dozen bars and restaurants, food shops, banks, proper facilities, and we'd also seen on the internet that it was, for want of a better word, a 'picturesque' place; several churches, squares, fountains and a market. It was also a gateway to the mountains with many walking routes starting and ending in the town. And only seventy kilometres from the airport. We thus set off one morning with great expectation. We drove down to the coast, along the A7 to Torrox and then turned up the A7207 towards the clearly signed Competa, fifteen kilometres away. And then we drove and we drove and we drove. Second gear, third gear, second gear, third gear, fourth gear for a hundred metres; third again, straight back to second, hairpin left, hairpin right, hairpin back left again. A well maintained road but tedious, tedious, tedious. Not a problem if you are on day out going somewhere, all part of the experience, but every time you wanted to leave the town the only way out was to go back to the coast along the road we had just negotiated or a similar one roughly parallel; and then every time you wanted to return you did it again in reverse. It seems a bit trite, if it's really a great place you can't be put off just because the access road is a bit of a pain. Well, yes you could. We had the whole of southern Spain to work with. Why choose to make life difficult?

I was starting to think along those lines when, forty minutes later (forty minutes to do ten miles!) we finally reached Competa and I didn't want to be negative but, it turned out as we discussed it later when Ania had recovered from her car sickness, the others had thoughts along similar lines. The shine had already gone off the place as we walked around though, it was indeed lovely. A traditional white walled Spanish town with narrow cobbled streets that opened into cheerful plazas, neat houses with balconies and much greenery, little shops and several larger more ornate buildings. Eventually we arrived at the estate agents but communication had obviously gone awry somewhere and it didn't seem as though they were expecting us; which resulted in a hushed argument between them as to who was taking us out and which properties they would show us. When they finally decided on what to do with us the places they showed us were, let's say, unimpressive and the general ambience wasn't helped by the agent continually moaning about how badly his colleagues had treated us. So, it didn't really go well at all and we went home disappointed, another high hope crossed off the list.

I thought the area I'd previously visited round Huescar was still a possibility and Morag and I did go to have another look but we quickly discounted it. Apart from being in the middle of nowhere it's on the edge of the only proper desert in Europe, not obvious in the snow but very evident by June, and the countryside and small villages around looked like places where somebody who liked solitude would be very happy. Which only left Alora, the 'ordinary' place that was to provide a bit of depth to our 'research' so that we could compare it to the places we were really interested in. We didn't have much hope but we've arranged things so let's go and look before we once more retreated to the UK to think again. Of course, Alora turned out to be a little gem.

I have to say that as we first approached the town it didn't look promising (perhaps we had sub-consciously convinced ourselves that we were unlikely to like it because of our experiences to date and our low expectations). The castle that had first attracted us on the internet looked quite puny in real life; more a cowboy and Indians fort and not at all like our local massive North Wales castles in Caernarvon, Conwy and Harlech. And my first impression as we drove into the main bit of the town was that it felt a little nondescript. But now I know it better I would say 'unpretentious' and I would say that was one of its best qualities. The setting was definitely striking, the town stands on three hills, one for the castle, one for a small church and one for a beacon that guides aircraft into Malaga airport, forty kilometres to the south. The hills are in turn are dominated by the El Hacho mountain that rises to about two thousand feet, towering over everything. The old part of the town with the castle predominate is a traditional pueblo blanco, one of the white walled villages that are a common feature of southern Spain. As well as the castle, within this ancient quarter you can't miss the imposing and very ornate Catholic Church of Nuestra Señora de la Encarnación which, excluding the ninety nine years it took to build, is over three hundred years old and supposedly, except for the cathedral in Malaga, the biggest church in the province. Miguel Cervantes, author of Don Quixote, lived in a house in what is now the church plaza for several years as the church was being built. The castle itself reflects the history of the area, built by the Phoenicians, extended by the Romans, destroyed by the Visigoths and rebuilt by the Moors before the Catholic reconquest of Ferdinand and Isabella in the last years of the fifteenth century. Although, at the time we first visited, it was being used as the local cemetery and was a bit scruffy and badly maintained, but the views were stunning.

The town grew slowly during the twentieth century and over the years has expanded northwards, where you will find the commercial centre and where most of the population of about seven thousand now live. If the buildings here are not as old as those round the castle they make for a comfortable, small Spanish town with plazas full of tables and umbrellas, bars, restaurants and many small shops. It's lively at the right times of day, in the morning and evening people congregate all over the place, but never overcrowded unless there's a festival on and dead as you like during the traditional afternoon siesta, still largely adhered to. The town is surrounded by a countryside of vivid and distinct colours and sits high above the Rio Guadalhorce, whose permanently verdant valley floor gives sharp contrast to the brown burn of the rest of the landscape in the summer bake. Beyond the river valley are many mountains and there are abundant walking routes in both the mountains and in the surrounding countryside, so that's one box definitely ticked. We start to really like the feel of Alora as we realise that it has lots of cultural character and lots of physical character, natural and manmade and the 'nondescript' feel was starting to morph into something more like 'pleasantly understated'. After a couple of hours walking about we started to become comfortable with the idea that this small but historic country town could become our base in Spain.

And we realised that it had a couple of other things going for it as well. Not only is it only forty kilometres from the airport, only half an hour on good roads by car, but you can get from the airport by train. One every hour, early morning until late night. This meant we wouldn't have the expense of hiring a car every time we came over. Proximity to the vibrant city of Malaga was also a bonus. And as Morag pointed out – you might have noticed one theme in this story that Morag curbs my overenthusiasm by pointing out sensible things – it was all very well we go and buy a house in a place where we would be quite happy spending our days walking and then sitting outside cafes and bars. But if we wanted the children to buy into it as they started to grow up, there had to be stuff to entertain them as well. From Alora it was just a short hop to the all the frivolities of the coast, by train or car. I had to confess that embarrassingly I had not given the children a thought as I engrossed myself in the idea of having a house in Spain. But she was right and it eventually came to pass that we got to know the coast pretty well. There's not a water park, zoo, theme park or fairground down there that we've not been to at some point; in the case of Aqualand Torremolinos and Tivoli World Benalmadena, numerous times (recommended if you have small children and are in these parts).

So we agreed that we would buy a house in Alora and, without much drama, that's what happened. We went back a couple of times but actually bought one of the houses we saw on that first day so, come that October, we were the proud co-owners of a modest, three bedroomed terrace town house on the edge of the town, overlooking the mountains referred to in The Introduction. And then we just got on with enjoying it. And as we spent more time in Alora, more and more delights that had not been obvious commenced to reveal themselves and I came to love the place and the local culture. For a start we discovered the Andalucian way of doing fiestas. They don't half like a party in Alora! At fairly frequent times each year they just close the roads, wheel out temporary bars and food stalls, put up a stage (or three) and shut down the town for mass revelry.

The first time we encountered this was when we visited the following Easter, or Semana Santa, week of Saints. Almost every night of Easter Week, but particularly Palm Sunday, Maundy Thursday and all day of Good Friday there are parades through the streets. But no wimpy Sunday School processions here. Very large and heavy floats, called tronos, each needing forty or fifty men to lift and adorned with elaborately decorated statues of Jesus and Mary, are carried round the very hilly streets. They are followed by marching bands, crowds and penitents in sinister robes. On the Thursday and Friday these are joined by the military, La Legion Espanola, with their haunting songs and rifle displays. It all comes to a head on Good Friday afternoon when the military, the bands, four of the tronos and about five thousand people all pack into the square in front of the church to watch La Despedida, the farewell of Jesus and Mary, culminating in anybody who wants to join in running, Running! the heaviest of the tronos up the steepest hill in town and back to the castle. If you are anything to do with health and safety, just don't look.

Other prominent parties are the feria in early August, when the funfair comes to town and for the best part of a week the celebrations start at 11 pm and continue all night. On La Dia de las Sopas the Ayuntamiento (local council) dishes out thousands of portions of Sopa Perota, a sort of soup/stew, to anybody who wants some. Why not? The flamenco festival celebrates a form of flamenco Malagueña invented in Alora and recognised by the gift of El Monumento al Cante Malaguena, an ornate fountain that used to dominate the main plaza but several years ago 'disappeared' during renovations and is now rumoured to be in the garden of a former Mayor. The grand parade of Romería de la Virgen de las Flores is a great way to end the summer and, the favourite of the children, the arrival of The Three Kings on Twelfth Night. This looked pretty tame by Alora standards when we first saw it; just three trailers each with a bloke in a vaguely regal costume, indicating that they were the kings. Not even horse or man drawn, just pulled by tractors. Why are all the children carrying empty plastic bags? It gets under way and each of the kings suddenly starts to shower their gifts, throwing out literally thousands of sweets to the crowd, several barrel loads on each cart. Mayhem, children running everywhere. Including ours, who took about three seconds to wise on to what was happening. What wonderful lack of sophistication, just throw a load of sweets about the streets and every child in town goes home happy.

It also soon became evident that, unlike Orgiva and especially Competa, it was well connected – and not just to the coast. Sevilla, Cordoba and Granada we knew of, all within two hour's drive but to this famous and nobly impressive Andalucian triumvirate I would unashamedly add Malaga, so often overlooked but with similar delights. You would probably also enjoy spending a while in Ronda, Antequera, Cabra or the World Heritage Site Osuna as well, all just an hour's drive. What else do you fancy that's nearby? The only natural flamingo breeding ground in Spain? The twisted limestone features of El Torcal? Prehistoric cave systems? Passion plays in an ancient bull ring in Carratraca? Add regular visits of The Vuelta de Espana (for the dramatic mountain top finishes); wine museums; Picasso's birthplace and museum in Malaga and the recently opened Pompidou Centre there and many other museums, the cathedral, castle and fortress, the historic botanical gardens and much more in this vibrant city. Since we started coming to Alora we have, and continue to, enjoyed enormously the variety this town and area has to offer. And to think I was half minded to have bought a place on the edge of a desert.

Enough of being the local tourist board rep, but two things relevant to the story should also be mentioned. The first of these actually took place way back in the nineteen twenties when the need to supply the growing city of Malaga with water was becoming an issue. A truly ambitious scheme to achieve this was hatched and unexpectedly this eventually played a part in my vineyard plans. Just to the north of the Sierra del Huma mountain, the most prominent mountain viewed from the house terrace, was the confluence of three rivers, the Rio Teba, Rio Turon and Rio Guadalhorce. The augmented Rio Guadalhorce then squeezed through a narrow gorge to exit the mountain and then continued down the valley to which it gave its name, flowing past Alora and reaching the sea in the centre of Malaga. When I say that the river squeezes through a narrow gorge, that's a bit of an understatement. I've never seen anything like this, even in The Himalayas. There are actually two linear gorges, separated by an 'inner chamber', a steep sided bowl about a kilometre in length. The gorges at either end are shear sided, each a few hundred metres in length but in places only ten metres wide and about four hundred, four hundred! metres deep. It's a truly spectacular natural phenomenon.

However, in heavy rain there used to be a build-up of water behind the gorges and consequent flooding. The village at the gorge exit is called El Chorro. In Spanish chorro means jet, both in the sense of a plane but also squirt, gush, blast, torrent, spurt, spew, erupt; all of which could be used to describe the way the water departed the narrow confines of the canyon, to the extent it was regarded as a, "danger to life and limb." When it rains in this part of Spain it can be truly phenomenal. I've known nine and a half inches to fall in six hours (they still haven't rebuilt one of the road bridges after that one). In such storms the three rivers to the north of Huma would flood very, very quickly and then hit the bottleneck of the gorge, prompting a sudden rise in water level of many metres, consequent severe flooding to the north and exiting at El Chorro like a gigantic water cannon.

So, to both resolved the water problems of expanding Malaga and the intermittent danger of 'El Chorro' it was decided to build a series of reservoirs to the north and south of the gorge. On a truly grand scale (given it was a hundred years ago) eventually four interlinked dams were constructed to the north to block the three rivers; and for good measure another three were eventually built to the south, two on the slopes of a small mountain to create a hydroelectric plant. Engineering on a scale way ahead of its time, much of the gorge labour done by specially recruited sailors, "because they were used to working hanging from ropes." All was eventually successfully completed but who could they ask to open such a momentous project? Well, it had to be the king, of course, and on 21st May 1921 King Alfonso XIII, sitting in the specially constructed Kings Seat, declared the complex open.

To help with the construction a rather precarious walkway had been built through the gorges. This was perched on the sheer sides of the cliff, a good hundred metres above the water. It was built by bolting brackets onto the wall and simply devising a way of laying a bit of concrete as a walking surface. A hand rail was then added but the path itself was only about two feet wide and remember, you are half way down a sheer cliff. I once went onto the old path and it's definitely not a comfortable feeling but nonetheless somebody had the idea that the King should walk along the path and through the gorge as part of the opening ceremony. It is not officially recorded what the King thought of this but it is rumoured to be along the lines of, "You must be bloody joking." Whatever, from that point it has forever become known as El Caminito del Rey – The Little Walk of the King. After the celebrations it was opened to the public and became a very famous tourist attraction (and Von Ryan's Express was filmed there), but it then fell into disrepair and was eventually closed in the 1980s because it was so dangerous. European funds were secured to re-build it about ten years ago and in 2015 a completely new Caminito was constructed a few feet higher than the old one, to a much better specification so that tourists would be allowed access. This has not only become another gem of the Alora locality but is now world famous and has done a considerable amount to restore the local economy after the financial crisis of 2008.

The second thing you should know about is that the best wine in Spain comes from Alora. Now that's some boast isn't it? And that isn't an idle one. In 2010 Perez Hidalgo planted a vineyard in a field outside of the town. I don't think many people noticed. He got on with things and went about his work without fuss. He acquired small premises on the edge of town, from the outside it didn't look to be more than a big shed, especially as there were no windows. I would guess he first produced wine in 2014 or 2015. I don't know, I wasn't aware of it. A while later I started to hear a bit of talk about a bodega in Alora. Everybody knew where it was because it was easy to describe the location. "The last building on the left as you leave the town going up the hill on the way to Fuente Higera." Not much seemed to happen there and the single door in the windowless façade wasn't very inviting. I was interested enough to ask in local shops for local wine but was usually offered Vina Malaga, a sort of sherry, or wines from Ronda, about 75 miles away, where there are many vineyards. I was told that you could go to the bodega but I didn't. I was also told you could buy the wine in El Cortes Ingles in Malaga; which was impressive as El Cortes Ingles is sort of the John Lewis of Spain. Then out of the blue it was given an award as the best wine in Spain.

There is a well respected wine guide in Spain called Los Supervinos. It has the very sensible and practical mission of judging all the wines in Spain available in supermarkets. That is, the wines ordinary people can afford and drink. In the category of wine under euro fifteen a bottle (this wine only costs euro seven) it judged the wine of Perez Hidalgo of Alora to be the best in Spain. Not only that, it awarded the wine its top classification of five lynx eyes (a somewhat bizarre form of categorisation), the first time for three years such an award had been made. Incredible, wine from the little bodega in Alora was the best in Spain. Cue much deserved local pomp and ceremony, newspapers, TV, pictures with the mayor and these days there are coachloads of tourists up from the coast, stopping at the little shed to hear the story and taste the wine. And I promise you, it's very good wine.

Alora has been a joy and I've never tired of it. Fifteen years on I still look forward to every trip, often taken on the flimsiest of pretexts, with delight and expectation. In 2016, when I started the quest to plant a vineyard there we had been enjoying this part of Andalucia for over a decade, I knew lots of people there, spoke the language to an extent and thought I knew my way around. With inspiration from the bodega, planting a vineyard there seemed, if not a perfect plan, certainly a reasonable one.

The Wider Picture IV:
Sustainable Vineyards

Viniculture could be said to be a sub-sector of the farming industry. Farming in the UK provides us with food but is also a vital part of our heritage, economy and way of life. Farmers contribute much to the fabric of our society and are custodians of a considerable amount of our beautiful countryside. Many are leaders in countryside diversity, animal welfare and proponents of renewable energy. However, farming and farmers are not without controversy and criticism is levelled at practices such as intensive farming of mono-crops; overcrowding of livestock; over use of pesticides and fertilizer; use of genetically modified crops, to name but a few.

This isn't a thesis on what is 'good' and what it 'bad' about farming (something I'm not qualified to write by a long chalk) but I would suggest that your opinion as to what is good and bad farming practice might vary depending on which end of a spectrum you tend towards. The need to get food on the table as cheaply as possible verses the imperative to preserve the countryside. Both are valid and vital aspirations and many would say that we can and should do both. Sustainable agriculture, let's defined it as the ability to meet this generations needs without harming the countryside and without compromising the next generation's ability to meet their needs, is generally lauded as 'a good thing'. But in general, sustainability increases costs and the majority of the public show time and again that they are not willing to pay higher prices for food. Economic and political reality also sit somewhere in there. Many people have to buy food as cheaply as possible to feed themselves and their families and cannot afford to pay more; many farms are barely economically viable and their main concern is to stay afloat. Looking after the countryside is a complex web of interlinked issues, filled with players with different goals and ambitions. And agriculture always provides lots of ammunition for a good political scrap, so don't expect much clarity from that direction.

Maybe we can look at the sustainability of vineyards in a similarly complex manner. Most people would assume that vineyards are beneficial to the countryside and I would agree. Whilst the 'monocrop' is the grapes the vineyards themselves are areas of great biodiversity, a good deal of the land area of a vineyard is after all a habitat for many species of wildflower and the diversity of insects and small mammals consequently attracted. The land is not intensely farmed and vineyards are generally atheistically pleasing, especially when you find one that is a green oasis surrounded by land that does happen to be intensely farmed. They also provide huge economic benefit, usually in rural areas where this is needed, with jobs and income being generated both by the business itself and enhanced by wine tourism, a growing phenomenon in the UK, providing enjoyment to many people. What's not to admire and encourage?

However, as with farming, all is not perfect. If we go back to the spectrum of the need to get food on the table (or in this case wine into the bottle) as cheaply as possible verses the imperative to preserve the countryside, I don't think vineyards can be criticised very much for failing to preserve the countryside. But there is a thought that we could do better. Concerns have been raised about issues such as over reliance on pesticides and fertilisers, excessive use of energy (especially diesel) in the operation of the vineyard, the draining of nutrients from vineyard soils and even the damage done to meadowland by the original ploughing to initiate the vineyard, dependent on what type of land is being ploughed. To promote more sustainable vineyards WineGB, the wine industry body in the UK, has set up the Sustainable Wines of Great Britain programme (SWGB). This promotes sustainable vineyard practice by inspection, auditing and certification. Its aims are to minimise use of pesticides and fertiliser, protect vineyard soils, conserve the environment and promote diversity, reduce water and non-renewable energy consumption and minimise the carbon footprint of member vineyards. They are laudable ambitions and my vineyard probably qualifies but I won't be joining.

There are vineyards in the UK that go even further than sustainability and aim to be completely organic. This is sometimes a marketing decision but often it's based on the philosophy of the owner. You cannot possibly fault, indeed must applaud, somebody who overtly tries go about their business in such a manner. However, I've been to several talks or participated in forums where the subject has turned to organic vineyards and the usual reaction has been to wish such vineyards the very best of luck but in the UK it's a bloody difficult trick to pull off. The two big barriers to organic vine production in the UK, particularly in larger vineyards, are weed control and pest/disease control. Without chemicals both are very, very difficult and are almost certainly costly, not least because whatever you finish up doing is likely to be highly labour intensive. It seems to me that the SWGB programme of sustainability tacitly recognises this by only seeking to reduce chemicals in its scheme, not to eliminate them entirely. In vineyards in the UK, in the constant battle to keep weeds, pests and diseases at bay at some point you are almost certain to need to use something inorganic that you wouldn't want to swallow. The SWGB stance is that if you are going to use it, please use as little as possible. A perfectly reasonable and valid viewpoint.

My vineyard probably not only meets the criteria to be considered sustainable but is likely to be organic as well. I haven't used chemicals on the vines. I've not so far had to use pesticides because I haven't as yet had any (serious) diseases to control (though I would if I had). I haven't used fertiliser as my soil is probably 'too good' – the field was a hay meadow for God knows how long, the top soil is about eighteen inches deep and full of nutrients. I'm forever fighting vigour and doing lots of 'summer leaf work', not seeking to promote it. I didn't break up the meadow ecosystem by ploughing when I first planted (though I wasn't aware of the issue then, it just happened that way). I use hardly any energy and no diesel in the vineyard, currently keeping the weeds down with an electric lawnmower. The field is fringed by wild flowers and surrounded by an ancient hedgerow, so I think I promote biodiversity (even if our cats don't). And as for water, it's Anglesey – everything I've ever needed has come from the sky. I think I manage things in a pretty responsible manner but I won't be seeking any accreditations. To become organic would tie my hands too much in case I have future problems and I do wonder if the SWGB sustainability scheme is a solution to something that's not really a problem. And once

I sign up you need to be inspected, a requirement for compulsory returns, and I'm sure that over time I'm going to have to keep proving that I comply. I do not need another layer of bureaucracy and regulation overseeing what I'm doing, and then the idea that I have to pay a fee to enjoy the extra hassle...

Let me tell you about my wasp problem. A couple of years ago there was a wasp's nest in a quieter corner of the vineyard. I'd noticed some wasps about but they were just the usual mere irritations, nothing untoward seemed to be happening. At the time the grapes started to ripen I happened to be away for a few days. When I returned I probably hadn't been in that quite corner for a week or so. When I did venture down there I realised that the grapes were full of wasps. I now know that, when the grapes are ripe enough, a wasp will just pick one to sit on and slowly gorge itself as it eats its way through it. I looked at the grapes, jumped back when I realised what was moving around in them, then slowly advanced for a closer look. There was little danger of being stung. I tapped a vine and all these wasps fell to the floor, drunk as skunks. However, it was too late to save the crop in that section which, from about twenty vines, was of course ruined.

We move forward to the following year and in that growing season the wasps seemed to appear earlier, though I might just have been a bit more sensitive to their presence. I posted a query on the WineGB vineyard email forum, asking how other people coped with the problem. The solution that was most suggested and the one for which people reported the best results for was to use wasp traps baited with a chemical called Agrisense Wasp Bait, an 'ecological, nontoxic chemical without impact on the environment'. Some suggested the same traps but baited simply with sugared water. The traps themselves are basic plastic domes with a hole in the bottom that the wasps can fly into but have great difficulty getting out, so eventually drown in whatever liquid you have placed in there to attract them. I bought the traps and the wasp bait (fifty quid for five litres so this better be good!) and deployed half a dozen traps spaced around the vineyard. As a control I also set up two further traps just baited with sugared water.

The result was spectacular! Within a couple of hours there were so many wasps in the vineyard that it was a virtual no-go area and

I certainly wasn't going anywhere near the traps, each with its own little swarm buzzing around. I seem to have attracted every wasp for miles about, which obviously wasn't the plan but there was no way I could get near the traps to take them down and stop the seemingly compelling attraction. It appeared that it was going to be a disaster but by the next day all had calmed down. The wasp traps were by then full of dead wasps and rest of the vineyard was wasp free. For the record, the final score was Agrisense Wasp Bait traps about two hundred each; sugared water traps, one or two. Fairly conclusive (and before you ask, no dead bees; the chemical is infused with another chemical to make sure bees stay away). I took the traps down. There was no chemical left in them as it had all been absorbed by the dead wasps. I dug a small hole and piled them in (is it possible that chemical infused wasps will cause damage to the water course, I wondered then dismissed, hopefully correctly?) and went back to tending my vines.

So have I acted in a responsible manner? I've solved my wasp problem but was the solution a bit over the top, considering it was near genocide at the local scale? Wasps are a pain in the bum but are a vital part of the ecosystem. Much though they are a huge irritant, the world would be a worse place without them. They pollinate plants in the same way that bees do, they scavage dead insects and they keep other insect pests under control by feeding on them. And without wasps all the figs would die off. My point is that, at the scale of a thousand or so dead wasps verses my grape crop, it feels like it should be my decision to take. If I was accredited as organic or sustainable, would I have invalidated my accreditation by using 'an ecological, nontoxic chemical without impact on the environment"; that wasn't applied to the ground or to my vines but merely remained in a pot? I don't know but I do know that I don't want the hassle of researching everything I do to make sure I stay within the rules. I think that I do things sensibly and responsibly and that's as far as I reasonably need to go (and I know what's going to happen at the first sign of wasps next year).

If you are going down the sustainable or organic routes then the very best of luck to you. But my business isn't a huge oil extraction process or some form of heavy industry. Is the negative impact of small vineyards on the environment such a big problem that it needs regulation? Every vineyard owner I have met has been pretty responsible about the environment. Me? I'm going to continue as I am in the way I see as accountable to current and future generations. Please drop in and buy my non-organic, probably sustainable – apart from the wasp thing – but definitely responsibly produced wine. Hmmm, perhaps that's a strapline that needs a bit of work.

CHAPTER 7

Inspiration

Okay, enough about buying houses and gallivanting round Spain, let's get back to vineyards and pull a few of these threads together. It was about the time of the abundant fifth year harvest from the vines in Anglesey that a collision of events and ideas occurred, some already alluded to, that crystallised the idea of planting a vineyard in Andalucia. The initial trigger was an innocuous conversation with Heather, a friend who had been head of a school in north London. I'd known her since my early twenties, when I was living in a flat in Onslow Gardens in Muswell Hill, in a large townhouse that had been converted into rooms and small apartments for letting. One flat had originally been let by friend Norman and it had become a focus of weekend life for this group of young blokes, most of us recently arrived to enjoy the excitement of being twentysomethings in London. Over several years the tenancy and shared occupancy passed backwards and forwards between several in the group, attracted by the convenience, conviviality and (appropriate) cheap rent. Across the road from this house was another similarly converted townhouse, the only difference being that all the tenants of this second house were young, professional women, one of whom was Heather. You can imagine that the two households gravitated towards each other and over the next few years such were the friendships, marriages and other relationships formed that even today, over forty years later, we still meet for 'Old Onslownian' reunions (often at the house of Antony and Ania, joint owners of the Spanish house, who were prominent).

If Old Onslownian sounds like a minor rugby club it's because that's what, at one point, it was meant to be. One of our chosen enjoyments as twentysomethings in London was going to

Twickenham to watch England play rugby. At the time I was playing club rugby and it was fairly easy to get hold of some tickets for the internationals. But we could never get enough. In those days ticket distribution was a rugby club closed shop and the tickets rarely went on sale to the public. The rugby clubs throughout the country were always allowed to apply for tickets before they went on general sale and this was almost always oversubscribed, so they were all usually taken up and the non-rugby public never got much of a look-in. For each game I could apply for a limited number, say, twelve and I might eventually be allocated six. But almost everybody in both houses, and others, loved to go and we never had enough tickets for all and, as I was the only one who actually played, I was the only supply line.

You will know that rugby culture usually involves a bit of drinking. After yet another enjoyable day on the terraces Norman and I hatched a brilliant idea to improve the supply line. We would form our own rugby club! Then apply for tickets via this club as an affiliated member of the Rugby Football Union. We had no intention of playing any games, just to have an AGM for the paperwork and to apply for tickets for internationals. The plan survived sobriety and we eventually contacted the RFU, where there was initial enthusiasm for our small expansion of the grassroots game. But the idea was soon scuppered by awkward questions such as, "what fixtures have you played in the last two years." So the rugby club never got off the ground but the name stuck.

Heather was at that time a teacher. She left London for a while mid-career but then returned and eventually became head of the school in which she had spent most of her professional life. I always knew her as hard working and conscientious. Well actually I've never seen her in a school, let alone a classroom but they don't do small schools in North London (not in the public sector, anyway) so you have to imagine that to be a successful head for many years she had to have plenty of ability and professionalism (and probably a bit of political nous as well). Certainly, it would not be unusual for me to phone her in the evening and find her absent from home, only to find out when I did manage to get in touch (this being before the days of mobile phones) that she had been at school every night that week. In her sixties she decided to retire. Proper regard was given and ceremony as befitted followed – and then she didn't work anymore. A few months after this, we were speaking on the phone and I remember clearly her saying,

"It's very strange, Kevin. I don't work anymore but they still pay me." This took me back a little, "What does she mean, what's going on?" Surely there's not been some administrative mistake and she's just accepting the money? Or some shady payroll scheme (not like Heather at all!). I tentatively enquired and she explained simply that she, of course, now received a pension. I was just that after she had worked so hard all her life that, as she adjusted to a life of more leisure, this just felt weird. These days she went to the theatre in the afternoon, or met her mates for lunch, or read a book but this 'salary' appeared in her bank account every month. Well, we had a bit of a laugh about that but after I put the phone down it did make me think. What I would do with my own twenty-five year end of career holiday to which my generation feels entitled?

It hadn't been something I'd ever considered before and it came as a bit of a jolt to find that at sixty two I was of an age that maybe it was something about which I should be thinking. That in two or three years I would have an important decision to make. But what would I do? I had the pleasant thought that, after forty odd years of working, it would be time to relax a little. And then the equally pleasant thought that maybe it was time to do just what I wanted? Doing just what I wanted seemed a nice idea for a few moments but then the reality of life brought me back to Earth. For a start, the children were both still at school, Lili with five years still to go; and Morag, younger than I, would be working for a few years yet. And then, well, there was the inconvenience of having to consider the money side of things. Okay, you can do whatever you want but it's not very sensible to spend everything quickly and then live for a couple of decades wishing you hadn't, is it? I'd been short of money enough times in my life to know that I didn't like it and I've already suggested that at my age if you spent too much (like ploughing thousands of pounds into a vineyard?) there wasn't much opportunity to replenish the funds. We'd done all right financially since we had been together and had been appropriately prudent and sensible, we had children to bring up after all, and there would be pensions eventually. We weren't going to be rich, we weren't going to be poor. A comfortable middle class perch with its constraints and responsibilities. So maybe it would be more realistic to plan that I could do what I wanted within the constraints of both finance and our responsibilities?

What do other people do at this point in their lives? Not something I'd given much consideration either. I thought about the retired people I knew from previous generations of friends and family. Some people did very little (and why not if they are happy). I have one friend whose family were very concerned about his impending retirement, given his super-active nature. They devised various schemes that might keep him occupied but when the time came it turned out that he was quite happy (and relaxed) doing nothing much; potter in the garden, visit the grandchildren, etc, etc. Good luck to him. I can't be the only one who knows people of retirement age who play a lot of golf, or more energetically compulsively bag Monroes or take long distance cycling trips. More power to their elbows (and knees). Others travel, again why not? This appeals, to an extent, but I have travelled quite a bit. There are certainly many places, even continents, I've not seen and I have an unfulfilled minor ambition to watch The Lions play rugby and/or England play cricket abroad (Australia, New Zealand, Sri Lanka, West Indies, Argentina, etc. I like the sound of that!) but these would be just interludes. And anyway, they would fall foul of the responsibilities issue for a good few years yet; children at school, wife still working.

All these activities are not mutually exclusive, a bit of everything? Not sure it fits the bill for me. Some people work for charities, or take more control of their daily lives by working part-time at a less demanding job. But that didn't feel right either, it felt a bit like I would be filling the hours for the sake of it. Some people, like some lottery winners, carry on working. I've often thought that winning the lottery would present something of a challenge (though I'm willing to give it a try). Suddenly, you don't have a routine and you can do whatever you like with little financial constraint, though presumably still responsibilities. What do you do? Same question as I'm asking myself and no doubt why some people do just carry on working. But no! Having escaped office life once I was, by necessity, back in another one, albeit with much more interesting work.

However, I wasn't going to spend an extra decade turning up to an office and working for people. But I wouldn't want to stop completely either, though nothing I'd come up with so far seemed right. At the back of my mind was also the thought that without enough focus I might slip into the habit of just sitting down with a drink a little too often.

All the above is a summation of random thoughts over a couple of weeks but eventually I came round to the idea of starting a small business, perhaps a project to turn something I enjoyed doing into something that made a bit of money. If it was a business it would impose a bit of discipline but hopefully not be overwhelming, something I would keep control of. I thought about the vines I'd planted on the bank. It hadn't gone very well but I recognised that the problem was me, my lack of skill, not that it was unfeasible, as I'd seen by visiting other vineyards in North Wales. Maybe I could build on that? Learn how to go about it in a more professional way, plant some more vines and turn it into a commercial venture. I wasn't planning to plant thousands, just in our acre field, sufficient to produce maybe a thousand bottles a year (another figure plucked out of the air). A small business just selling to local pubs and restaurants, etc.

And then my thoughts became a bit more expansive. What about planting the vineyard in Alora? This idea popped into my head at some point but I dismissed it pretty quickly as a flight of fancy (but enjoyed the daydream of thinking it through, like I enjoy the daydreams of scoring centuries for England at Lords, or tries at Twickenham). The obvious attraction of planting in Spain was the climate and my thoughts were based around the perception that it would be so much easier to produce and ripen grapes there, which you would have to say is true. I've explained that the limiting factor in Anglesey is that we could do with a bit more sunshine. Surprise, surprise, this isn't an issue in southern Spain. I knew several people who just planted vines on a bit of land around their house and grapes, well, just grew (big, fat and juicy), sufficient to keep their family in wine for the year. Harvest was in August, two months earlier than here in the UK, and you have to say that there's nothing wrong with the end product. As the daydream continued, I figured that we wouldn't want to move to Spain, even after our responsibilities had lessened, so this is when I hatched out the scheme to do it remotely. I knew the area around Alora well, knew lots of people there, thought I knew my way around. Well, it's an idea, it would certainly be fun trying to pull it off. Whatever, daydream over, and as regards planning something more feasible for eventual retirement, I've got two or three years to think it through before it all comes to a head. Something will come out in the wash. But I didn't have two or three years, a month later I found out I was going to be made redundant.

After setting myself up as specialising in designing and writing data capture systems for field research projects, not surprisingly a lot of my work started to come from the University in Bangor, where you will not be surprised to be told they do quite a bit of research. After working on a few projects focused on the environment I also came to the notice of a department doing medical research at the university, and I was able to win some work from them. Research is research and from a computing point of view collecting and storing data acquired by interviewing patients is much the same as collecting and storing data acquired by measuring things in a field, it's just less muddy. Before I knew it I was getting my head around the unique and complex privacy restrictions involved in doing research with health data; and I must have done so reasonably successfully as they kept giving me more work. One thing led to another and eventually I was asked to become salaried staff in the university Clinical Trials Unit; first two days a week, then three, then four and finally full time. I missed the flexibility and buzz of working for myself but the salary was more than I had earned in my best year working freelance in North Wales; and you got holidays and a pension thrown in, so what the heck. And I found working for a university was, for want of a better word, 'softer' than working in industry or business (or banking). There was no paranoia about being there exactly at 9 o'clock, or what you wore, or working from home if a child is sick. You were more generally treated as an adult, you had a job to do and got on with it, reporting progress at sensible intervals. I settled in and did get on with it and a regular pattern of life developed, conducive to having a young family.

The downside of working for a university is that many employees there don't have job security. A lot of academic funding is for three or four year projects. The way it happens is that an academic gains a grant, they assess the skills they need to do the research the grant is paying for and so they hire appropriate staff, but it can only be on a three or four year contract because that's how long the funding lasts. It's a sort of academic 'super-gig' economy. Like the more conventional gig economy, it suits some people. It worked for me, but for people who need proper financial stability I always thought it was a shitty career. I was always grateful for the work and the stability it provided (thank you especially Rhiannon and Nefyn) but in the fourteen years from the start of my first job there, to the day when my luck finally ran out, I didn't once have a contract on which the exit wasn't date-stamped.

When the axe did finally fall it came as much more of a surprise than it should have done. We all knew when the funding period ended and the money ran out. Equally, we all expected it to be renewed as usual but when the renewal was announced a few months in advance it was a shock to find that funding had been cut by almost fifty percent, so some people had to go. But I'd been through this scenario several times in this department and previously something had always come up. It felt like the re-run of an old drama. If this sounds a bit blasé, I also knew it wouldn't be the end of the world. I had been in similar situations previously, Morag was still working and I was confident that if I had to I would find something. However, with about a month to go it became obvious that this time nothing would 'turn up' and the redundancy was definitely going to happen. I had better start thinking seriously about what I would do next. There was, however, going to be one small silver lining. I worked on so many contracts at the university that, despite never having job security, they legally had to enrol me in their pension scheme and even make a redundancy payment. So, a few weeks later, like Heather, I didn't do any work for them anymore but they still paid me, albeit not that much. But I was a bit shocked to find that I was a pensioner, and I even had a bus pass (you get them at 60 on Anglesey).

But then what? The middle class perch was still comfortable and we certainly wanted it to stay that way. I was able to get intermittent freelance work but continuing in such a manner didn't look very hopeful, or enticing. It felt like a period of being in limbo, without any real direction. At the university I had been involved in some fairly big developments and now I wasn't, back to tinkering round the edges of projects for money. And the vineyard idea kept playing in my mind. Eventually, I realised that I really had had enough of turning up to an office and working for other people and I was going to do something that fitted better with the idea of having a bit of fun (within my constraints and responsibilities). Then one day you just decide, don't you? Right! I am going to plant a proper vineyard and what's more, I'm only going to do it once so let's have some proper fun. I'm going to plant it in Andalucia!

The Wider Picture V:
Welsh Vineyards

North Wales not warm enough for a vineyard? It's a veritable wine producing region! Well, that's a bit of an exaggeration but if you include the rest of Wales and thus the thirty or so vineyards that have been planted throughout the principality, it's not so far fetched. When I planted my vines in 2017 there were only two other commercial vineyards in North Wales: Gwinllan Conwy at the head of the Conwy Valley and Pant Du, south of Caernarfon. Now there are six, pretty soon it will be like the Loire Valley up here, a field of grapes round every corner. There's even the suggestion of a North Wales Vineyard Trail. And why not? More and more people are heading our way, curious to look at what we are doing and sample what we produce. So okay, it's a bit much to say that North Wales is as yet an out and out wine producing region, but it's certainly an area where you will find quite a few very pleasant vineyards to explore (and please read the later chapter focusing on what the future might hold!). During the period I lived in London, Young's brewery in Wandsworth, who had about one hundred tied pubs, issued leaflets listing all their hostelries. When you visited one and had a pint there the landlord would sign your leaflet and if you continued and eventually bagged all hundred odd you were invited to a party at the brewery. Maybe soon we will have our own leaflets printed. Visit the six vineyards of The North Wales Vineyard Trail and we'll throw a party every St. David's Day for those who cross the finishing line. By the time you read this it will be a well-worn path (maybe).

Getting back to reality, you have to say that the Welsh vineyard industry is still fairly small and nascent but, pro rata by head of population, it's comparable to what's happening in England. The expansion of the vineyard sector here in Wales, as with the rest of the UK, is moving on apace and there has been strong growth in the last ten years or so. The whole thing did seem to start a bit later here than in England. I suppose it would have taken a couple of more decades for the then more challenging climate of Wales to improve sufficiently compared with, for example, counties nearer The Channel. But pioneers stepped up here as well, and I guess with much the same motivations of enjoying a project or taking a serious hobby and maybe seeing if they can make it work commercially. Here are a few stories...

Glyndwr was the first and is thus now the oldest established vineyard in Wales. Planted in 1979 by Richard Norris and his family, it was at the time the fifth generation of the family business growing and selling potatoes, dating from way back in 1842. Richard says that he was used to the annual cycle of planting and lifting the spuds but became a little frustrated that you had to start again from scratch each year. He slowly developed the rather pragmatic desire to farm something that 'stayed put for a while' and eventually, with the benefit of advice he calls 'inspirational' from some of the owners of newly planted English vineyards, came round to idea of planting grape vines. And so it came about, with this practical but slightly unusual motivation, that a Welsh division was added to the emergent UK wine industry. Now the Glyndwr Wine Estate is another UK vineyard that can more than stand its own with any continental site. As well as boasting seven acres of vines that produce award winning wines they sell into Waitrose, Sainsburys and many fine restaurants, including in the House of Lords, it has its own restaurant, shop, accommodation and is a wedding venue. I forgot to ask him if they still grow any spuds!

Parva Farm Vineyard is another of the early vineyards planted in the modern day but historically can claim to be a lot older. I've mentioned vineyards in Britain in the days of The Romans and some of the workings found at this site suggest that it's quite possible that there was a vineyard here in those times. I've also mentioned the link between monasteries and vineyards and that too is the case here; this was almost certainly the site of the vineyard of neighbouring Tintern Abbey. The current vineyard was, as Glyndwr, planted in 1979 and is now owned by Colin and Judith Dudley who acquired it in 1996. It's now a thriving estate of four and a half thousand vines producing respected wines but when they took it over in 1996 it had all been somewhat neglected. It must have been a daunting prospect to take on, not least because they inherited seventeen difference varieties of vine (with seventeen different sets of problems), were dealing with vines in poor condition and disease was rife. They gave it four years and if they couldn't make it work in that time they would grub them out and keep sheep and cattle. They got to work, streamlined the varieties and just made it (with a small extention), getting their first decent crop in 2001 and producing their first wine, a medium dry blended white. Several other white wines followed, together with a rose, two reds, sparkling white and sparkling rosé and even a spicy mead and several fruit wines. Many national and international awards have followed over the years.

I started to enjoy these little stories and as I got to know my peers here in Wales, I found them by no means unusual. Every vineyard seems to have a little tale that is in some way similarly optimistically cheering and heart-warming. And in looking at the motivation behind the initial planting there's usually a familiar theme, 'Change of lifestyle'; 'it will be fun'; 'More control'; 'Doing something I will enjoy'; … As I became more integrated into the vineyard community in Wales the stories just kept popping up.

During the last two decades of the twentieth century and the early years of this one the slow but steady increase in the number of vineyards in Wales continued and by 2013 there was enough confidence to form The Welsh Vineyards Association. When I planted I had no idea there would be such a thing or for that matter, enough vineyards in Wales to warrant an association. When I heard of them it seemed sensible to try to join and eventually I was put in touch with chairman Robb Merchant who, together with wife Nicola, run White Castle Vineyard near Abergavenny. Both were born in and stayed local to Abergavenny, Robb a manager at The Royal Mail, Nicola a district nurse. There must have been some yearning to have a less conventional lifestyle because in 1993 they bought the small holding where the vineyard now stands. Then Nicola started thinking, "Wouldn't it be great to plant a vineyard here?" And eventually, in 2009, they did. And it worked well enough for Robb to take it on full time in 2014. After another couple of plantings they now have 7000 vines of seven different varieties and their thriving business produces a full range of white, red, rose, sparkling and fortified wines; gaining Protected Designation of Origin status and for good measure restoring a Grade II* listed 16th century barn in which to hold vineyard events.

However, I was pretty wary when I first got in touch with Robb. I was a new and very small vineyard approaching the rather official sounding Welsh Vineyards Association. What would they think of me? I mean, I didn't have much of a track record, did I? Wouldn't I be too small to be taken seriously? Did I have enough vines to even officially be thought of as a vineyard? Would they ask embarrassing questions like, "How much wine have you produced (at that point, as noted, two bottles a year for the last three years)?" Or ask my opinion on some technical issue that would totally bamboozle me? However, when I eventually talked to Robb on the phone he was extremely welcoming and encouraging. And he told me that the Gwinllan Conwy vineyard was only about twenty miles along the coast from me and happened to be run by then Association Secretary Colin Bennett. Why didn't I go and have a chat to him? I emailed to introduce myself but with increased trepidation. After all, not only might I be too small and amateurish to be taken seriously, wouldn't I be a local competitor?

As it turned out, in the spirit of several of the tales I've told you about established vineyards helping out tenderfoots, he couldn't have been more welcoming. We had a long talk on the phone. I had hoped that maybe I would be able to go over to his vineyard and have a look at how he went about things. Before I know it, he's not only invited me for a tour round his place but arranged to come all the way over here to Anglesey to talk more about my plans. We soon meet and I'm still a little anxious that I would be seen as somebody muscling in on his patch but *he* is the one that brings up the issue of competition. He tells me that he told one of his friends that he was coming to see me and they had has asked him why he would want help me, for the very same reason, why help the competition? He then explained that as far as he was concerned, the more vineyards in Wales, the better. Simply, the more of us there were, the bigger the wine producing sector, the more people there will be who will realise there are vineyards in Wales and the more people who will then come to Wales to visit the vineyards and buy wine. Brilliant! What a great way to do business! Which business school promotes the idea of helping your competitors as much as you can as a strategy for success? And doesn't it wonderfully carry on the traditions of the earlier pioneers, lending a hand to other people starting up? In the nascent position the vineyard industry finds itself in here in Wales I've come round to it completely and if somebody wants to set up half a mile away I'll go and help them plant and lend them my equipment. Indeed, I've now had several people visiting here to pick my brains as they make plans to start up. Why not? The more the merrier. There's no shortage of people wanting to tour vineyards and buy wine in France, is there?

At some point Colin told me how he and wife Charlotte came to start their vineyard and I couldn't help but recognise some of the same arbitrary fortune that had guided me. In his own words,

"In 2010 we bought a small holding outside of Conwy in North Wales. The site had a sloping south facing field and it was our dream to plant a vineyard. With no prior knowledge of viticulture, but plenty of experience of drinking wine I mentioned my idea to the farmer who was selling us the property."

"Grape will grow just find here," he said!

"How could you possibly know that!" I replied!

"Then he led me across the field to a remote corner where to my astonishment, there was around a hundred mature vines! Some years earlier a retired gentleman by the name of Edward O'Neil had asked the farmer if he had a small plot of land that he could rent to plant a vineyard. Feeling sorry for the man in what he believed was a hopeless exercise he let him have rent free, a quarter of an acre plot, steep and rocky and of little use. The vines took perfectly and after four years they produced their first crop. Sadly, Edward then had to give up the vineyard due to ill health and it became overgrown and abandoned. Years later we discovered it and it was the best proof that we could have that vines really would thrive in this area of North Wales. This small site is now part of a three-and-a-half-acre vineyard producing award winning wines and has become a key tourist attraction for North Wales! If ever there was something meant to be! But most importantly, a heartbroken gentleman who had to abandon his dream can proudly gaze up on this hillside and see that his dreams also turned into reality, beyond his wildest expectations!"

I hope by telling these tales I'm giving the impression that there's I real community spirit amongst the vineyards here in Wales, and it's also heartening to see that the government is recognising the potential of the industry. No, not that one, the one here in Cardiff, which is starting to take a very hands on approach to assist and it turns out that our current small numbers are greatly to our advantage. WineGB as the industry body for the wine industry in the UK does sterling work, representing all vineyards and wine producers, lobbying government, fighting our corner, setting standards, providing education and training, supporting research and development, and much more. But it's by necessity a sizeable organisation with many voices, many members with sometimes conflicting requirements and it's difficult for individual (small) vineyards to get themselves heard. The Westminster government is supportive, as it is of all sectors but the size of both the government and the wine sector in England can be cumbersome and prevent specifically targeted assistance.

In Wales it's different. Business development is a devolved issue and is handled in Cardiff. Because of the smaller scale of both government and the wine industry here assistance can be a lot more flexible and specific without breaking the myriad of competition rules regarding state support for industry. And the Welsh government sees great potential in the vineyard industry in Wales, particularly the economic benefits of employment in vineyards and through wine tourism. As there are only thirty or so vineyards it can be a lot more focused with its help. I don't mean that it can bung us all a few thousand quid each (unfortunately, that would almost certainly be against competition rules) but it can act strategically to help the sector as a whole. And this it has done by setting up a Special Interest Group to help grow the sector. And that's what's happening. We meet regularly and, because we are small and focused, we can get things done, rather than it being something of a talking shop. As I write the industry is going through a consultation process channelled through the Special Interest Group to decide (Welsh) government policy in the wine industry, to promote it, to grow it, to encourage new entrants, to encourage farmers to diversity, to work out how best to invest funds to enhance an industry sector that is becoming a Welsh success story. Watch this space (and read the later chapter on where it all might lead!).

I planted a vineyard mostly because I had the opportunity, the timing was right and I thought it would be fun (and I fancied the idea of turning up at dinner parties with a couple of bottles of the latest vintage, to general admiration and envy). An unexpected bonus was to join the burgeoning vineyard community of Wales. That's a privilege. It feels like I'm a member of an exclusive club, the proud, independent (believe you me, they are all independent!) Vineyards of Wales. But as the number of vineyards increases that club will obviously become less exclusive. Great. The more the merrier!

CHAPTER 8

Learning the Trade

If I was going to take planting a vineyard seriously I realised that I needed to enhance my skill set somewhat. After five years working at it I've taught myself, and put into action, some of the basic principles of vine growing and grape production but I'm not exactly doing great, am I (two bottles a year for the last three years)? On the plus side, the vines are healthy and maturing. I severely prune them each winter, as I should, and when the season starts they look the part. They continue to so do throughout the early season but I'm starting to eventually realise that maybe I'm not doing the pruning properly: I definitely leave too much foliage on during the middle of the growing season and I need to be bolder there. And during those early years when I wasn't doing enough, each year around mid-summer everything seems to get a little bit away from me and somehow (with hindsight, not surprisingly) I just don't get enough ripe grapes to turn into wine. Two weeks summer holiday, always taken in July/August because we are still constrained by school terms, doesn't help either as the vines are at that point left to their own devices when they probably need a bit more attention. In truth, at this point the whole project was still something I did on a whim and I hadn't been taking it that seriously. For those five years I still had a full time job and there many other interests – I'd rather spend half a day out on my bike than half a day bud rubbing in the vineyard (Ooops, I guess that's still true!). Yes, I have seventy-five vines but you could say that they are just an extension of the vegetable patch. I may as well have planted seventy-five gooseberry bushes and be making jam. If I am going to try to do it properly and plant my vineyard in Andalucia I needed to up my game.

I found out about Plumpton College. I can't remember if I just came across it on the internet or somebody told me about it. Formally Plumpton Agricultural College, it's now part of The University of Brighton and is recognised as the UK Centre of Excellence for Wine Education. They offer foundation degrees and a three year Bachelor's degree in both the Wine Business and Viticulture & Oenology. It's the only place in the world that offers undergraduate degrees in wine production and the wine business in English. And if getting just one degree doesn't sate your thirst for wine knowledge you can then also go on to do a Master's degree. If at first glance doing a whole degree course in wine seems a little overblown, that's not the case at all. The wine business is huge and complicated and the traditional wine growing regions of the world have been offering equivalent qualifications for decades. The South of England (and spreading steadily northwards) is to all intents and purposes now a major wine region, growing in importance. Vineyards in the UK are now way beyond the point of a few pioneers planting some vines in a field and maybe needing a bit of casual labour every so often. The industry needs trained chemists, plant scientists, marketers, horticulturists, wine makers, administrators, accountants, soil scientists and more, all with a deep knowledge of how their subject relates to vineyards and wine. Back in my thirties when I threw in the banking job to go to university, had I known about it then I wonder if I would have chosen a degree at Plumpton instead of the Geography course I eventually alighted on? I would certainly love to do it now but it's obviously never going to happen: finance, the required years of study and that it's 350 miles from the family home are just the start of the issues. However, it turned out that they also deliver five-day short courses, one in the growing of grapes and one explaining how to subsequently turn them into wine. You can do this in one five day block or five separate days throughout the year. Given the distance I had to travel I did the intensive five day course in Principles of Vinegrowing, again reasoning that Winemaking could wait for a year or two.

I got in touch with them, exchanged a few emails about suitability (them for me and me for them), booked my place and so on a bright and sunny Tuesday morning in late August (bank holiday weekend so the course runs Tuesday to Saturday) I find myself walking into the Wine Department at Plumpton College; and both the College and the Wine Department are truly impressive. They have been teaching agriculture here in one form or another for nearly a hundred years. The main building was the oldest on the complex and the wine department the newest, both striking. The main building ivy clad and quietly grand; the wine centre building, opened in 2014, modern and stylish. The facilities in the wine centre, I can safely quote from their website without doing any of my own research, are the best for teaching, training and researching the wine trade in the UK. There are, of course, teaching rooms and lecture theatres to a standard required in any higher and further education facility but it's the state-of-the-art commercial winery, research winery and laboratories that are pretty astounding. Add this to a ten hectare vineyard, partly used for plant trials but also producing some forty thousand bottles a year; winning awards and selling many UK stores including Waitrose, and you have a truly impressive teaching facility.

I join my fellow students and we see all the above as part of the introductory tour and then we settle down in the classroom to start, appropriately enough with a lecture on evaluating sites for suitability for the planned planting of a vineyard. There were just over thirty of us, about a dozen were embarking on the Masters degree in Vinegrowing and Onology and this was a voluntary introductory course. The other twenty or so of us had either just planted or were about to plant vineyards; or in the case of one gentleman, had acquired his vineyard with a house he had bought in Italy and he wanted to know what to do with it. The new vineyards were or were going to be all over the UK, as far north as the Scottish Borders and in North Yorkshire; and varied in size from the small scale I was planning to serious investment in five or ten hectares. But, of course, we all had one thing in common, a strong desire to know more about what we were doing.

I'm wearing two hats on the course and as I start to listen to the lecturer. One hat is on behalf of the planned adventure in Spain and one is on behalf of the vines still growing in Anglesey (I was going to plant in Spain but I wasn't going to grub up the vines in Anglesey, they would still need to be looked after). Even with my basic (lack of) knowledge I knew that growing vines in sun soaked Andalucia would require different (hopefully easier) techniques than growing them in rain rich north Wales. That was, after all, the motivation for the Spanish escapade. With my Anglesey hat on this first bit about selecting sites is irrelevant, I had already planted the vines where they were on the bank and that's that. I know I made lots of mistakes or just didn't do things I should have done but I had a different mindset then, I was just messing about. I was now going to get more serious. For 'Anglesey hat' I would list my failings as they arose but hopefully start to learn about how I could mitigate my mistakes and improve the vines with better management.

Wearing the Spanish hat was more worrying. This was the part I had to get right, the point of me spending the money to come on this course. By this time I had already been across to Andalucia to look at land a few times so had 'evaluated' a few sites in my own amateurish way (reference the Introduction and Chapter 2). The lecturer was talking about starting a vineyard from scratch and looking at climate, soil, aspect, topography, wind, altitude, etc. etc. before taking the plunge. I know he was explaining what was ideal, the perfect combination of characteristics you could wish for in a site and that the eventual selection is almost certain to be, in reality, a compromise. My growing concern was that around Alora I was running out of sites to view and I hadn't yet seen one that had felt remotely right to me, even before I had sat through this lecture listing the perfect combination of characteristics I should be looking for. There were relatively few sites available and, as alluded to earlier, my list of compromises was growing. I didn't have the luxury of considering climate, soil, aspect, topography, wind, altitude, etc. etc. when I planted in Anglesey and it was beginning to look like that was the case in Spain as well. As I said in the Introduction, my criteria had become access to the road, not in the middle of nowhere, water and not too steep (or have other problems to make it hard work). I was betting the success of this project on the idea that the climate was so ambient for viticulture in the south of Spain that the grapes would grow (almost) anywhere so long as they had water and, pragmatically as regards site selection, I couldn't see how I could consider all these other desirable characteristics. But if I'm not going to take any notice of what they are saying on this course, just go ahead and stick with what I think I've worked out, then what the hell was I doing there in the first place? Then came the first big lesson of the week.

The Director of the Wine Unit was lecturing, a man with decades of experience of viniculture in the UK, France and elsewhere. He was, as you would expect, very knowledgeable of all aspects of growing vines and the production of wine. Indeed, he had written many scientific papers covering almost every facet of the subject. However, when he answered questions at the end of the lecture he didn't, I thought, really answer with the precision you might expect from somebody so eminent, especially as the questions seemed to concern fairly basic issues that people new to the subject might ask. Then he told us something I didn't expect, that in one aspect he was really going to get on our nerves as the week wore on. He explained that he knew that we were all new to viticulture; that we were all enthusiastic and had many, many questions and he apologised that many of his answers might seem to lack clarity. He then said that,

"Most of my answers and those of my colleague are going to start with the phrase 'It depends...'."

The course title was 'Principles of Vinegrowing' and that's what they could teach us, *principles* of vinegrowing. It was up to us to take away the principles and apply them to our own situation. If there was one thing I came away from the course with (rightly or wrongly) it was that mostly you had to work it out for yourself, at your own vineyard.

"That's a very valid question, Mr Mawdesley,"

"Oh, you want an answer?" Well, it depends on the soil; it depends on the climate; it depends on the variety of vine or the rootstock; it depends on how much rain there was last week, or how much sun last month; it depends on how you pruned the vines in the winter, or how you pruned them in the winter depends on how vigorous the variety of vine is, or it depends how the rootstock interacts with your soil to promote vigour... It depends, it depends, it depends, to most questions there is not one answer that fits all circumstances.

It even depends on your overall philosophy, the type of vineyard you decide you want to have. For instance, most vineyards have regular chemical spraying regimes but I've mentioned that some vineyards are organic, how do you then deal with pests and plant diseases? Wooden trellising (looks better, especially if you plan to encourage tourists to visit) or metal, easier to install and lasts longer. I've seen grapes growing in poly tunnels. Some people think this is cheating. I know of vineyards where not one single grape that they have not watched grow all summer will go into their wine; others that quite happily buy in a tonne or more grapes to supplement their own. So many aspects of your management regime depend on your philosophy (and don't forget the theory I have that if you get ten vineyard owners/managers together in a room you are likely to get at least five views on any particular subject).

After I had thought all this through and when we had finished for the day it made me feel much better and for me puts the course into context. Learn the principles, learn about what's important, learn about all the things I need to consider, learn about the things that so far I'd done wrong; then go away and apply the principles in your situation. Or in my case, situations. The course was about growing vines in the UK which, certainly as you get further north, is still a marginal wine producing area and often requires that everything possible is done to encourage grape production and ripening. I would take away the principles and I would have to apply them to the vines in Anglesey. In Spain I would be applying the same principles but I would apply them differently in a climate much more conducive to viticulture.

Another high point early in the week was a rather oblique reference to something that suggested that my idea that the grapes would indeed 'just grow' in southern Spain was perhaps not far from the truth. One lecturer was talking about different growing systems and touched on the idea of bush vines. In almost all parts of the world, as I'm sure you know, vines are grown by training them to cling to trellis systems, which require considerable effort and expense to install. In some areas of the world, where conditions allow, they just don't bother with such systems. They simply let the vines grow like bushes because conditions are so favourable they will just grow anyway, so why bother with the expense an effort of trellising. When you first plant a vine it will send out shoots in all directions from its base. In the UK and most other wine regions you don't want that. You select one (or two) shoots and prune all the others away. You want the plant to concentrate on putting down roots and growing one strong shoot. If you don't prune away the shoots from the base the vine just grows like a blackcurrant bush, as I've proved with some of the vines on my bank. However, in the right climate what is mismanagement in Anglesey is reasonable practice. The grapes form, ripen and you pick them like, well, blackcurrants.

This jogs a memory and I recall that I've seen this growing technique in southern Spain, several years earlier. We were walking, I can't remember where, and we came across this small field full of bushes with grapes on them. At the time it was something of no more than a mild curiosity but I must at some point have asked somebody about them because I now know that they were being grown to produce Vina Malaga. Malaga 'wine' was once famous and sought after but has these days fallen out of fashion. It's not a true wine but a sweet fortified drink like sherry, but nothing like as well known. Production is still considerable though, and now increasing. And if you are ever at a loose end in Malaga you should spend half an hour in the delightfully dark and dingy Antigua Casa de Guardia. Here Vina Malaga is served straight from the cask, the waiter diligently marking your consumption in chalk dashes on the bar in front of you, to be totted up and paid for when you leave. Most vines for 'normal' still wine in southern Spain are grown on traditional trellis systems but if there are already people growing bush vines in the region, think of all the work and expenditure I would save if I used the same method for my own vines. And the fact that they were already growing in this haphazard manner surely showed that the grapes would indeed just 'grow themselves' in Andalucia (if they had water). At the next break I asked the lecturer what he thought of the bush vine idea if I was planning to plant my vineyard in such a hot climate. He warned me off the plan both from the point of the inefficiency (low yields) and the that it was backbreaking work to tend plants so low to the ground. Okay, fair enough, but he did agree (with a few reservations) that the climate of southern Spain was favourable for viticulture, so it was likely my grapes would probably 'just grow' there.

The week progressed and so did the course. Planting, how to trellis, pruning, propagation, nutrition, managing and improving the site, sustainability, canopy management; and this is where I learnt about Growing Degree Days and saw the graphs that so starkly represented climate change and indicated that climate was moving inexorably north. We spent the mornings in the lecture room and the afternoons in the vineyard. Very much a hands-on course, testing the soil, pruning the vines, handling the machinery. My emotions fluctuated with the days (hours). At some points I was thinking, "Jesus, I know so little." Then the next lecture I might think, "actually I didn't badly with that." But then at the next one, "this is so confusing and there's so much to take in I'll never remember it." Thankfully there was also the occasional moment of clarity, "so that's what I should have been doing in Anglesey."

As the course continued my confidence grew. Then we arrived at the final full day, vineyard pests and diseases and the management of them, which frightened the life out of me. All that work and then something comes along and kills everything. It was like having a headache then Googling "What is a headache a symptom of" and actually reading the results. Calm down Kevin, it's not that bad and you need to know about these things and what to do about them. Then the last half day was a review and then a short multiple choice exam. I get a merit pass (I wanted a distinction) and a sticker to say that I've trained at Plumpton. I'm proud of that, proud to have been associated, however briefly, with this wonderful place.

I've been on many courses in my working life and they have been of varying degrees of worth. Some, after the first hour you wonder why you're there. Some, particularly if you are there to learn a new skill, perhaps a new computer language, were very worthwhile and you come away with what you want. Maybe it's because of the circumstances, that I paid for it myself and that it's about things that I need to know and I want to hoover up the knowledge. I come away feeling that it was the best, most relevant, interesting, informative, useful, enlightening course I've ever been on and I happily set off back to Anglesey to correct all my mistakes, thinking about how I will apply my new found learning in Spain.

I've said that by no means do I consider myself to be a viniculture expert, I think I've made clear where I stand on that spectrum, and the things I write about are what I think (or thought at the time) and the way I see things. I've also said that one of the dreads of writing this book is that I will expose to my peers the glaring mistakes that

I continue to perpetuate, or some of the facts that I'm spouting so knowledgeable are just plain wrong. I meet other owners through the Welsh Vineyard Association and do get chance to talk to them about technical aspects. But that's only two or three times a year. Mostly I'm working on my own and I'm aware that if I get a mistaken idea in my head, I can be doing something that's just plain wrong and then blithely continue to repeat the mistake, year on year. My many years of mis-pruning is the perfect example of this. So please understand that I'm writing about things as I understand them, for better or worse.

Since I opened the vineyard and have been doing tours, occasionally there are people who are tempted to have a go for themselves, to plant their own vineyard. Perhaps on a small scale, for instance there was one couple who had an allotment and were wondering how many vines they might fit in; or on a much grander scale. Indeed, I've said that I've even been approached by a few people who are actively planning to plant, maybe even quite a sizeable area. They've seen my website and wonder if they are about to start the same journey as I've been on and ask if they could come and pick my brains, for what that's worth. As has been previously indicated, you are all more than welcome to visit but excuse me if many of my answers start with the words 'it depends'. This isn't because I want to sound as though I'm as knowing of the world of wine as the people at Plumpton. I'm not by a long way. It's because I'm still not sure that I'm going about things as best I could, because what works in Anglesey might not be right for where you want to plant and because I don't want to tell you with certainty to do something that turns out not to work for you. What I will and have told people with certainty is that if you are going to plant a vineyard YOU HAVE TO GO ON THIS COURSE. Throughout the week on the course occasionally a point would be made by one of the lectures and I'd notice perhaps a sharp movement from one of the other people in the classroom; an intake of breath, maybe a pensive or even worried look. At one point somebody actually said,

"I wish I'd known that before I planted."

I've said before that if you do decide to plant a vineyard and you don't have prior experience, you have to make your biggest decisions when you know least. So I will also say to you with certainty that if you are going to plant a vineyard you have to go on this course and GO ON IT BEFORE YOU PLANT!

The Wider Picture VI:
Vine Varietals Suitable for the UK

The number of vine varietals that are suitable for cultivation in UK vineyards is increasing. This is mostly because global warming is making the climate more amenable. More and more varietals that couldn't be relied on to ripen in the UK because of our cool climate now cope much better with the environmental conditions here. But in relatively recent times new varieties, better adapted for the cooler UK climate, have also come on stream (well, some of them are not that new but they've not been around for centuries like many traditional vines and they are coming into their own in the UK now). I'm referring mainly to vines that produce grapes for still wines. The varieties of vine that produce sparkling wines have remained much the same when planted in the UK but are becoming more prominent here because of climate change. I planted vines to make still wines and the reason I can do that in Anglesey is mainly because of climate change but also because of the new varietals, adapted to cooler climates, that have been developed in the last few decades.

So, how do you go about creating a new type of grape. Well, you know how cattle, pigs, turkeys, etc. are selectively bred to produce more meat, more milk, bigger birds for the Christmas table (have you ever seen a drawing of a turkey from the eighteen century? Wouldn't feed a family of church mice). As you probably know, animals with the desired characteristics are selected for breeding and are encouraged to get on with it. Sometimes this works and sometimes it doesn't but eventually, if you stick at it long enough, the species 'evolves' and you get an animal (or bird) with the characteristics you want. In layman's terms, that's basically what you do to breed a new type of grape. And if 'breed' sounds an odd word to use in the context of grapes, no. Almost all the major wine producing countries have grape breeding institutes and have had grape breeding programmes for more than a century. Two of the most famous, and the ones I'm indebted to, are the Staatlichen Weinbauinstitut grape breeding Institute in Freiburg, Germany, and the Geisenheim Grape Breeding Institute in the Rheingua region of the same country. They were responsible for developing, amongst many others, both the varietals I now grow.

The Geisenheim Institute was founded in 1872; Staatlichen Weinbauinstitut has been undertaking practical research into viticulture since 1920, so both have over one hundred years of experience. Their principal purpose is breeding and cloning vines to develop disease resistance and other desirable attributes but Staatlichen Weinbauinstitut is also very active in soil and ecosystem development within vineyards, as well as progressing new techniques for both making and analysing wine. Geisenheim, through its collaborations with the University of Applied Sciences in Wiesbaden and Giessen University, is the only academic institution in Germany to award higher degrees in winemaking. Solaris, the vine variety that was thankfully recommended to me when I first planted, was created in 1975 by a Dr. Helmut Becher, who worked at both Institutes. It was developed to be early ripening, hardy, high yielding, disease resistant and with good vigour, which is what I need in Anglesey. In my experience Solaris doesn't ripen early in Anglesey but its 'early ripening' qualities mean that it does ripen by the end of the growing season, many varieties wouldn't this far north. Hardiness is not so important as our proximity to the sea and our maritime climate ensures that we don't get many extreme temperatures, hot or cold, so that's not vital. As far as high yielding is concerned, my yields have up until now been modest but my vines are not yet fully mature, yields are increasing and I'm waiting expectantly for the higher kind. Disease resistance has been a definite boon as so far I'm chemical free. Good vigour cuts both ways. I've mentioned that it's known to require 'continued summer leaf work', that it would rather produce foliage than grapes. Continued summer leaf work can be a pain, it sometimes feels more like a battle. But rather a plant that is too vigorous and requires a lot of leaf work than one that doesn't thrive at all in this climate.

From asking folk who have come here for my vineyard tours, it's true to say that Solaris is not a wine variety that many people have heard of, but I'm confident that you soon will. A fair percentage of UK vineyards planting for still white wine have now planted this grape and as more and more vines in UK vineyards reach maturity there is going to be more and more Solaris wine available in the shops. Because never mind early ripening, hardy, high yielding, disease resistant and good vigour; its most important characteristic, I'm sure you will be pleased to hear, is that it produces a delicious wine (though you might say that I would say that, wouldn't I? Well, you are welcome to drop in to allow me to prove myself right).

If you were asked what type of wines were produced in the UK what would first come to mind would probably be still and sparkling white wines; perhaps rosé. That's what I would have said five years ago and I'm sure many people would say now. You don't really associate red wines with cooler climates; you tend to think that they need a lot more sun. However, one of the biggest changes over the last couple of decades is the amount and quality of red wine that is now produced in the UK. Again, we have the combination of climate change and new varieties to thank for this. Rondo, the second variety I eventually planted, is a dark skinned grape that produces a rich, ruby red wine. It was developed in the nineteen sixties in, as it was, Czechoslovakia by Professor Vilem Kraus but passed on to Dr. Becker at the German institute, who did further work to improve it. I often take my wine to Food and Craft Fairs and the like; setting up a stall and offering free samples in the hope that people will then buy a bottle. I usually just take the red wine because it's easier to just have one wine and because of the problems keeping white wine at the right temperature. When I offer the sample the three surprised reactions I most frequently get are (in order),

"A vineyard in North Wales?" Said with slight scepticism,

"Yes, would you like to try the wine?" There's possibly a dubious pause here, followed by a tentative sip.

"Wow, that's nice" is usually (but not always) the second surprised response, followed by the third,

"and it's red wine!" My experience so far has been that the Rondo vines are actually more suited to the climate up here than the Solaris. It produces a bigger crop and ripens earlier; and my Solaris vines seem to have a tendency to be a tiny bit fragile around flowering time. Like Solaris, Rondo is probably a wine that many people have not yet heard of but again, you soon will. More UK vineyards are also planting this grape, so eventually there is going to be more and more Rondo wine available in the shops. And, as with Solaris, its most important characteristic is that it produces a delicious wine (you might again say that I would say that, wouldn't I? Well, you are again welcome to drop in to allow me to again prove myself right).

Many of the varieties now grown in the UK, such as Seyval Blanc, Pinot Noir, Madeleine and Reichensteiner, have been around since vineyards started to reappear in this country after the second world war (but they produce better fruit now). Others, like Solaris and Rondo, provide examples of the newer varieties that have started to flourish here. Pheonix, grown for white wine; and Regent (red) are two others. And now there's a new kid on the block that people have high hopes of. Divico is a hybrid grape that was invented in Switzerland at the Agroscope Agricultural Research Centre in Pully, on the shores of Lake Geneva, by Juan-Laurent Spring. It was successfully bred for the usual cool climate characterises of hardiness, frost and disease resistance and early ripening but has one other great quality. Red Wharf Bay Vineyard Rondo, whilst delicious (have I said that already?) is, as is usual in the UK, quite a light red wine. It is hoped (expected?) that even in the UK climate Divico will produce a heavy, full bodied red wine. There has never been a vine variety that regularly produces such a wine in the UK and if Divico lives up to expectations it will be a huge step forward for the UK wine industry. I keep seeing the word 'gamechanger' in reports. The first UK Divico vineyard was planted in 2018 by our old friends at Halfpenny Green (still pioneering). A trial organised by National Institute of Agricultural Botany is being run there as well as at renown vineyards Bolney, Nyetimber, Chapel Down and Gusbourne. The first wine is due in 2022 – look out for it.

Climate change and new varieties developed for cooler climates, a powerful combination driving the flourishing UK wine industry. I'm not saying everything is viniculturally perfect up here in Anglesey but more and more, year after year, the whole thing is improving.

CHAPTER 9

The Perfect Plot

And then I found the perfect plot! Well, not exactly 'perfect' perfect but I thought perfect enough for what I needed. In the end it took six months of searching but as soon as I walked on to it I knew it was right straight away. I'm back in Bermeja where this story started. A neighbour across the road from Dave and Paqui has put a small plot of land behind her house on the market. Literally across the road from them. Dave had told me about it over a beer the previous night and here I was, up bright and early in the morning to have a look. Dave and I walk down the road about fifty metres to the entrance, access is via a thirty metre dirt track, perfectly serviceable for vehicles, so no problems with access to the plot from that decent highway connecting Bermeja to Alora. We walk down the dirt track around the back of the roadside houses, and there it is. A well maintained little parcel of land nestling in the bend of a small stream. It's not quite as large as I would have liked, maybe space for 800 vines rather than the thousand I was thinking of, but that's okay. It doesn't have the scenic vista that you get from the other side of the road, where you look across the river to the nearby mountains. This is in a rather enclosed small valley that cuts off anything but the view of the immediate scrub hillsides, which is a pity. No sitting in the evening after a hard day's toil, sipping a beer whilst looking out over the land into the glimmering distance. But I want to produce grapes and make wine, not sell postcards, and I think it's perfect for that.

The plot is divided roughly into two. In looks well drained and I guess the stream, incised into a small gully, provides the natural drainage lines. The flat area nearest the stream couldn't be better. Its grassland already cleared of everything else, no wild vegetation, scrub bushes or anything that needs work, even around the edges. It would just need ploughing and planting. The top half would not be quite as easy but there are no real problems. It's slightly elevated and slightly sloped and has some lemon trees, again all well maintained and nothing I saw as a great problem. The plot was roughly square, the top side backing onto the gardens of the road houses, the north side onto somebody else's land with the other two sides bordered by the stream. The stream is small and looks ephemeral, I doubt it runs in the summer. There's also no well but this doesn't matter (What! I thought we had taken on board the need for reliable water?).

I told you about the reservoirs at El Chorro, a few kilometres to the north, and said that they were relevant to the story. When the reservoirs became operational, just sending the water down the river to the city would have been a bit hit and miss so a series of irrigation canals were constructed for that purpose. The main canal is quite a grand affair but many subsidiary ones are just concrete channels only a foot or so wide. And just such a little canal went through the middle of the plot I was going to buy. So what, you may think. You may suggest that I can't just hack into a publicly owned water supply and divert it onto my land at my pleasure. Well, the beauty of this plot was that to an extent I could. When the canals were built all those decades ago the planners realised that they couldn't just drive them over privately owned land without compensation so a deal was done whereby everybody who finished up with a canal built across their property would have the (valuable) irrigation rights in perpetuity. And those rights were passed on to the new owners whenever the property was sold. And that was the case here. This land was allowed six hours of irrigation water each week, which was plenty for what I would need for the vines. And it was a guaranteed water supply. Well, as guaranteed as any water supply could be in this part of the world. So long as Malaga didn't run out of water, neither would I – and there were four reservoirs of the stuff at the head of the valley. Dave told me that there was this delightfully informal system whereby I phone up Juan at the reservoir and said that I wanted to take my water for that week and he just diverted it down my branch of the canal, then I opened a sluice gate and flooded the land. All this needed checking of course but that seemed to be the system in the rest of the area and I had no reason to doubt it. As things transpired, I never got round to finding out.

I attempted to quell my initial euphoria and tried to put on a harder hat to consider things more meticulously. The plot had water that was as guaranteed as could be; the price was in my budget; it had good access to the road and the road was a straight run into Alora; it was a decent sized plot for what I wanted; looked easy to work; was already half cleared and at first glance looked fertile enough. There were bars, restaurants and other services in Bermeja, which would be useful; I would be a neighbour of Dave and Paqui and they would keep an eye when I wasn't there; I'm sure they would store things for me until I got organised; and I would have goodwill in the village. What else could I want? Surely the perfect plot for what I needed?

Playing devil's advocate with myself, I tried to think of problems. One unknown was the quality of the soil but I had decided that this didn't matter that much, as long as it was well drained, not heavy clay and not in any way toxic. Vines seemed to thrive almost everywhere around here. I've said that initially I drew up a list of criteria and of course decent soil was on that. But that I then realised that I couldn't be too fussy and that the essential criteria were water; that the land would be reasonable to work; accessibility to the road and Alora; and price. I was by now fairly confident that in southern Spain the production problems were almost the opposite of the UK, where, "every little helps." In southern Spain you perhaps do the opposite of all the little things you do in the UK to encourage growth, in order to slow things down. By now I firmly believed that the grapes were going to grow and ripen anyway so long they had water and this plot had plenty. I decided that I would have the soil tested but, unless there was some compelling problem thrown up by the test, I would take my chances with everything else. So, stop prevaricating, Kevin. This is it! I went to see the owner and we agreed a price. I went to see my Assessoria (a sort of paralegal who would do the conveyancing) to set things in motion and then a few days later I was back on the plane to the UK in high spirits. It looked like it was finally all going to happen. Think of it, our own vineyard in Spain.

Back home I impatiently continued researching, making plans and enjoying that 'beginning of a project' buzz. For a start, I needed to decide what variety of grape to plant? Then what equipment would I need and where would I get it from? Where would I get the trellising and how would I install it? Did I need help with the plot preparation and the planting? Where will I find a commercial nursery with a good reputation within a reasonable distance of Alora, to source the vines? And then there were mundane things like getting the money in place to transfer to Spain and other such issues.

My first thought had been to plant Tempranillo vines for red wine. I know, I know, I've said that this variety won't flourish in Andalucia because the winters are too warm and it was during this little phase of research that I found that out. At the time I liked the idea of it because it must be about the most famous grape in Spain, the most widely grown red grape variety in the county (but mainly in the Rioja region in the north) and the thought was to play safe in my choice. Whilst I thought I could pull this project off, I could see that planting the vineyard in southern Spain but looking after it from the UK was going to produce logistical challenges, so let's make everything as simple as I can. Deciding on an exotic vine variety was perhaps extending the limb I was going out on a little too far, so Tempranillo initially seemed a good idea (though the wine couldn't be called Rioja as such wine has to be made in the Rioja region). My thoughts at the time were that unaged wine from just Tempranillo grapes can be a bit bland so maybe I would plant a second variety, with the idea of making a blended wine? And should I just stick with red wine varieties? Maybe a white or a rosé as well – or maybe I'm making things too complicated? As regards sourcing the vines, there must be plenty of commercial growers given the number of vineyards in Spain, time to get on Google again. Reputable? Surely not a problem in such a major wine region but I'd heard stories of the occasional batch of diseased vines and I didn't want to be caught out. It can be that you don't realise that there's a problem with the vines until they fail to establish several years down the line, which would be a disaster. There were lots of similar little conundrums and logistical problems circling round in my head but mostly I was just relishing working through things and enjoying thinking about what was going to happen.

About a week after I had returned home I was still happily researching and planning what I needed to do when I came across an article in a magazine about British vineyards and their continued expansion, which you can imagine I was interested in and started to read. It detailed the mini-boom in the vineyard industry in this country; the increase in the land under vines; the improvement in the quality of the wine; the general positive vibes about the industry in the UK. I'm aware of most of what's being stated and I'm skim reading as I get to the sentence, "such advance in new planting in this country continues to be possible because the UK remains exempt from the ban on planting new vines in mainland Europe." My brain slowly registers that there's an important point in there and then suddenly kicks properly into gear. What? That is surely not possibly true! A ban on planting new vines in mainland Europe? My first thought is that some people who are paid to write professionally sometimes write absolute drivel. How can there possibly be a ban on planting vines in Europe, in the major wine producing regions in France, Spain, Italy and the rest? It's nonsense, how can this guy have written something that is so blatantly wrong? Then I think that the rest of the article showed he was pretty clued up. But the idea that some of the biggest wine producing areas in the world have a ban on planting vines, that's patently absurd. He must be mixing something up. Maybe there's a ban on planting certain varieties because of over production or something like that, or maybe restrictions in certain areas of Europe? But I'd better see what I could find out about it and after five minutes on Google I find it's true, more or less anyway. Since way back in the nineteen seventies in Europe there has been a ban on planting vines on new land, to curb the number of vines and the supply of wine. This is unbelievable, unconceivable, unthinkable, no, unimaginable! How can this possibly be and what do I do now?

At the root of the problem was The Common Agricultural Policy. Do you remember that there used to be lots of surplus farm production in the EU, referred to in the British papers as butter mountains and wine lakes and the like? Well, as far as I understand it, and I'm not pretending I'm the world's expert as it's a very complex and emotive subject, very heavy going but I hope I'm getting the essence of it here. As far as I understand it, the Common Agricultural Policy (CAP) is a series of subsidies for farmers both to iron out the fluctuations in the supply and demand and to encourage farmers to look after the environment. I'm not going to get into the rights and wrongs of the policy, and believe you me one of the mountains caused by the CAP is the amount that's been written about it. Many studies have been undertaken to test if it's 'a good thing' or if it's 'a bad thing'. Within these studies you can find support for whatever view you want to promote and, the issue being muddied by the politics at the heart of nearly every country in Europe, every possible view is promoted. You can usually spot the naked political posturing but trying to separate sensible research and commentary from the clever politicking is more difficult. But as I understand it, as far as I can make out these are main arguments.

On the plus side, as I've said before, farming is a vital industry that provides one of our basic necessities, food. However, it's a low income business working on narrow margins and highly susceptible to the vagaries of supply and demand and, of course, the weather. There is obviously a time lag of some months between sowing and reaping, the problem being that when you sow in the spring you have to guess how much you can sell after you reap in the autumn. Farmers, as far as I can make out, are pretty good at making such decisions, based on years of experience of their land and their trade. But compare the circumstances of farmers to that of industry. Like, for example, if you own a factory that produces the mythical widgets. If demand for widgets suddenly increases you can quickly put in place measures to produce more, to take advantage of the buoyant widget market. If widgets go out of fashion and demand falls, on an equally rapid timescale you can introduce measures to combat that. Slow down production, store the widgets until they become fashionable again, make something else, etc. In either case, you can react fairly quickly to market fluctuations. But farmers can't. In the spring they have to make a reasonable guess as to demand in the future, at harvest time, but they can't control everything and sometimes they get it wrong, probably because of a change in external conditions which leads to scarcity or surplus. Most years all goes well and they sell most or all of the crop, great! Money coming in, no problems and the circle starts again. But in the years they can't sell the produce, storing perishable crops isn't as easy as storing widgets and maybe the crop is rotting in a barn and no money comes in? Two or three years of such circumstances and they are in big trouble.

In the mid twentieth century this was a serious issue, as there was little in place as regards a safety net. But this is where the CAP came in because as its base the CAP declares that by law the EU must step in and buy the farm produce that cannot be sold on the open market, the main benefit of which is that it prevents the scenario above where farmers, particularly small farmers, were going bankrupt when they couldn't shift their produce. However, the negative side of this is that it can distort the market and surpluses start to accumulate, especially if growers realise that they can make a profit by just growing to sell to the EU, who are lawfully bound to buy the stuff. It's a guaranteed market, so I'll plant loads, by law the EU has to buy the surplus and it's not my problem what they then do with it! Let's illustrate this situation with the fictitious example of the celebrity Brussels sprout diet.

One spring, not so long ago when we were still in the EU, after the introduction of new varieties and a favourable press had resulted in the unprecedented high consumption of Brussels sprouts the previous Christmas, the benefits of Brussels sprout were being promoted everywhere. You couldn't avoid stories about these delicious green orbs, with stuff all over the internet and social media. TV adverts and the supplements of all the weekend papers were full of it. It seemed that every self-publicising TV or film celebratory, internet influencer, premier league footballer and the like could be seen drinking Brussels sprout sushi or eating Brussels sprout ice cream; workouts were accompanied by energy giving sprout snacks; hundreds of diets were quickly devised (eat only Brussels sprouts for a month and lose a stone – probably true); celebratory chefs were making every imaginable dish from Brussels sprout pate, Brussels sprout souffle, Brussels sprouts cheese cake to Brussels sprout chocolate sponge. As it gathers momentum a Brussels sprout juggler, balancing seven sprouts on her nose and one on each breast whilst simultaneously juggling another ten behind her back, wins Britain's Got Talent and performs at The Royal Variety Show. Over the proceeding winter the world has not been able to get enough of Brussels sprouts and come sowing time, as a farmer planning your crops for the coming summer, you see the market developing and you decide to plant sprouts in all your fields instead of the usual wheat, barley and other cereal crops.

It's early August, the fervour for Brussels sprouts is still at its height and there's still a month or so until you expect a plentiful harvest and your mega payoff, the weather's been good and you're looking at a bumper crop. In many years a bumper crop can actually be a bad thing because everybody else also has a bumper crop, the market is flooded and the price hits rock bottom (but the CAP sets a floor price and the buys in the surplus so you can always sell to them and you don't suffer too much). However, this year it's different. The Brussels sprout diet is more popular than ever and despite the bumper crop there's going to be a shortage. You anticipate selling all the crop at record prices. Everything is looking wonderful. That night you're watching the final of The Great British Bake Off and the winner is going to be decided by the best Brussels sprout based dish. In a novel twist, the winner isn't going to be decided by the usual judges but a six year old boy. He might be the son of a famous footballer; or the son of a film star or one of the cast of a prominent soap. He might even be the son of a minor Royal. It's all live, he's wheeled on at the start and he displays to the cameras, with the delightful oblivion that only young children can pull off, that he's not happy. The programme moves on and the big moment arrives, four Brussels sprout dishes to test and the one he likes best is going to be the winner. He's handed a spoonful of the first dish, a Brussels sprout gateau with blueberries and angostura bitters, cooked three ways. He takes hold of the spoon and yelling,

"I hate Brussels sprouts, they're 'orrible."

He throws the mush at the presenter, hitting him on the cheek below his left eye, where it sticks for a second before slowly sliding down his face, then dribbles lazily down his white shirt. Overnight it has 28.6 million views on YouTube, the majority from people who think, "you know what, the kid's got a point, Brussels sprouts are 'orrible'." The Brussels sprout fad has ended and the forward price of sprouts plummets. As a farmer it's a bit of a disaster in that you have lost the expected mega Brussels sprout payday and in times gone by, your Brussels sprouts would have rotted in the ground because it wouldn't even be worth your while harvesting them. However, these days the EU will come to your rescue. In a month's time the market is going to be flooded with Brussels sprouts that nobody wants to buy but the EU is legally obliged to set a floor price and buy the lot. You're peed off that you've missed out on the big payday but happy that because of the CAP you're not going to go bankrupt over the winter. But in the government commandeered warehouses of Europe, the Brussels Sprout Mountain has come into being.

Okay, this is a bit of an extreme example but it illustrates that the CAP can be a good thing in that 'it levels out the vagaries of supply and demand, maintains the food supply capacity and ensures that produces, particularly small producers, don't go bankrupt in bad years'. But it does distort the market and by ignoring the basic rules of supply and demand and as such it can be hugely wasteful, leading to overproduction (and surpluses have been known to be dumped on developing nations, undermining the livelihoods of farmers there). Additionally, there is always the temptation for suppliers to 'play the system'. Surpluses don't build up in the frivolous manner I describe above but sometimes they do because there is not the harsh discipline of the market to effect behaviour change. If too much milk was being produced in the EU and the CAP didn't exist, dairy herds would be slimmed down and farmers would move into the production of something else. However, a lot of investment has gone into building up a dairy herd, both from the financial point of view and in many cases emotionally as well. The herd may be the culmination of the work of generations. Change is expensive and it's pretty much impossible to flip and flop from one thing to another each year. Even if you know that there's too much milk, what the heck, you know the price that you're going to get for it from the EU and you can make a profit on that, so you just go ahead and produce the milk anyway. So we get milk quotas and more market distortion. And if you add into all of this that agriculture is such a huge and vital industry in most countries that politicians want farmer's votes (and there are a lot of them, politicians and votes) you finish up with the hugely complex wasteful/beneficial overbearing system that is the CAP today.

In the case of wine the system is further complicated. Let's say you are growing potatoes, or wheat (or Brussels sprouts). So, you get some decent seeds, prepare the land, plant the seeds, keep the land weed free and make sure the plant gets sufficient water (and maybe a bit of fertilizer) and a few months later, unless you are very unlucky, you harvest your crop and take it to market. With grapes, once you harvest the crop you are, of course, only halfway there. There then comes the complicated and time consuming second stage of turning the grapes into decent wine, which requires skill and expense. Ideally, you make wine that people are going to enjoy. But if you are 'playing the system', or just not very good at turning grapes into decent wine, or weren't producing grapes of sufficient quality to make decent wine, maybe you would skimp a bit on this second stage? If you were 'playing the system' and you thought you could make a profit at the price the EU was paying for wine, maybe you would just ferment the grapes for a bit so some alcohol is formed and its legally wine, bottle it up and send it to the EU warehouse. Don't bother tasting it but here's my invoice and bank details, just transfer the money there, thank you very much. Maybe there were also too many vineyards, too many bumper harvests or whatever but by 2005 there was certainly too much wine and the wine lake was getting bigger and deeper every year. At least with butter mountains and the like the product could be put in refrigerated warehouses and maybe sold eventually. A lot of the wine lake was apparently undrinkable and was mostly turned into industrial alcohol. It then became really silly when the EU decided to pay some vineyards to just distil the grapes straight into industrial alcohol so that the EU themselves didn't have the expense and bother! Chateaux de Floor Cleaner, great for your pipes and drains!

It was realised what was happening, that this state of affairs was unacceptable and reforms would have to be made. But you can't change things overnight. Some of the measures put in place were pretty drastic, including not only a ban on planting new vines in the major wine producing countries but also in some cases paying vineyard owners to grub up their vines (and if they are paying vineyard owners to grub up their vines you can't have somebody like me planting a new vineyard in the next field, can you?). Britain, as an emerging wine producing nation, was exempt and was soon to leave the EU anyway – but Spain certainly wasn't. And even though by the time I came along with my grand plans of planting 800 or so vines in Spain, things had been relaxed a little and each country could increase the land under vines by 1% per year, I was caught up in it and it wasn't looking very hopeful.

It's a wonderful example of the consequences of distorting the market. World wine consumption is growing year on year. You will be aware of all the new major wine producing regions that have sprung up, seemingly from nowhere, over the past few decades. More are still emerging and don't they produce rather good wine? Wine is one of the main industry sectors of the EU and they want a share of the expanding market for their own producers. So they are simultaneously wanting to increase production for export whilst reducing production to curb over supply. I can see that they want to increase production of good wine that sells for a premium and reduce the mass production of the crap. But who decides which wine is good enough (it's not a problem you have with carrots or lettuce)?

I got in touch with my Assesoria and it wasn't something he knew much about. However, he's a well-connected guy locally and he arranged an appointment for me to see the person responsible for agriculture on the town council. I'm back on the plane again. This isn't the kind of trip I was thinking of when I was plotting to pop over on all those jaunts I was planning. I went to the council late one afternoon, the man I saw was very understanding and tried to be helpful but there was no way forward. He explained that by law I would be allowed to plant up to the very precise number of three hundred and thirty-three vines outside of the CAP restrictions. But these vines had to be used to produce wine to be consumed by family and friends only (as previously mentioned was being done by some of the people I knew). None of it could be sold commercially; neither could the grapes be legally exported. To plant more than this and to operate commercially I would have to go into the tendering system that was used to allocate the 1% increase in vine production allowed each year. We then discussed this system in detail. I would have to put in my bid in the autumn and then wait to see what happened. But I had no knowledge of the 'playing field' and how level it would turn out to be. Would small producers be looked on favourably or would my bid to plant 800 vines be simply not taken seriously. As a new producer would I be at a disadvantage to the established producers who were looking to increase their holdings. They would certainly know 'the system' better than I, who would be going into it blind. Would there be the Spanish equivalent of an 'old boys' network' of people who had worked in the industry for years. Even worse, would people resent this foreigner trying to muscle in? I had no way of knowing but the refreshingly straightforward man I was talking to was pretty pessimistic about my chances of success and it was obvious that if I bought the land it might be many years before I received permission to plant my vines. It was also explained to me that the results of the tender were released each January. This seemed obtuse. Even if I took the gamble and went ahead, which by then I knew I wasn't, I couldn't work with that. I've already explained that vines have to be ordered in the autumn for delivery for planting the following April. How can I order in the autumn if I won't know until January if I'll be allowed to plant? I can't keep ordering in the autumn and cancelling in January; I can't take delivery of 800 vines every year hoping to sell them on if I can't plant; I can't keep them for the next year. Maybe if you are big enough you can make some kind of arrangement with the nursery, or maybe they have their own nursery. Whatever, I couldn't operate in this system. If I bought the land I wouldn't know if I would be allowed to plant in one, two, five years or whenever. This project was dead.

With great embarrassment I went to see the owner of the plot I was planning to buy and explained that I would have to withdraw my offer. I'm grateful to her in that she was actually quite understanding, if disappointed. However, I felt like an idiot who had wasted a lot of people's time and let them down and a couple of days later I got on the plane and went home, feeling somewhat less happy than the previous time I told you about. You might ask, why did nobody tell me about all this? And the simple answer is that nobody knew. Why would it even cross the mind of the people who had been helping me that it was not permitted, or it was severely restricted, to plant new vines in a major wine producing country like Spain? The estate agents? Why? They were used to selling houses or plots of land that people wanted to build on. As regards agricultural land, there had been a flurry of people looking for land to plant avocados (perhaps why my choice of plot had been so limited) but if anything Margaret and Paul were doing me a favour trawling round the countryside with me. As I've said, what kind of commission were they going to earn on the sale of a small field? The Assessoria, whom I only involved at the last minute anyway? He deals in tax and conveyancing and accounts. As far as he was concerned I was just buying a piece of land. There was nothing to suggest to anybody that there was a problem. On the contrary, plenty of Spanish people planted vines on their land, no doubt less than three hundred and thirty three and for their own use; and there had recently been a vineyard planted just outside Alora (best wine in Spain, how did he navigate the bureaucracy?).

On the plane home I'm thinking about, "What now?" I've put a lot into this and until the last week or so it's been great fun, going on the course at Plumpton, making lots of plans, frequently gadding over to Spain with a purpose but enjoying myself as well (my cycling had noticeably improved over the last six months). But I'd put a lot of emotional energy into it as well and it's not worked out. This wasn't just a bit of a project that had gone wrong. This was a lifestyle choice and something that was going to keep me occupied for the next decade or more, until one day, I suppose, it would all get physically too much. My last big job/role/project and it didn't come off. Though as I write this, with three or four years hindsight, I now look back and think that it might be a good thing that it didn't happen. Thinking about the work I've had to put into the field here in Anglesey, a similar size to the one I'd settled on in Spain, I wonder if I would have been able to manage to pull it off in Spain, working from a distance? Not just the amount of work but the timing of it and being on hand to spot problems. Maybe I would have found that I needed to spend longer and longer over there and it would become a millstone rather than an enjoyment? If the purchase had worked out, could it be that I might now be the proud owner of a very nice plot of weeds in Andalucia? For Sale; will accept half the price I paid for it. Who knows? And it's easy to ponder with hindsight, at the time I was pretty despondent.

So I'm on the plane home thinking, "What now?" I had my seventy five vines in Anglesey to look after and I've been on the course so I should be able to make a better fist of it. Not the same though, is it? But remember we have a field. I could plant some more. I know a lot more about how do go about it now (I think) and I'm painfully aware of the mistakes I've made with the vines on the bank. Why can't I plant a vineyard in our field in Anglesey and make a proper job of it? And this is what I think of as the true conception of Red Wharf Bay Vineyard as a commercial enterprise. On the plane coming back from Malaga, fed up, thinking about what next? It's not going to be the same as a vineyard in Spain though, is it? No, but easier to manage. Well, easier to do the work, and I won't be planting bush vines because the climate is such that they just grow and it will take considerably more care to nurture them. But I have my Principles of Vinegrowing badge, so I should be able to make a better hash of it. And as I'll be starting from scratch in the rest of the field, with my enhanced knowledge from the course I should be able to do things in the correct manner from the initial planting, which should generally improve the standard of everything. The existing vines are healthy, just mis-managed, and as I've said, I've been to other vineyards in North Wales and know it works if you do it properly. So why not?

What about the travel to Spain? That after all, to me, was a hugely advantageous part of the plan. So what about bringing stuff back from Spain to sell in a small vineyard shop? We had once speculated about importing Spanish ceramics to sell in garden centres and crafts fairs and the like but the idea hadn't gone much further than the bottle of wine that spawned it. But why not? But what's the link, why should a vineyard in Anglesey sell ceramics and other stuff – what? Leather, cowbells – from Spain. Does there have to be a reason? Yes, it's a bit lame if there isn't. I know, I wanted to plant my vineyard in Andalucía but in the end couldn't because of the Common Agricultural Policy; so I decided to plant my vineyard in our field in North Wales and bring a bit of Spain back to Anglesey. Yes, Red Wharf Bay Vineyard: Linking Anglesey and Andalucia.

I get off the plane and drive back down the A55 with my head buzzing. I get home,

"Morag, I've had an idea!"

The Wider Picture VII:
Wine Quality

What makes a good bottle of wine? I have my own ideas about this, a philosophy I would suggest everybody adopt. Personally, I start at a pretty basic level. I've said that to me if you have a glass of wine in your hand and you are enjoying drinking it then you are appreciating a good bottle of wine – and if it cost £7 from Tesco, all the better. If you are enjoying the wine, surely it's better to be enjoying a bottle that cost you a few pounds rather than having to pay twenty quid to satisfy your quaffing standards? If you were enjoying a pint of beer, you would call it a good pint. If you were eating a decent steak you would call it a good steak. I would say that it should be the same with wine but with wine it's not that simple, is it? There seems to be a lot of baggage thrown in.

A while ago there was a story well covered by most media about somebody having a meal at a restaurant being served a £2,500 bottle of wine by mistake, rather than the somewhat lower priced bottle they had ordered. The general take on the story was a sort of mix between, "What a cock-up" and, "Wasn't he/she/they lucky." A little reported nuance of the anecdote was that the beneficiary had 'only' ordered a £250 bottle of wine, to which my first thought was, "Who orders wine at two hundred and fifty quid a pop?" Then further thoughts went along the lines of, "What extra quality is there in a bottle of wine that costs two hundred and fifty quid a pop?" And then, "what's the difference between a two hundred and fifty quid bottle of wine and a two thousand five hundred quid bottle of wine (aside from the obvious answer of two thousand, two hundred and fifty quid)?"

Are the wines from Red Wharf Bay Vineyard of good quality? Well, the short answer is, "yes" but we've covered that I would say that, wouldn't I? And as I've said before, come and try them and make up your own mind. The most compelling evidence I can offer you to support my assertion is that most people who taste them seem to like them. But it's not universal and occasionally I get a pulled face. That's fine, people have different tastes and taste things differently. As I understand it, we are all born with a certain number of taste buds and, like brain cells, spend our lives killing them off. The way you taste is mostly dictated by the number of tastebuds you have left. I remember a story about a lady who in her adult life had retained as many taste buds as most babies have and earned a six-figure salary from a company that made baby food because she tasted the food just as a baby would. So people will taste things differently and the number of people who have killed off just the right number of taste buds and say, as they taste my wine, something to the effect of,

"That's really good" is gratifying. "Wow, nice wine from a vineyard on Anglesey!" As ever, I forgive the surprise in their voices.

So how do Red Wharf Bay Vineyard wines compare to the wine that cost £250 quid a bottle (or for that matter the one that costs £2,500 quid a bottle)? I don't know. I know there are people who could tell me, dedicated and skilled experts with years of training in the tasting of wine (and I know it's possible that their conclusion would not be the one I wanted). I've seen people taste a wine blind and know immediately the country of origin, region and grape varietal (I might even manage that with a few more popular wines but I would get it wrong more than I would get it right). And if you are taking this tasting lark seriously, that's just entry level stuff. I've heard of people who can identify not just the region from which the wine originated but the actual vineyard and even the vintage. Incredible! This requires not only considerable skill but also prodigious memory (but, I can't help thinking, how much wine have they had to drink to get there?).

The wine industry obviously needs people with such skills. I would say in particular good sommeliers, who should tell you which wine to drink with the food you have ordered; and people in the production process who can 'taste and adjust' as the wine is developing. I once went on a distillery tour at one of the major Cognac producers (not wine but similar tasting principles). It finished, of course, with a tasting session and as part of that we were told of the daily tasting tribunal, when the experts gathered to assess the progress of various barrels at the appropriate stage of production. Each would be tasted and the apposite next action decided upon to ensure they maintained the standard of perfection required. Somebody asked how the tasters came to be in their positions and the lady talked of years of practice and training. I wondered if this was enough. When I played rugby, no matter how hard I practiced and trained I was never going to play for England (or even get a regular berth in the first team of the club I played for) and I said something along those lines.

"Yes," she agreed. To operate to their standard it wasn't just practice and training but there also had to be, liked the baby food lady with the tastebuds, an anatomical advantage you were born with.

You don't have to drink much wine before you start to realise the difference between a seven pound bottle and one costing ten, fifteen or even twenty pounds (I'm referring to the supermarket retail price of imported still wines, perhaps it would be £40 or £50 for sparkling wine, and maybe you have to add a premium to that for UK wines because of our costs of production – see the later chapters on economics). You and your tastebuds start to discern the types of wine you prefer and you buy and drink accordingly. I would suggest that there is a rough correlation between increased price and increased enjoyment in the prices ranges above. But only a correlation, not an absolute link and I suspect it would tail off towards the top end (I don't know, I've haven't drunk enough wine at that price to give an informed opinion). But above £15 or £20 quid for still wine (and even approaching it) for most people is it worth it? Being flippant (maybe), if you take it too seriously are you not training your pallet so that you become more and more dissatisfied with most of the wine you drink? There has to be a reason why a bottle of wine will command a price of fifty or a hundred pounds. I don't know what it is and I don't want to find out. Do you (and who makes the rules anyway?)? Do you want to train your tastebuds so that spending ten, fifteen or twenty quid on a bottle of wine leaves you thinking that it's okay but doesn't have the X, Y or Z factor of that fifty quid bottle you forked out for last week? And where does it stop? Do you treat yourself to a hundred quid bottle next month? And are you vaguely dissatisfied, or not satisfied enough, with any wine you drink until then? Then finally you get to the Premier League and you're discussing the merits of a £2,500 bottle over a mere £250 bottle. But unlike the Premier League you are not getting paid millions for your skill but paying rather a lot to feed your expensive habit. The 'lucky recipient' of the £2500 bottle in the restaurant cock-up mentioned above didn't even notice their good fortune. In the extremely unlikely event of me finding myself in the same situation, I doubt I would either.

Back in the real world I would guess (my favourite form of research) that eighty or ninety percent of the people who drink wine just want to enjoy the glass that's in front of them. They've had a hard day/week/month and they just want a pleasant drink to help them relax when they get home, or a drink with a couple of mates on the way. Or they are going out for the night or are on holiday and just want a glass of wine, they're not going to think about it much. They know roughly what style of wine they like and they will happily order it and enjoy it – so it's a good bottle of wine. A more economic way of enhancing your enjoyment of wine is maybe to start to learn which foods to pair with which wines. After all, if you spend ten quid on a bottle you can get a lot of cheese with the change from the fifty quid somebody else is spending on a more expensive bottle. Again, it's more important that you find out which wines you prefer with which food, they're your tastebuds. You can easily find lots of advice, though I recently enjoyed an article that bemoaned the point at which advice becomes rules and suggested pairing a green chili cheeseburger with a crisp Chablis. If that's what you like, go for it and don't let advice become rules. But mostly, just have a glass of wine and appreciate it for what it is. If you're enjoying a good bottle of wine, great – be happy!

CHAPTER 10

Finally, I Plant a Vineyard

So, here we are. This is supposed to be a book about a vineyard in Anglesey and we're through to Chapter 10 and I'm only just getting round to planting it! But after a fairly circuitous journey (it feels like a series of random and arbitrary events have happened over the years and now there's a vineyard – arbitrary fortune) I'm finally there and now it was time to get down to the task of turning our hay meadow into a functioning vineyard. I've explained previously that when you plant vines for the first time, as with my initial efforts on the bank, you make your biggest decisions when you know least: where to plant, what to plant and how to plant. Because if you decide in a few years that you got those fundamentals wrong, frankly it's too late. Well, by the time I came to plant the main vineyard I knew a bit more about things but I'm still about to make those fundamental vineyard decisions and I'm nervous.

I'm walking round the field trying to think things through. It's a sunny day and the view is as glorious as ever, but I'm not giving it my usual regard as inconsistent thoughts bounce round my head. When I decided that, okay, I'll shift my thwarted Andalucian plans to Anglesey I had imagined just going for it and planting the whole of the field. However, as I deliberated further it struck me the it might be better to do it in two stages. As I walked round I was confronted with the reality of the amount of work involved and I began to think that if I started with, say, planting about a third of the field I could still manage it all 'by hand' (by that I mean with my gardening tools). If I planted the full acre, maybe twelve to fifteen hundred vines, I would probably need machinery to help me with the work. But what machinery? I couldn't spend a fortune gearing up with every bit of kit that might be useful only to find I didn't need or use half of it. But how would I know what to spend money on and what I could continue to do off my own bat if I didn't test it out first. Perhaps it would be better to plant, say, three hundred vines, and work my way into it, as they had said on the course, to get to know my own vineyard.

"It depends..." and included in this concept of variable methodology is simply finding out what works on your land. What will thrive and what won't work under your own unique set of conditions? But how do I go about working this out, how do I take it on board in practical terms? Do I just, "suck it and see"? It all seemed straight forward in the classroom but now I'm bombarded with thoughts, doubt and indecision. A lot of my working life has involved testing things, whether this be in an IT system or on a research project. Fundamental to the process is to isolate one variable and then make controlled changes to test how that variable reacts; or make controlled changes to the variable and see how each change effects the rest of the system. The key is to isolate the variable of interest but in vineyards there is such a huge combination of interacting variables that this seems impossible. The soil, the vine variety, the rootstock (there's more than one type of American rootstock), management (particularly pruning), the weather and much else. And when you do try to test things out in a vineyard, mostly you only get the results of any experiment once each year, at harvest, and the first one of those won't be for three years. If I decide to test a different pruning method and it seems to work, or doesn't, how do I know the improvement (or deterioration) in performance isn't down to some aspect of, say, the weather that year? I know of vineyards in close proximity to each other where a vine variety will thrive in one and fail in another for no obvious reason. Why would that be and how do you work it out? If I was planning this as an academic project I would divide the field up into small parcels and plant different varieties/rootstocks and use different husbandry methodologies in each parcel, all controlled and minutely measured and annotated. Then in five years I would study the results and I would have the data for an interesting academic paper, but I wouldn't have a functioning vineyard.

I continued to ponder as I walked round. It struck me that another reason for starting by just planting part of the field was that

128

I wasn't sure what mix of varieties I wanted to finish up with, several years down the line. There was always going to be Solaris for still white wine as I already had seventy five of these vines and I'd tasted the product from better managed vines than mine. I looked across at the vines I had mismanaged for five years. They grew well enough and were healthy, I just wasn't looking after them properly to make them produce and ripen sufficient grapes. I knew that if tended better the vines would thrive, the grapes would grow and ripen and then produce a decent wine. I had already decided that I also wanted a grape for still red wine as well the Solaris and, after a bit of research, mostly asking people on the course, had more or less decided that probably the best bet would be the Rondo variety I've already told you about. So that's a red wine and a white wine; solid and fairly safe choices. But what about producing a sparkling wine or a rosé? Most UK vineyards plant one of the vine varieties suited to producing sparkling wine, the attraction being the premium price that it can command obviously offers the potential for a better profit margin. But making sparkling wine is a more involved process than making still wine and it usually takes two years from after you harvest the grapes to when the wine is ready. Do I want to invest in the extra equipment and will I have the additional skills needed to make such wines? Rosé? I'm not sure what the market would be like. But even if I stick to just still red and white wine, should I plant more than one variety of each to either make different still wines or a blend a wine from two or more grapes? If I plant just part of the field I can 'see how things go' and decide accordingly when I'm ready to plant the rest. I more or less resolve that I'll plant just a third of the field but defer a decision on exactly what I'll plant and give up for the day.

As I thought it through further over the next few days other considerations came into play. A pleasant and unexpected benefit after my ignominious retreat from Spain was the realisation that, whilst I'm currently struggling to think things through and make decisions, I'm much more relaxed about the whole thing now that I'm literally planting in my own backyard. As I think my way further into this enforced change of plan suddenly, despite my indecision and pondering of all the variables, somehow there seem to be generally a few less unknowns. Maybe it's just that when I wake up at three in the morning thinking about things (I do occasionally but not obsessively and generally I sleep well, thank you for your concern) I will be able to just go into the field at breakfast time and think through properly whatever has crept into my head that night, so I can stop worrying about it, rather than letting it fester for a few weeks until my next trip to Spain. Maybe it's just that I'm more familiar with how things work here and I won't have to battle with a different culture and language? Occasionally, something a bit worrying had happened as regards the house in Spain, for instance an unexpected letter from the taxman or the local authority (I'm not going to incriminate myself by talking about regulations I've inadvertently broken in Spain simply because I didn't know they existed). Whatever it was that had happened had go on the list of things I had to sort out the next time I was over there, and then it would be a niggling worry until the next trip that something serious/costly was amiss. As I was mulling things over I had already wondered if I might have 'missed a bullet' when I had to pull out of buying land in Spain but it was still too close and raw for me to admit that.

Additionally, I'm beginning to appreciate that there's a further dimension to having a vineyard in Anglesey that wouldn't have been possible if the vineyard had been in Spain. In Spain I was just going to grow grapes as an 'absentee landlord', then turn them into wine to sell. In Anglesey I've realised that I can open the vineyard to tourists and host vineyard tours. I'm looking at the view over the bay and it's suddenly blindingly obvious that people would love to come to this delightful place for vineyard tours and wine tastings. As I'm in permanent residence here I could organise such tours and wouldn't somebody on holiday on the island love to be shown round the vineyard and then sit on the patio overlooking the bay, drinking wine? If I'm going to add that string to my bow this can't just be a scruffy field with vines growing in it. It's got to look the part and I need to take that into account as I'm setting things up.

Additionally, a very clear advantage over most business start-ups is that finances are not a great worry. At this point I was still doing a small amount of freelance IT work, just the contracts I felt obliged to not abandon. I'm not distressed that this seems to be drying up and I wasn't actively looking for more. Morag has a proper career and is planning to continue working full time for a few years yet. So that's one regular income and we have another small one in that as I've explained I'm now a pensioner. It's not a desperate business gamble and there's no need to go 'all in' and look for the maximum financial return in the minimum time. More and more I'm coming round to the idea of why not work my way into it slowly? I said at the beginning that this is not one of those stories where we give everything up to embark on some wide, heartfelt venture and eventually, against all the odds, bask in the glory of our success. The middle class perch is still comfortably under our feet and we would like it to stay there. I had already decided that I was going to use the money I earned from my last freelance contracts to set up the vineyard and I had promised Morag, once I had made the initial investment, that it wouldn't become a money pit. If it 'keeps me out of trouble' and I'm enjoying myself, fine. If it does no better than breaking even I'll be a bit disappointed but not unhappy.

At some point in this period of perusing I casually set myself the target of maybe eventually earning perhaps five hundred pounds a month to supplement my pension. Not exactly shooting for the moon and based on nothing more than, not for the first time, just plucking figures out of the air. But if I can do that and enjoy myself for the next decade or so then, I might not hit The Sunday Times Rich List but I'll think it, in my terms, a very successful endeavour. After a few years, when I've shown it works, maybe I could buy the adjacent field and plant a few thousand more vines. That would triple? Quadruple? wine production; and I'd have better access and could build a proper shop, perhaps a café with a car park and maybe even a coach park; and a proper winery? No, no, no; ignore all that. Too much hassle and going back to being like having a job again. It's never going to happen.

On the other hand, whilst I'd come round to the idea playing the long game and planting in two stages, I was keen to get started. We were now in October and if I didn't get the vines ordered quickly I wouldn't have any for next spring and would miss the next planting season, thus have to wait another year. I might be more relaxed and taking the long view of how things would eventually finish up but I was much too impatient to delay the actual start for a whole year.

I'm again in the field having what I hope will be a final look around and think about things before I place the order for the vines.

The aspect is wrong, I haven't tested the soil, the climate is a bit marginal, is wind going to be a problem? Is proximity to the sea a problem? I look across to the vines I already have. I know that the Solaris grows here. If the vines will grow in the unfavourable conditions on the bank they will grow in the field, I just need to manage the vines better to make better grapes. To hell with more testing, it will just delay me for a year. I make the decision and walk off the field then dive straight in and order another three hundred and twenty five vines, bringing me up to four hundred in total. I decided on another hundred Solaris, making one hundred and seventy five in total; and two hundred and twenty five Rondo for still red wine. I cannot for the life of me remember why I picked these odd numbers rather than making it two hundred of each.

I placed the order, transferred the deposit (you usually have to pay half on order, half just before delivery) and sat back to think about how much of the advice from the Plumpton course on site selection and planting a vineyard I had just ignored. I justify myself by thinking that if I'm going to plant on Anglesey I'm going to plant in our field. I didn't select the site, it selected me. I'm not going to look around for a better place that I could no doubt find but involves me traveling five miles every time I need to do a bit of work (let's forget that a few weeks ago I was planning to have to travel fifteen hundred miles to do the weeding). If we are going to have a vineyard in Anglesey I'm going to wake up every morning overlooking it; I'm going to walk around it in the evening looking at what's happening; I'm going to be working in the field in the afternoons, occasionally stopping to admire the view of the bay; and I'm going to sit in the garden on sunny days and drink the eventual product raising a glass to the vines that spawned it.

Yes, the new vines will be on a gentle north east facing slope, probably the worst aspect. I've said before that Anglesey is on one of the western extremities of the UK and pretty far north. Days are longer here in summer than almost everywhere in England and Wales. And if anything, the soil is too good and encourages 'the wrong kind of growth', too much vigour. I've explained that in most of the field the top soil is at least eighteen inches deep, it having been a hay meadow for decades or longer, so it's full of nutrients. The problem with vines is they mostly just want to grow, to produce canes and foliage rather than grapes, and it's always a bit of a battle with them. As previously stated, vines generally produce grapes when they are stressed ("Help" I'm going to die, I'd better produce seeds to create the next generation). Solaris and Rondo are very vigorous vines. One of my problems with the Solaris on the bank was that I hadn't wielded the secateurs as strongly as I should (Oh dear, I might kill the vine) and I'd let them put too much energy into producing foliage. You wouldn't believe how much wood I hack off a vine in winter if I've let it get a bit out of control. I think they are going to grow here and it's managing that growth that's going to be the issue. If the vineyard is going to be in Anglesey it's going to be in our field so let's just get on with it and see what happens. Suck it and see after all.

Winter passes and suddenly it's April and it's getting towards time to plant, so I need to prepare the ground. The nursery I'm buying from is in Herefordshire and I'm in touch to talk about delivery. They already have my vines safely in cold storage there. I was keen to get them as soon as possible but they were nervous and advise me not to plant them too early as, once the buds start to burst, a late frost is disastrous. They seem overcautious but they explain that they had had a heavy frost down there the previous night, minus two centigrade. I check the local forecast, in Anglesey the overnight low was seven centigrade (It depends...). However, I realise that there's no point putting myself under unnecessary pressure and a delivery date of 3rd May agreed, giving me a few extra weeks to get the field ready. When they arrive I will need to get them in quite quickly or there is a danger they will dry out and die. If you are sure of what you are doing you can keep them safely for quite a while before planting but, whilst I know the theory, I've never done it on this scale before and I'd rather err on the side of caution. The most I had previously planted in one season was the batch of fifty Solaris and they all went in the ground the day they arrived. Similar rapidity wouldn't be possible this time. They come out of cold storage at the nursery and, I presume from the excellent condition in which they arrive, are sprayed with water before being sealed in plastic to keep them wet on the journey, by next day courier. Ideally, as soon as they arrive, if you can't plant them you put them back into cold storage until you are ready to use them but

I don't have the facility for that. Keeping them damp (not soaking) and dark is vital and if kept properly they will be okay for X days. But out of the ground they seem to be quite delicate and I don't know what value to give X. As an example of their fragility, when planting previously I had taken a bunch of twenty five, split them next to the planting site and just started. I was lucky. On the course we were warned that we would not be the first to find that on a sunny day it's likely that if you do just leave twenty five plants lying around they will dry out before you plant the last of the bunch and that the final few will have desiccated and won't take. I guess it wasn't sunny when I had previously planted but I'll need to be pretty nippy to get in three hundred odd without mishap.

To prepare the land I need to lay out the field, to decide where the rows are going to be planted and how far apart they should be spaced. I also need to prepare the ground and I need to install the posts that will eventually support the trellising systems. I'm making decisions that should be easy but I'm nervous because they are irreversible and I've never done this before, or never done it properly before. As I've suggested, once we've rammed in a hundred plus posts and planted three hundred and twenty five vines I can't just change my mind, can I?

There's one question I've heard countless people ask, including me, before they plant their first vines. How far apart do you space them? How far apart should the rows be and by how much do you separate the vines within the rows? You would think that there would be a pretty straightforward answer to that but guess what? It depends...... If you plant too far apart, either regarding rows or plant spacing, you are wasting that valuable commodity, land. If you separate rows by an extra half metre and also space the plants an extra half metre apart you will roughly half the number of vines you can fit in any one field and thus half the eventual yield per acre of the vineyard. But if you are planting a large area you are going to eventually need heavy equipment for maintenance and you need to make the rows wide enough for it to get through. Even in smaller vineyards it's likely at some point that you will acquire a small tractor. I know that I've planted the vines on the bank too close together, they shade each other out and it's very difficult to manoeuvre to work them. However, in some places (not Anglesey) such close spacing can actually be a good strategy. In Spain, for example, where you have plenty of sun and the shading out can be beneficial. I've seen many vineyards where the plants are packed much closer than you would position them in more northern areas because the climate allows it, the extra vines thus substantially increasing overall yield of the field. Even in more northern areas of Europe (perhaps France rather that North Wales) I've come across the theory that if you plant the rows closer together it traps in the heat of the sun and helps the grapes ripen (you put ten vineyard owners/managers in a room together...). Also, different varieties could need different spacing along the row to stop them overlapping, vigorous varieties needing more room to grow.

I stand in the field and agonise about this when I should just make a decision, cross with myself because despite the above considerations, I suspect that unless I do something really stupid there's probably not a wrong way of doing this. Or then again, what if there's something I don't think of and I do something inappropriate that stands as evidence of my ineptitude for years to come? I haven't got a lot of space, so maximising the number of vines I can fit in is a big factor. I will never have really big machinery so I don't need to worry about that; though I might one day have mini-tractors and the like so there needs to be a decent row width (and I don't want them shading each other out); and I want room to work, not like on the bank. Also, if I'm going to do tours there needs to be space between the rows, both for aesthetics and for people to pass through. I decide to do a trial layout using canes. When I do this for real each new vine will be planted next to a cane for support so I already have a stack of about 350 these. Once I have planted I'm going to be looking at the vineyard for a good many years, so half a day testing to see how it might appear seems a prudent measure.

I also need to decide quickly about trellises. For a start, wood or metal? It appears that most vineyards are coming round to the idea that metal is best; cheaper, easier to install and longer wearing. However, wood looks better and the tourism idea is coming more to the fore. Even though it's more expensive and more difficult to install I'm only doing a small area so the extra expense and effort is not overmuch. The trellis wiring can wait until the following winter but the posts themselves will be 2.4 metres long, 75 cm of which has got to be rammed into the ground. This needs a JCB with a post-rammer and I won't want such a heavy bit of kit plus attendant folk tramping around the vineyard after planting, especially when the new vines are fragile. So I have to get the posts in before the new vines arrive. I've already hired Dave, a local contractor, and his son (and JCB) to do the heavy work. All I have to do is mark out the site, so fairly imminently I have to come to a decision about the row and plant spacing but I manage to continue to fret over it for several days. You obviously need a post at each end of a row, then you also need interim posts every 7 or 8 metres or so to support the trellis wires. There will be eighteen, nineteen, twenty rows, depending on how I space the vines and I reckon between 8 and 25 vines in each row (such numerical variety because the field is an odd shape). Finally, they should run north-south (so each side of the vine gets cooked equally by the sun each day) and have space at each end to turn equipment and so the bloke who cuts the hedges each year can get his tractor round.

I start the trial layout. I'm armed with tape measure, canes (those marked with red tape are the trellis poles, the others for the vines) and have a compass round my neck to keep me on my north south axis. First row, lay down the tape measure, check the orientation. Stick in the red cane at the end, let's say the plants are going to be 1.4 metres apart, so five plants between each post; first plant cane 0.7 metres from the post; cane, 1.4 metres, cane, 1.4 metres, cane, 1.4 metres, cane, 1.4 metres, cane, 0.7 metres, cane with red tape for the next post. Simple now I've started and I just get on with it but it's surprisingly easy to get confused in the middle of the field. Sticking in canes to mark where posts will go is not greatly intellectually challenging and my mind wanders. After a few rows are finished the canes go north south but you can also look from a different angle and they line up from different aspects as well. I find I go off on more than one dogleg, each time having to start again, which is a bit embarrassing even if I'm the only one that's aware of it. Can't stick in sticks in a straight line, Kevin? I've decided the rows should be 1.6 metres apart and I get about six rows in and pause to have a look. Are they too narrow? This is test so let's try different distances. I start again at plants 1.6 metres apart; rows 1.8 metres apart. Too far spaced? I change my mind, then I change my mind again. And each time I change my mind I don't take all the canes up, for comparison. But this just makes things more confused. I then realise I've make a complete mess of it, take them all up and decide to go and have a drink and do it tomorrow. I eventually decide, somewhat arbitrarily but as I had originally thought, that the rows will be 1.6 metres apart and the plants will be separated by 1.4 metres, which I stick to meticulously as I successfully lay out all the canes the next day.

Now armed with figures for exactly how many posts I wanted I had to go out and buy them. I needed 'tree trunks' for the end posts, less substantial ones for the interim poles. A visit to the local agricultural contractor went without hitch as he had all the wood I needed in stock. As I was leaving he asked if I would be interested in a new product he has just started to sell called, unimaginatively, Postsaver. It's a bitumen based sleeve, guaranteed to prevent wooden posts rotting for twenty years, which seems an impressive boast to me. Wooden posts usually rot near the base, at soil level, caused by the interaction of the wood, the damp soil and the oxygen in the air. The idea of this product was that you fitted the sleeve to the post at that level and melted it in place with a blowtorch, the protective properties of the bitumen severely curtailing any ensuing rot. The guarantee amused me as it seemed slightly preposterous. Did they fit a sleeve to a post, ram it in the ground and wait twenty years to see what happened before they started marketing it? If the post rots after nineteen years, where do I claim my refund? Nonetheless, I buy enough Postsaver to cover all my posts, and a blowtorch. It's pretty cheap, seems scientifically solid and if it adds only a few years life to the posts it will be worth the afternoon I spent playing with the blowtorch (never used one before). We shall see what happens, feel free to contact me in 2037 to ask.

Finally, I needed to get the ground ready. Most will plough the area before planting new vines and, with hindsight, maybe I should have done. But that would mean finding a farmer willing to do it for me and I'm a bit daunted by the idea of that. I don't think finding somebody who can and will to do such a piddling little job would be easy, especially as all the land around here is grazed by sheep and, I think, rented by a farm twenty miles away. How much do I pay him; when can he do it? With the vines on the bank I keep the circle around the base of each clear but otherwise let grass grow along the row in between, cutting it regularly. I know that it's a pain to do that on the bank but it would be easier on the flatter field, where the vines are better spaced. I decide I'll stick with that, it's the easier option to organise and will look better for visitors. I found out much later that there is a school of thought that it would be 'criminal' to plough ancient hay meadows because there are so few left in the country and it destroys a unique eco-system, so I win some accidental brownie points there. However, I still had to find a way of initially cutting the grass in the field to prepare for planting and then subsequently keep the grass down over a quite extensive area. I can't just use the lawnmower. Inspiration as to how I would achieve this this came obtusely.

I've mentioned Nefyn, with whom I used to work. I was talking to him one day as plans were advancing and he told me he had friends who owned a vineyard in Herefordshire. This was a coincidence as not only did Antony and Ania, with whom we shared the house in Spain, live in Herefordshire but a couple of weeks later we were going down there to visit them for the weekend (another Old Onslownian reunion). I was eager for any relevant input and I asked if he thought it would be possible for me to go and have a look at his friend's vineyard when I was down there and after a quick phone call they kindly agreed to show me around.

Sunnybank Vineyard is run by Sarah and Richard Bell and it's a very unusual vineyard in that the grapes are most definitely of secondary importance. Sunnybank is the National Collection of Vines, awarded full collection status by The Royal Horticultural Society in 2010, and they have (as at the day I visited) 478 different varieties of vine growing there. To support the collection they sell vine cuttings (mostly small quantities to individuals rather than to commercial growers). Grapes do inevitably appear and then ripen each year, so at harvest time they lump them all together and ship them off to a winery to be made into uniquely blended wine, Bacchus/Bianca/Muscat Ottonel/Noblessa/Pinot Blanc/ et al, et al, et al..... rosé. No blend is ever the same but it comes back a very drinkable wine. We get on well as they show me around and decide that, I can't remember if I asked or they invited, I would come back in a few weeks to spend a day helping with the winter pruning. For me, the more hands-on experience I can get, the better.

Winter pruning is actually the most important job of the year. It involves cutting away most of the previous year's growth to set the vine up for the next season. Grapes will mostly only grow on wood that was new the previous year. If you can imagine a typical vine with a trunk of about two to three feet high. At the head of the trunk canes emerge and you usually select the best two of these (with possibly a couple of stubs left for the following year) and cut away everything else. You are trying to create a balance between stressing the plant sufficiently to produce grapes, neither leaving too much on, which can mean that the plant doesn't have enough energy to ripen the grapes; nor leaving too little and decreasing your yield. If you knew what the weather was going to be like in the months to come it would help but depending on (it depends...) variety/ climate/vine age and other factors you select your cane and count about five buds along and then cut. When completed this leaves a traditionally shaped vine, a trunk of two or three feet coming out of the ground and two canes at right angles which will eventually be tied to the bottom wire of the trellis system. As spring arrives the buds you have left on the canes will burst and produce the new canes, foliage and grapes for that season. Of course, vines don't read textbooks and don't all grow as instructed therein and with some of mine you would struggle to recognise anything like a traditionally shaped vine.

Sarah and I spend a few hours doing the pruning, memorably accompanied by a magnificent red kite who seems to regard these fields as home territory, hovering low over the vineyard. I've never seen one before and I'm enthralled. Richard then shows me the equipment they use to keep everything under control. They have about two hectares, so more to look after than I but he but offers much useful advice, including about keeping the grass down. I had got as far as thinking that maybe I would be able to get some kind of second hand sit-on mower for perhaps 500 quid and I mention this. Richard didn't think this would work very well, such movers being fine for nice flat golf courses and hotel lawns but not up to the more rugged and sloped terrain of a vineyard. He showed me the small tractor they used, which was perfectly suited to the job and even had a cutting boom that sensed the vines and retracted accordingly as you moved along. He simply drove slowly down each row, the cutting boom deployed behind him. When the boom sensed the vine it retreated back towards the tractor to avoid damaging it, extending again as soon as it had cleared the trunk. Each row cut in one pass, turn and go back along the next one, brilliantly efficient.

However, he had paid £3,500 for the kit, second hand. Annual maintenance wasn't cheap either. This is out of my league as I'm expecting the installation of the whole vineyard to cost less than that. You might be surprised at such a low budget but vines from a commercial nursery are less than £3 each, so about £1000 for 325; materials and installation of trellising about the same, plus the same again on sundry expenditure. I'm doing most of the labouring myself and I already have the land, so no expense there and so in total not as much as you might think. £3,500 for a mower would just about double my expenditure.

The conversation with Richard had focused my thoughts though and when I return home I'm still considering it. I wonder if I'm overthinking this for my little patch? The vines are ordered and Dave will be here in a couple of weeks to sort out the posts but grass is definitely growing. This is before I've laid out the canes but I've marked the rough boundary of how far into the field I will plant, so know the area I have to clear of grass. Okay, maybe I could just use the lawnmower? The obvious flaw in that plan is that it's an electric mower with limited cable length. I go to the electrical supply shop and buy a very long extension lead and I join this to a second cable to get sufficient reach. I sort out the inevitable tangling and get on with it and despite the amusement of the children,

"Mum, mum, come and look, dad's mowing the field!

In two hours I've finished. I'm triumphant! I doubt the old lawnmower will last the year (it didn't) but what's a new lawnmower every year or two compared to the cost of the alternative? And that's how I've done it, so far, ever since.

It's finally time to plant. The vines have arrived, the field is mown and laid out and all the posts are in. Dave and son came the previous Saturday and it's such a pleasure watching and working with people who really know what they are doing. Working as a team, one in the cab, one on the ground the post is tapped in, check with a spirit level, tapped in a bit more, check, tap, check, tap, finished, move on to the next. In one day they rammed in one hundred and twenty eight posts; all perfectly lined up not just in the rows that I've laid out but, by 'adjusting' a few of my canes, in lines perpendicular to the rows as well, to make it more aesthetically pleasing. And as a bonus they dug a hole for the children's trampoline. The safety equipment had broken last autumn and a new set of nets was going to cost about £160. Instead of that they suggested I let them spend ten minutes with the JCB digging a hole and lay down the trampoline safely flush to the ground, so there was nowhere to fall off? Simple but inspirational and indeed completed in ten minutes. If only everyday went so well.

If I'm going to plant three hundred and twenty five vines a fundamental requirement is to dig three hundred and twenty five holes and I will need to dig them quickly ('no', it needed a bit more subtlety than digging a pit for a trampoline). Previously when planting I've done the digging by just taking out a spade and getting on with it but that was only twenty five, then fifty holes and both times there had been a decent amount of rain and the ground was soft. The holes need to be about one foot deep by roughly nine inches in diameter. I had a test dig but the weather had been dry and the ground was harder than when I'd done it before. Also the grass of the hay meadow was matted and interlocking and difficult to cut through, so hand digging didn't feel like a viable option. You might think that this shouldn't be a panic as all I need to do is to get the holes dug well in advance of the arrival of the vines. But on the course we were told not to do this as the soil water will drain away and dry out round the side of the hole and the air will also dry the little pile of soil you have left exposed, both to the detriment of the vines when eventually planted. The normal method is to use a wide bore soil auger, dig the hole, apply a bit of water, put the plant in immediately and fill the hole. During the weeks of preparation I had been pondering where I might buy or hire such a thing as a wide bore soil auger but it turned out that I didn't need one.

Claire occasionally keeps a horse or two in our field. The field isn't big enough to permanently graze horses but they come for a couple of months at a time, which will still continue with the unplanted land. I know her because her daughter is the same age as Lili and they go to school together. Her husband Hayden is a hotelier and mends boats, which is an unusual combination of livelihoods but indicates his range of skills. The horses were back and he and I were building a fence along the last line of Dave's poles, to segregate the horses from the pending vines. I told him about my problem with the holes and the need for a wide bore soil auger, hoping that within his extensive connections he would have an idea as to where I might source the auger. I was surprised when he said not to bother as he would dig the holes. His brother had just bought a mini-digger (a very small JCB sort of thing) for his business and Hayden was itching to have a reason to have a go and I thought, why not?

On the day the vines arrived so did Hayden and the digger. He starts digging and I wait for him to get a few holes in front before I start planting. The digger is only small but very powerful. It rips into the soil and only needs one scoop for each hole. Dig, scoop, lay the soil next to the hole and move on to the next one. The digging bucket was about a foot wide, a little bigger than ideal but that shouldn't be a problem. The problem was one of finesse, it was very difficult to keep the holes to the size I wanted. Sometimes he could just about manage it, a delicate hole about one foot by one foot and the required one foot deep, with a neat pile of soil beside it. Mostly it just didn't happen like that. The scoop width restricted the hole width to the required one foot but the hole could stretch up to three feet long and might be two feet deep. That's a lot of soil and the field was soon covered in mini mountains, as though we were suffering a plague of demented giant moles. I'm very grateful that he's getting me out of the planting dilemma but I'm starting to have concerns. We carried on for a while, it was taking me a lot longer to plant the vine and fill the larger than expected holes than it was taking him to dig it. After a while I looked up and I'm seriously worried: I've got to get these vines planted and suddenly the devastation in the field is now on par with a first world war battlefield. I wonder if I can get ever it back in shape. Morag comes round the corner of the house,

"Bloody hell, I thought you were planting a vineyard not digging a mine." However, I'm committed, I have no plan B. I've got to get on with it and get them in. Hayden finished digging in half a day but it took me four days to insert a vine in each hole and fill it in again. At least there would be lots of air around the plant roots. All this was not helped by it being one of those rare May weeks when the sun just shone. I kept the unplanted bunches in a cool room and kept spraying them to keep them damp and that thankfully that worked. When I split the bunches I kept the vines under the shade of a bush at the edge of the field with a little spray can nearby, so the need to traipse back and forth didn't aid productivity. But when we had finished the field was flat again. There was soil everywhere but I knew the grass would eventually just grow back through it and it would get back to normal. And there were all these little stick things protruding from the soil, all in nice neat little lines. I finally had a proper vineyard. It might be the consequence of some arbitrary fortune. It might be situated fifteen hundred miles from where it was planned to be in a place in which I had landed more or less at random. It might be behind a house we obviously couldn't afford and in a field we initially didn't want and the original vines might been planted on a whim and totally mismanaged. But now there it was, quietly starting to grow.

The Wider Picture VIII:
The Route to Market

How do you start a commercial vineyard business? A fairly fundamental question and one we were asked at one point on the course at Plumpton. The Director of the unit was again lecturing and as always he was refreshingly happy to expand into wider aspects of the subject, as appropriate, and we were equally happy to soak up his words and hopefully benefit from his acquired wisdom. At one point, as an aside, he started talking about setting up a wine business and asked the above question,

"How do you start a commercial vineyard business?"

However, nobody replied. Perhaps, as I was, they were daunted by the enormity of its scope and unwilling to put ourselves so casually on the line. I certainly didn't want to get up in front of the class and say what my plans were. I mean, I had an idea in my head as to what I was aiming at but nothing so formal that you could actually call 'a plan', let alone a business plan and the strictures that invoked. My thoughts basically revolved around planting and nurturing the vines and eventually producing grapes. Then to make wine that I hoped would be of reasonable quality (then take some to friends' dinner parties and say, "this is from the vineyard," to general approval and envy). Then to build up a business selling it to the public, probably starting with local shops, pubs and restaurants. There's a large Spar attached to the local petrol station that has a brisk tourist trade and I envisaged turning up there to see if I could strike a deal. I knew it was going to be relatively expensive wine (see the bit about micro economics that comes later) and the scope for return is thus squeezed because both myself and the store have to make a profit. However, I'm a local producer with a product that will catch the eye, so it should work. Hopefully they take some to try, find they can sell it and we are up and running. I'll then try at a few bars and maybe a restaurant or two on the island. Wine with meals is sold at a premium compared with that sold at retail outlets, so there's a bit more scope for profit. It would be the same pitch and again, hopefully they take some to try, find they can sell it, and I have another customer. Carry on in the same manner, working the various outlets and casting my net ever wider, and eventually there will be a viable business. However, I wasn't so assured of what I was planning to do as to stand up there and talk with confidence about what I was aiming at. It was a new venture, a totally new experience. I lot of it was again 'suck it and see', and anyway, isn't that something he should be telling us (I guess he was about to)?

After asking the question the director surveyed the silence briefly and with nobody forthcoming then said,

"Okay, let me guess what your plans are." I can't remember this word for word but what he said was more or less what I've proposed in the previous paragraph. He suggested that we were on the course to learn about viniculture so that we could go back to plant our vineyards, or go back to our recently planted vines, with enhanced knowledge as to how to nurture them. Fine, that was the point of the course. We would diligently work for three or four years and wait until we eventually achieved our first decent harvest, at that point we would finally make our wine and then proudly start selling it, probably initially by hawking it round local shops, pubs and restaurants. Well yes, we all agreed. It was obvious from the reaction to what he had said that he had fairly accurately described the bedrock of not just my but most other people's plans. How else would you go about it, particularly as a small vineyard?

"No," he said, to the concerned attention of everybody there, "that's not what you should do at all."

I didn't think I was being particularly remiss in not producing a formal business plan. This wasn't a complex multi-faceted endeavour with a huge capital outlay, just a one-man band. I was enjoying this adventure and was going to see it through, come what may. I had a fairly accurate picture in my head of what I was spending. Where's the fun (or the need to confront reality) in producing a bunch of figures that suggest the plan might or might not work out? I was going to try it and to see what happened anyway. I promised Morag that it wasn't going to be a money pit. If it started losing money I would just cut my losses and quit. Probably stop the business side of things and just carry on making wine for family and friends. I did eventually produce a proper plan but only under duress from HMRC. They insisted on seeing a proper business plan before they would accredit me as bonded premises and, despite thinking it a bit excessive, I produced one because they said I had to. It was an interesting exercise but it only put down on paper what was in my head, as stated above. How else would you go about it?

The contention the director then put before us was that maybe we should just buy in grapes from other vineyards, then make some wine and bottle it with our own brand and sell that to the people we were planning to target as our eventual customers. Indeed, why even bother buying in grapes and making the wine. Buy in readymade wine and just label it with your own brand and then sell it. In this way you are building up your brand and customer base and are ready to start your business almost immediately, no need to wait three years for the vines to produce grapes, plus another ten months or so to make the actual wine. As well as steadily building a business, at the same time you are finding out what people like. Then, once you have worked that out, eventually plant your vineyard and then grow the grapes to produce the wine that you know people want.

"Isn't that cheating?" was my first thought, selling wine that's not made from grapes you have grown at the vineyard. But, "No," and it's more widespread than you might think. There are very strict rules about labelling wine properly. Amongst other things, if I buy in grapes or readymade wine the source of the grapes or wine has to be stated on the bottle. There are other rules about the vine varietal and the vintage that have to be very strictly adhered to, are checked regularly and woe betide... But branding is different. If I want to buy in readymade wine and market it as something like 'Kevin's Big Bonza Red' there's no reason why I shouldn't, provided that I explain on the label where 'Kevin's Big Bonza Red' originated from. And if people start to like 'Kevin's Big Bonza Red' there's no reason why I shouldn't carry on buying wine in, labelling it up and building up a business. Then eventually, instead of buying in the wine I save the cost of that by planting the type of vines that make 'Kevin's Big Bonza Red' and at some point in the future I have a commercial vineyard. However, I dismissed this idea out of hand and I suspect all of others in the room did the same. It was much too big a jump from the fun we were having as nascent vineyard owners. Put the plans on hold for a couple of years whilst we set up a business buying and selling wine? No, we were much too committed to our grand strategies. It was certainly too far removed from my own plans to contemplate, I just wanted to plant a vineyard and to produce some wine to sell.

As it has turned out, if we jump to the present I have never yet approached local shops, pubs, restaurants or anywhere else to stock my wine. There's one small shop, run by a couple that moved here for a lifestyle change. They asked if they could stock it along with the other local products they sold. I instinctively liked them and their ethos seemed right so I said, "Yes." Otherwise, I sell all I produce from the vineyard or at craft fairs and the like, so what's the point of complicating things. I don't have to go through the process of getting further accredited by HMRC to act as a wholesaler and I don't have to share the profit with the eventual retailer (so can keep the price lower). Indeed, the last thing I currently want is a retail outlet that suddenly starts selling, say, five cases a week. I would run out of wine half way through the year, which would be a disaster. I can't just go out and get more. I would have to close for months until the next vintage was ready (I was once talking to a group of other owners about this problem and the need to always plan eighteen to twenty four months ahead to ensure sufficient supply and that you always had wine in stock. There happened to be a local gin producer listening and somebody asked him if he had the same problem. He said that if he put a batch of gin on at 9am he would have 50 litres by the same evening. Some things are just not fair).

So there was no way I was going to abruptly change plans, no matter how convincing an argument he came up with. However, the way I've finished up going about things is not quite the way that was suggested way back on the course in 2016 but it wasn't a million miles away from it and my eventual business was certainly a lot closer to his model than to my original plans.

CHAPTER 11

Making Wine

But, what now? I had a vineyard, but there won't be any grapes until the end of the third growing season. Do I just twiddle my thumbs for two and a half years? They had to be looked after of course but with only four hundred that certainly wasn't a full-time job. If you have, say, ten thousand vines then everything is a big job. Take bud rubbing – rubbing off the buds that the vine will invariably produce in places you don't want them, particularly on the trunk. This might only take thirty seconds a vine: thirty seconds, move on to the next one, thirty seconds, move on to the next one, etc. If you have ten thousand vines that's a pretty daunting task – not a day you walk into the vineyard looking forward to. Indeed, it's going to take one person about eighty four hours, or two weeks of work. With just four hundred vines it takes me about three and a half hours. Even with tasks that took a bit longer, at that point there wasn't anything I had to do that I couldn't knock off in, say, a little over half a day. Which was fine as I was getting to know the vineyard and fitted in well with the bit of freelance work IT work I was still doing (despite resolving never to go to an office to work for other people again there were still a couple of projects I felt I had to finish) but I was itching to get going with things that pushed the project forward. I planted in May 2017 so the first harvest from the new vines would hopefully be in the autumn of 2019 and I should have some wine by mid-2020. I will, of course, in the meantime be getting grapes from the now better managed vines on the bank but, in the remedial years, still nothing like sufficient to do anything serious with.

I reasoned that if I'm now going to do vineyard tours and wine tasting as well as just producing and selling wine I was going to need two somewhat fundamental ingredients, a vineyard that looks like a vineyard, rather than a few sticks in the ground, and wine for people to taste. Both of these prerequisites seemed depressingly far down the line but if I'm not going to have wine until mid-2020 then I suppose that's the date to aim for to open for business. At least by then, after three year's growth, the vineyard should certainly look the part (and I'm definitely glad I got the vines in the ground asap rather waiting another year). It all seems a long way off but I'm conscious of the tasks looming on the horizon, so at least there are things for me to get stuck into. For a start, as I've hinted at before, I'm worried about the wine making side of things. What about all the equipment I'll need to do it at the scale I'm thinking of? And I've only ever made white wine but I know making red is trickier. Sure, it's a long way off but how will I learn and practice before I have to do it in earnest and get it right with my own grapes?

However, it turns out that several instances of arbitrary fortune set in motion an unexpected train of events that more than resolve the wine making issue and also speed things up considerably. The first card in this sequence had already been dealt, though I didn't realise at the time. It started with a small party Morag had arranged the previous summer. She was the supervisor for several PhD students in her department and decided to invite them and their partners over for a barbeque at the end of the academic year.

"You might be interested to meet Sioned's partner Antonio," she told me. "He's involved in wine in some form or other but I've never met him and he doesn't seem to be about much."

When Antonio arrived it turns out not only is he a professional viniculturist and wine maker but had trained at Plumpton, taking the three year degree. And he hadn't been about much because he was just back from New Zealand where he had had a contract with a vineyard to oversee the harvest and the start of the subsequent wine making. He was back in North Wales for a while before flying out to take on a similar contract in The Azores. Itinerant winemaker, following the sun round the globe! We got talking and I asked him something about wine making at the scale I was hoping to undertake, once I was producing grapes in sufficient quantity (which would be miniscule compared to the wineries he was working with). He then started talking about his family who made their own wine in their cellar. He was born and bred in Manchester but was of Italian extract, his family having emigrated from Sicily several decades ago. It seemed that each autumn their cellar vinification was sufficiently productive to keep the extended family in wine for the whole year. He talked about the grapes they used and about the issues working with Sicilian grapes and it suddenly struck me,

"How on earth do you get that quantity of Sicilian wine grapes in Manchester?"

"Aargh!" He said, "You've probably never heard of The Wine Grape Club."

The Wine Grape Club (Google it, there's only one!) has actually been on the go since 1978 and is run by a very enterprising chap called Chris who each autumn rents a refrigerated warehouse in Hatfield, just off the M25. He then ships in lorry loads of wine grapes from Spain and Italy, 'to supply people in the UK who love making wine with high quality, freshly picked Mediterranean grapes - enabling them to follow ancient traditions of wine making in their own homes.' And thus facilitating a Sicilian winery in a cellar in darkest Manchester. The club is free to join, he does, after all, want to sell you his grapes, and has several hundred members who converge on the warehouse each September and October to select their preferences. What a wonderful thought, all these people arriving in the exotic wine centre of Hatfield to 'harvest' their grapes and drive away with them. And that each winter in garages, basements and sheds up and down the country there are people busily fermenting tonnes of Mediterranean grapes to make their own, hopefully delicious wine. I want to join them. I get in touch the next day, no problem, anything from a couple of boxes to a couple of tonnes. He can have it delivered but it's expensive for small qualities and best just to call in. It's a long way to go but I want to see it anyway and a few weeks later, when he tells me the grapes have arrived, I'm off for a visit.

I get there and from the outside it's every bit as you might imagine a warehouse in Hatfield to be, a nondescript brick building in a small industrial estate. But you walk in and it's a wonder to behold, a large refrigerated room stacked high with palates on which were boxes and boxes of delicious looking grapes. A cup of coffee, a quick tour and a resume of the qualities of each grape and forty five minutes later I'm heading back up the M1 with twenty kilos of juicy Tempranillo grapes in the boot to start my red wine making career. Chris even put me in touch with a restaurant owner called Marco, someone else of Italian extract who buys grapes in quantity to make several hundred bottles a year. Marco kindly invited me round to his house to show me how he went about it and I was very impressed by the slickness of the operation he had running in his garage. Large fermenting bins, bottling equipment and the rest, all spotless and well ordered. And very nice wine.

When I get home and set about getting the equipment I'll need to process my precious twenty kilos. It's obviously going to need something a bit more sophisticated than the jerry-rigged lemonade bottles I've used so far but I'm not yet ready for something on the scale of Marco or the Sicilian operation in Manchester. After a quick trip to the local home brew supply shop for fermenting bins, demijohns, chemicals, airlocks, etc. I set about making the wine and all goes to plan. After several months I bottled it and it was, well, alright. Not brilliant but, well, alright. More importantly though, what this little escapade did do was highlight a few home truths. Throughout the process I've been having nagging doubts about how I will get on with this side of the business when it gets to the serious issue of producing wine commercially. Over the months I've been experimenting these have crystallised into two main concerns. Firstly, equipment, if I'm going to do all this at the scale I eventually envisage I'm going to need to a more professional setup. I'm thinking that five, ten years down the line when the field is fully planted and the vines are mature I would want to be producing perhaps fifteen hundred or two thousand bottles a year. I'll need to gear up to something much more complex than what I'd seen in Marco's garage. I wouldn't have to buy all the equipment at once but after a quick search online I realise that a) it's going to be expensive; b) I'm going to need a new building to put it in and c) I'm not sure exactly how I would go about doing things properly at that scale. I am, after all, going into this with rather limited experience.

Which brings me to the second of my concerns, my own abilities. It's one thing for me to mess about with a few bunches of Solaris in a lemonade bottle, or even to ferment twenty kilos of Tempranillo in the spare bedroom, and in each case produce some wine that is, well, alright. It's another thing entirely to start a small production unit. True, I planted the original vines without having much prior knowledge of growing the things and I've learned as I went along, but that includes several years of mistakes. If I'm going to make wine as part of a business there's no room for making mistakes and learning as I go along, it's got to be right first time. Imagine putting all the harvest into the fermenting bins, diligently processing it for six months and then finding the result is not up to much or even undrinkable? Oh well, try again next year. Talk about putting all your grapes in one basket. The obvious first step to rectify this would be to go on the other Plumpton course, the winemaking one, but would that be enough? It suddenly strikes me that proper winemaking is very skilled, as much an art as a science. I'm starting to lose confidence in my ability to do this and it is after all a pretty vital part of the whole enterprise. There was also a third main concern that I should have had but didn't think of at the time. It's okay for me to make my own wine and if it so happens that it poisons my family and friends, then that's unfortunate. Making wine to sell to the general public is a different matter and subject to strict food production regulations and testing, which will be complex and expensive.

Skip forward a year. Things have fallen through in Spain and I've just planted in our field in Anglesey but I'm no further forward as regards how I will eventually make the wine (but it's a worry that's still at least two years into the future). As you know, I had become aware of The Welsh Vineyards Association (WVA) and, in that first summer of growing, this sets in motion another train of events. I have talked about connecting with Colin Bennet and that he came here to Anglesey for a look round. I've told you about how he welcomed me into the community of Welsh vineyards. And that he also gave me lots of useful advice, particularly about things in the vineyard of which I was unsure. A subsequent meeting generated further pearls of wisdom, including the most important advice he gave me. When my concerns about wine making grew to the extent that I started asking how others went about it, his suggestion manages to turn my plans on their head. Basically he suggests, "Don't bother." Get somebody else to do it for you. He didn't mean to hire in a professional like Antonio to make wine for you on site but just take the grapes to a winery. This would cost a bit but outsourcing negates the need to buy a lot of expensive equipment, I won't need a new building to keep it in and they are professionals, they know what they are doing. I won't run the risk of turning out some vintage vinegar and closing down for a year until I can maybe do better the next time. Outsourcing also neatly circumvents the issue of testing and regulations, that all falls on the winery to where I eventually send the grapes. Just take the grapes to them and they send wine back to you in bottles, ready to sell. They even put your own label on it for you. It turns out that most small commercial vineyards, and a good number of larger ones, don't take the risk of making their own wine but outsource it by sending their grapes to a winery. Don't bang your head against a brick wall. I listen with interest and growing relief. In an instant this is the solution to a persistently niggling and potentially expensive worry and in consequence, a few weeks later I find myself at Halfpenny Green winery, mentioned previously, talking to Martin, Clive and Ben about contract winemaking and hoping this really will work in the way Colin suggested.

I came all the way to Staffordshire because this is where Colin recommended as it's the winery he uses, but also its actually the nearest winery to Anglesey. I don't think the distance will be a problem but when I first arrived I did worry that I will be too small for them to be interested, at least in the initial years. We talk and they will obviously have no problem adding my relatively miniscule amount of grapes to their overall production (remember their production figures, quoted previously). However, they have a minimum fermentation batch size of half a tonne of grapes and there's no way I'll be producing anything like that amount in the first year or two. I would eventually hope to be producing anything up to two tonnes a year from my field but it's going to take a few years to get to that level. But they explain that there's a way round this, they can sell me the grapes to make up the batch size. I didn't realise at the time but this is quite a common practice. There's only one harvest a year. If you don't produce enough grapes to fulfil what you expect to be the demand for your wine in the year after the wine is ready, as I've said before, not an easy calculation, your only option is to buy some in. If another vineyard realises they have overproduced that year, they have too many grapes for their own requirements, they are happy to sell their surplus and a natural market develops. I now know that in many wine making regions some vineyards are even simply 'grape farmers'. They have no intention of producing wine but just become supply conduits for larger vineyard operations. Halfpenny grow both Solaris and Rondo and would have no problem supplementing my own harvest. They could even, if I wanted, produce a Red Wharf Bay Rondo for me from the current crop, which would be harvested a couple of months later.

This triggers the memory of the lecture back at Plumpton when the Director started talking about setting up a wine business. You remember that he speculated that most people in the room would be planning to plant their vineyard, wait until the grapes were ready, produce the wine and eventually start selling it, probably initially by hawking it round local shops, pubs and restaurants. We all agreed that was the case but he said that what you should do is buy in wine or grapes to make wine and then bottle it with your own brand and sell that to the people you are targeting. Find out what people like, build up your brand and then grow the grapes and produce the wine that you know people want. I had dismissed this out of hand as too big a jump away from what I thought I should do but maybe with grapes from Halfpenny Green, the same type of grapes that are growing in my field, I could follow something similar to that path?

We go up to the tasting room at Halfpenny and they offer me a sample of the Rondo from the previous year's harvest. It's delicious! If I wasn't sold on the idea already that I would have my wine made here, I certainly was then. This was several levels above the 'it's well, alright' wine I had produced myself and it was wine made from British Rondo grapes grown in Staffordshire, roughly the same latitude as Anglesey. You would be proud to serve this wine. I had planted my vines in May 2017 and it was now August (they are doing fine, thanks for asking). Going back to the question I posed near the beginning of this chapter, what do I need to run vineyard tours and wine tastings? I need a vineyard that looks like a vineyard and I need wine for people to taste. I didn't expect that I would have the latter of these two vital elements in place until mid-2020 but if I bought grapes in from Halfpenny I could have wine next year, two years earlier than expected. Back at the vineyard, after a few months growth, there was already a decent amount of foliage on the vines and they looked a lot more the part than the few sticks on show just after I'd planted. Maybe by June of the following year it would be starting to look like a vineyard, albeit an immature one? And of course, there's the more mature vines on the bank. Maybe that could be part of the story?

I asked if they made some wine for me from this year's harvest, it could it be ready for next June? They said a bit early but possible. So I thought why not go ahead, so long as I was honest about where the wine came from when I started to show people round? This is my vineyard, this is the story so far and this is wine from the same type of grape that's growing in the field but until my vines are mature enough the grapes are from Staffordshire. I don't see why that's not viable and it means I can start running vineyard tours in mid-2018 instead of mid-2020. That's exciting but if it's going to happen I'd better start getting my proverbial finger out regarding all the licensing, regulatory stuff and the rest. What if I go ahead with the Halfpenny wine and one of the authorities I'm going to have to deal with says, "No," licensing, planning or whatever? For instance, if I'm charging for vineyard tours and part of that is wine tasting I am effectively selling alcohol to the public and will have to be licensed. I'm going to have to go to Anglesey Council and ask,

"Can I open a pub in my back garden, please?"

That's going to be an interesting conversation and I've been worrying about it for a while but what the heck, I have to take the plunge at some point and I agree with Halfpenny that I will buy half a tonne of Rondo grapes from them and they will make them into bottles of wine for me, to be delivered June 2018 or as soon as possible after.

So parallel paths of arbitrary fortune, nurturing a vineyard and sourcing some wine, are coming together quicker than expected but this episode has one final twist as these twin courses of coincidence converge. You will remember that when the venture in Spain fell through and I decided to plant in Anglesey, I had decided to give the vineyard a Spanish ethos and bring products back from Spain to sell during the tours, ceramics, leather goods and the like. I was starting to think about going to Spain to try to source things, though I hadn't a clue how, other than surely it must be possible to buy and bring products back from Spain? A week or so later I was thinking about this and something brought The Wine Grape Club back to mind.

They bring grapes back from Spain to sell in Hertfordshire and it was coming round to that time of year again. Halfpenny Green turn grapes into wine. Why not buy half a tonne of Spanish grapes from The Wine Grape Club and take them to Halfpenny Green where they will make The Red Wharf Bay Vineyard Spanish red wine? That would be different, wouldn't it?

I get on the phone to the grape club and talk to Chris and he has no problem with the idea. Half a tonne is a normal sized order for him and, so long as I trust him that the grapes will be okay (I do) I wouldn't even need to trek all the way down there again. It would cost me about sixty quid to just put the half a tonne of Tempranillo on a pallet and have them delivered to Staffordshire. I then get on the phone to Halfpenny and talk to Clive and he doesn't see why they can't make wine out of them and even suggests that that they make a third wine, a blend of the Rondo and the Tempranillo. I'm nervous that I've just doubled up from half a tonne, about four hundred and fifty bottles, to a full tonne and I'm worried about the expense and scale of getting a tonne and a half or about thirteen hundred and fifty bottles in my first year. He says that's okay, he'll split the tonne into thirds: one Rondo, one Tempranillo and one the blend and we agree to go ahead on that basis. That will be three wines for people to taste, great! Three wines seems a much more rounded package to be able to offer to people on a vineyard tour/ wine tasting.

I planted in May 2017 expecting to wait three years (or maybe even four, depending how things went) until the next phase, actually opening the vineyard to customers. Suddenly things have moved forward so quickly (and as you can see, I've moved a lot closer to the route to market suggested by the Director of the unit at Plumpton). I started this episode vaguely chewing over what I might need to eventually get in place for mid-2020 and now in less than a year's time I'll have a three hundred bottles of each of three different wines, at which point I'm planning to open a vineyard and invite people in for a vineyard tour and wine tasting. I had indeed better get my finger out!

The Wider Picture IX:
Wine Myths

There's a lot of bollocks talked about wine (some would point the finger at me, perhaps with justification). I thought that I would spend a few hours on Google seeing what myths and generalisations I could find. There's nothing scientific about this survey, nor anything particularly discerning. I was just having a bit of fun looking around to see what was there and I'm just reporting what I came up with. In no particular order, without comment (or not much anyway):

Red Wine goes with meat and white wine goes with fish: If you like.

Putting ice in your wine is a faux pas: My wife sometimes does this, if that's what you like...

Never chill red wine: Beaujolais? Pinot Noir? In southern Spain in the height of the summer you will often be asked if you want the glass of Rioja you've just ordered from the fridge or at normal temperature. The first time you're asked you quietly scoff and find you are drinking something with the texture of bull's blood, the second glass you have from the fridge.

Screw caps are inferior to cork: Wasn't this put to bed years ago? Though Argentina and Portugal seem to stubbornly resist.

Serious wines, laid down for years, always have a cork: Hmmm. If you are going to lay a wine down for ten or fifteen years it must be a bit of a jump to abandon the corking method used in your vineyard for generations and go for screw caps, to find ten or fifteen years later that it had worked or it didn't work. Dunno, I don't have enough (any?) experience of opening wine that that has been laid down for ten or fifteen years.

The design of the label reflects the quality of the wine: This does seem to be nonsense, design is just marketing. But if you are really being honest, if you are at the off licence and decide you want to try something new. How much is your choice influenced by the gravitas of the label?

Few professional wine tasters really know what they are doing: I'm just repeating stuff I've found

Only red wines are worth cellaring: If you are buying wine to lay down for drinking in X years' time (is it worth the wait?) then you're out of my league. But if you are so doing might you not add some Champagne, maybe some Rieslings and a few bottles from the Loire valley to your cellar?

Wine that are blends of different varieties are inferior: Champagne? Bordeaux? Crooked Field Red from Red Wharf Bay Vineyard (that's what I called the wine from the mix of Rondo and Tempranillo grapes)?

Boutique wineries make wines that are more authentic: In the context of this, what does authentic mean?

Great wines have legs: More likely to indicate alcoholic strength and thus go to your legs

Champagne is just for special occasions: Or never, try an English or Welsh equivalent

The bigger the bottle, the better the wine: As I understand it there's a difference (better?) in wines in bigger bottle sizes (magnums, jeroboams, etc.) compared to the same wine in a standard bottle because the bottle size changes the way the wine matures. Antony, co-owner of the house in Spain, has a small collection of jeroboams and when he gets one out he likes to open it by taking the neck off with a Russian sabre. I've never been sober enough to judge if there's a difference in the taste.

Sancerre is a breakfast wine: I hadn't previously come across the concept of a breakfast wine but I love the idea of deciding to purchase a bottle or two just for that purpose. Sancerre? I suppose, if you've run out of Champagne (English and Welsh sparkling wines being too fine of quality for this early in the day)

The larger the punt the better will be the quality the wine: I thought a punt was a flat bottomed boat, or the hoof of a rugby ball, or a bet on a horse race. Apparently it's also the big wodge of glass at the bottom of the bottle.

There are no sulphites in white wine: Read the label!

In a restaurant it's best to order the second cheapest bottle: I'd never heard this before but apparently it's so widespread a notion that some restaurants inflate the price of the wine in this position on their list. If there's nothing you can see that you know about or particularly fancy, I'd go for the house wine. Any half decent restaurant should have a decent house wine.

Sediment means the wine contains colourants and isn't as natural: Doesn't it mean that it's not been filtered and thus could be said to be more natural?

Champagne should only be served in flutes: Even at breakfast?

You don't get a hangover if you drink [ ]: Fill the gap with whatever you've heard this said about but if it has alcohol in it, make sure you have some paracetamol in the cupboard. I have this naive theory that there's a strong correlation between the amount of alcohol you consume, in whatever form, to the severity of your hangover.

To keep Champagne fizzy, put a silver spoon in the neck: And when it's a full moon, find the north star and howl at the point twenty three and a half degrees to the west whilst rotating the bottle anti-clockwise.

Boxed wine is poor quality: If you are enjoying a glass of wine then it's good quality wine. Please read the chapter on wine quality

Wine has to be expensive to be good: If you are enjoying a glass of wine then it's good quality wine. Please read the chapter on wine quality

In a poor vintage year, no wines are any good: If you are enjoying a glass of wine then it's good quality wine. Please read the chapter on wine quality

Big wine companies can make good wines but not great wine: If you are enjoying a glass of wine then it's good quality wine. Please read the chapter on wine quality

All Wines get Better with Age: Like people? Some just get old and disagreeable.

Sweet wines are inferior and for people who don't really like wine: In general, a lot of people drink sweet white wine when they are young. Often they then decide dry white wines are rather nice as well. After killing off a few more tastebuds they start to appreciate reds and finally realise that sweet white wines are delicious with pudding. All generalisations are wrong, including this generalisation about generalisations.

Knowing about wine is really sophisticated, you know, like James Bond: There's a lot of bollocks talked about wine.

CHAPTER 12
Jumping Through Hoops

Having decided I can open in 2018, hopefully in June, I have about ten months to organise whatever I think I need to organise to make this a legal and proper business operation – and one problem is that I'm still unsure of all the things I might need to do to achieve that. Obviously, everything has to be above board and I have to make sure I'm trading lawfully, whatever that entails. Top of my worry list is getting a licence to sell alcohol. What does that involve (will I be granted one)? If I'm going to offer food there must be regulations to make sure I don't poison anybody. There's duty on wine so I'll need to pay tax. How does that work, weekly, monthly, annually? How do I register? What about local planning regulations, will they even allow me to do vineyard tours? Do I need extra insurance? I'll need a website, at least that will be straightforward but there are probably things I've not thought of (yes, there were). There would seem to be many organisations to contact but I can see that all have a sensible purpose. It does get a bit frustrating at times though.

Ten months may seem like a decent amount of time but I have the idea that organising many of the things I need to organise could drag on, so the sooner I start the better. It turns out to be a bit of a roller-coaster and I jump through enough hoops to qualify as an Olympic hurdler. You just don't know what's round the next corner or what going to turn up in your inbox each morning. I just have to get on with it and when dealing with the various agencies I adopt the mantra, "Tell me what you need me to do and I'll do it." In several instances the difficult part was getting somebody to kindly address the first bit of the previous phrase but, as it turned out, not so with the one I feared most, getting an alcohol licence.

Step forward our local county Licensing Officer, a local business hero if I ever met one. If there is a more helpful person working for a regulatory organisation then I've yet to meet him or her. I had no idea how you went about getting a licence for alcohol but I was aware that if I didn't finish up with one it would scupper a large component of the project, one that I had now come to think of as now fairly integral. I had realised that I certainly couldn't do vineyard tours if I didn't have an alcohol licence because people would pay for the tour and part of the tour would involve me supplying them with wine to taste, effectively selling them alcohol. But I was going to have to go to Anglesey Council and more or less say, "Can I open a pub in my garden, please?" Licensing laws seem more relaxed these days than in my youth. Do you remember pubs used to have to close in the afternoon, much to the bemusement of foreign tourists, bizarre? And you had to go home at eleven at night (not something that's bothered me for about thirty years) and even ten o'clock when I lived in Scotland for a brief while. Everything was very strict and strictly enforced by the police. Pubs lost their licence for transgressions, how do you get to be one in the first place? Didn't the licence have to be granted by magistrates? How many stories do I read in the local press about unruly behaviour and worse outside pubs? Are they going to be conducive to the idea of a pub in an Area of Outstanding Natural Beauty? I suppose it's not like I'm opening a 'pub' as such. I just want to have wine parties at the back of the house (does that make it more or less likely that I'll get approval?).

In the square in the middle of Pentraeth there's a board detailing a little of the history of the village. It tells me that about two hundred years ago there were seven pubs in the locality. Our latest local census numbered the current inhabitants of this parish at eleven hundred. That must be at least double the number from two hundred years ago so seven pubs between no more than six hundred people is going some. I believe that before alcohol licensing came along some of the more enterprising people would brew their own stuff and just gather their mates around in their front room and sell it to them. This still happens in many parts of the world but I don't think it would be looked upon benignly in Anglesey these days. And there are still two busy pubs in Pentraeth. Won't they object?

I contact the local council and they direct me to said county Licensing Officer. I tell him what I'm planning and ask if I could come and see him.

"No," he said. He would have to come to me as he needed to inspect the site to be licensed. That is of course sensible but feels ominous. I don't know what's going to happen but there's no way to avoid this.

It's a beautiful day when he visits. I get him a cup of coffee and we sit in the garden. I'm asking that they license the conservatory and a cabin outbuilding, together with the garden in between, all overlooking the bay and the vineyard, so this seems a good place to take drinks with visitors. He seems very relaxed about things and says he loves the view, then turns to the field. There's a small hillock at the far end and he says, "Kevin, I can just see a yurt on the top of that hill. People will love to come here." This isn't what I expected and neither is the rest of the meeting. Things have moved on since my youth and, in principle, he will have no objection at all to me having a licence for the vineyard. Today they want to encourage tourism and employment and how could a vineyard not do that? The only issue they have with alcohol licences is to make sure that there isn't disturbance, noise, unruly behaviour, etc. especially late at night, and that's not going to happen here. They also frown on illegal activities like drugs and underage drinking but I think I can safely make sure neither of those happen. A few people coming round every so often for a couple of glasses of wine is going to be all very civilised and unremarkable. I will be duty bound to prevent crime and disorder; adhere to public safety and protect children from harm, none of which I think will pose a problem.

So, in principle it's fine but then he starts talking about the process and produces the licensing application form. It's twenty seven pages long including notes and it has to be sent to eight different people/organisations. However, he then sits down and spends forty five minutes going through it with me, explaining each section and pointing out pitfalls I might inadvertently fall into and delay the awarding of the licence. I will also have to advertise the application in a local paper and display a summary of the application at the premises, like the planning notices you sometimes see. I won't necessarily have to go in front of the magistrates, only if somebody objects and he doesn't foresee that. He even tells me that other licensees, i.e. the pubs in the village, can't object just because of my proximity (and in reality I suspect I'm not going to dent their businesses at all, maybe even enhance it).

I was a bit taken aback when he says that I will have to take landlord's exams. My first thought is that he must be joking but he explains that the law was changed about 15 years ago. It is no longer the case that a person is licensed to run a particular pub, as on the sign you used to see above the entrance, "John Smith is Licensed to …". The problem with that was that if John Smith left for some reason (or died) then the pub immediately lost its licence and had to stop trading until that could be sorted out, which could take a while. These days you have to have a Premises Licence, as I was applying for, and the person in charge of each licensed premises has to have a Personal Licence. This makes the person running the place interchangeable with anyone else who has a Personal Licence, which is obviously more flexible. To get a Personal Licence I had to go on a one day 'landlord's course' and pass a 'landlord's exam' at the end of it. It was a bit of a pain, another worry and more expense but a sensible and well ordered way to go about things. The course was actually fun, apart from the nagging apprehension that I had to pass an exam at the end of it. It was full of straightforward facts, licensing law, good practice about your duties and responsibilities when you are running a pub, literally separating fact from barroom myth. Even some interesting points, did you know that it's legal for sixteen year-olds to drink in pubs in the UK? I didn't but it is, provided they are just drinking wine or beer, with their parents and sitting down eating a meal.

The officer left and I got on with the application. The eight different organisations I had to make copies for were the Police, the Fire Brigade, Public Health Wales, Consumer Protection, Planning, Environmental Health and Social Services, as well as the Licencing Department itself. I couldn't but notice that the final five were all situated in the same Council Offices in Llangefni, the county town. The officer said that if I wanted him to look the application over before I submitted it just make an appointment, which I thought best and did. I duly completed the form but there didn't seem any point making eight copies before we met, in case I had to change anything. We had the meeting and he thought it was all okay, so I said that I would drop the eight copies in the next day but he said,

"No." If I could wait fifteen minutes he would get the copies done there and then and distribute them himself. After all, mostly they were just going upstairs, weren't they? You just don't get civil servants going that far out of their way to be so helpful – Local Business Hero!

After the application went in the police visited and the local police Licensing Officer was as relaxed about everything as the council Licensing Officer had been; the Fire service checked the premises but there wasn't really much to check. I won't have to go in front of the magistrates as long as there are no objections from the eight people who receive the application or members of the public who see my advertising. Nobody so far has foreseen any problems and if they had have done they would have flagged them up to the other bodies involved, so all is okay. There remained the nagging worry that a member of the public would object but nobody does and twenty one days after I put the application in I own a pub!

Concurrent to this and continuing long after there's a steady stream of notifications, applications and official visitors. I inform the local planning office and ask if I need to make an application to them, another big worry because presumably they could also just say, "No" and stop the whole thing. But I quickly receive an email in reply to say that at the scale I'm planning to operate they are happy to let things ride as they are, so that's another big one ticked off. The rudimentary issue of insurance suddenly becomes frightening when the first quotes come in at over two thousand pounds but the Farmers Union of Wales come to the rescue with a more sensible offer. I know that I must register for business rates and have a lurking fear of doing this. I've no idea how this works but I have a feeling that it might be very expensive, perhaps to the extent that it will make the whole project uneconomic. I kept putting it off but eventually bit the bullet and phone the council. The council tell me to contact the Valuation Agency Office in Bangor and this I do, arranging an inspection. 'Inspection' again sounds ominous. As with many of the other things it all feels part of a nebulous 'system' into which I've been tossed to flounder, that at some point one of the many people I'm dealing with might just turn round and say, "No."

Or, in the case of business rates, send me such a large bill that I have to give up the whole idea and just make wine for my own consumption. However, once again my fears are unfounded. A very pleasant lady visits and I tell her my plans. She tells me that the vineyard is agricultural land and thus exempt from business rates and that, whilst the tasting area might be rateable it will be such a small rateable value that I will qualify for something called Small Business Rate Relief and have nothing to pay. I hear nothing else but I'm happy, I've done what I'm supposed to do by informing the agency and there's nothing to pay. Perfect outcome!

I'm planning to serve small amounts of food at the wine tastings. Over the decades I've fed a lot of food to a lot of people and as far as I'm aware I've never poisoned anybody but I'm sensible enough to know that if I'm serving food to the general public there are surely regulations I have to comply with. I again contact the council and indeed there are, and then some! They put me in touch with Food Standards and, in outline, I will need to register my food producing business with the council, go on one or more food safety courses to qualify (and pass more exams) and have the kitchen and serving area inspected (there's that word again). But again, all with very sensible underlying principles and God forbid we go back to the days of slack regulated free for all. Still daunting though and I'm now glad I'm no longer going to make my own wine as that would have opened a whole new bundle of testing and regulation.

I talk to the local FE college and we decide that I need a Level 2 Food Safety Certificate and a few weeks later I'm back in the classroom. The course frightens the life out of me. Do you know how many ways you can kill or harm people by cooking for them? As the day wears on I get more and more worried about the procedures I'm going to have to put in place. It's not so much that I'm likely to harm anybody (as I say, I haven't so far), it's more that in the unlikely event anything untoward happened, I have to show that I've taken proper precautions. The problem is that it seems to me, as the day progresses, that said precautions are designed to keep an industry/restaurant scale kitchen safe and hygienic and I will have to comply with the same rules, even though I'm thinking along the lines of something like a barbeque a couple of times a month. I sort of realise that this is reasonable, germs don't know how big or small the kitchen is, do they? But on a practical level how will I cope with the complexities of implementing a full-blown food safety regime? I get inspiration towards the end of the day. Why bother with cooking? Almost all the problems with food hygiene occur when you apply heat to uncooked food. I'll just serve cold food, then it's just about storage and serving, which is a lot simpler. What about calling the food 'Anglesey Tapas'! That fits I with the Spanish ethos. Everybody knows that tapas are small snacks served with alcohol, Anglesey Tapas can be portions of Anglesey produce, maybe a cold platter of cheese, bread, farm shop produce, etc. served with the wine. We get to the point of sitting the exam but it's fairly straightforward (once you have been on the course) and I pass and go home with my certificate to prepare for the kitchen inspection. I implement all the things I've leant on the course, separate fridge, procedures book, tick list for each event, etc. and the subsequent inspection passes without incident (I'm told that because I'm now just going to serve cold food I'm considered very low risk) and we are pleased to eventually get one of those little green notices, you know, the ones you see on the door of every restaurant, in our case with five stars on it.

Food Standards I expected, I didn't know that there were also Wine Standards – and they are not in the least bit interested in the quality of the wine I produce. From the Plumpton course I know that if you plant more than one tenth of a hectare of vines in the UK you must inform Defra, and this I have done. Wine Standards follows on from that and they are concerned that I run a proper and legal wine business, fully registered with HMRC, having the correct licences, paying duty when I should, etc. Another worrying process but they are a pleasure to work with. I have said that my attitude to all the regulatory and other hoops I have to jump through is that if you tell me what you need me to do then I'll do it. It's the only way really. Even when I find some things frustrating or perhaps slightly absurd, I have to run a legal business and I can't fight the system, so I have to comply. When it comes down to dealing with individuals they are always very helpful. Wine standards don't make the rules, they are there to make sure I comply with UK and, as then, EU law. And they start by sending me a couple of documents laying out in simple language exactly how I do that. Thank you.

I duly register the vineyard and this prompts a visit from the very helpful and friendly regional inspector. He takes me through various aspects, taking my plan to import Spanish grapes and blend them with UK grapes in his stride. He is particularly concerned with labelling and that what is said on the label truly reflects what is in the bottle. This is very precisely regulated. For instance, I can't use the word 'Tempanillo' on the label of the wine made from the Spanish grapes even though it is Tempranillo unless I can produce Spanish certification to establish the traceability of the grapes and confirm the varietal. I don't know if this will be possible given the provenance but even if it is possible, it will be longwinded, so I opt to drop it. My options then are to call it 'European Union Wine' or 'Wine obtained in UK from grapes harvested in Spain.' The former is very impersonal so I opt for the latter as at least it mentions Spain but I query the phrase, 'Wine obtained in UK...'. It seems very clumsy, can't I say, 'Wine produced in UK...'. But no, the law is very proscriptive in the wording and it has to be word for word. He also tells me about minimum font sizes for the bottle volume and wine alcohol content. I'm mildly amused that the minimum font size of the volume is bigger than the minimum font size for the alcohol content, surely the strength of the drink is of greater concern? I remember visiting Brusselss several decades ago and that all wine was sold in 70cl bottles rather than the standard 75cl normal in the rest of the world. Maybe the EU bureaucrats thought they were being sold short at their lunches and this is their revenge? Whatever, what I have to do is laid out in black and white and that's all that matters. The officer even offers to review and okay my labels before I have them printed, which is what happens. Again, thank you, it was such a straightforward process.

The final regulatory piece in the jigsaw was HMRC, which wasn't so straightforward but we got there in the end. You have to pay duty on the sale of alcohol, fair enough but it was a bit of a shock to find that I would be liable to pay the duty on all the wine the moment it left Halfpenny Green, before I had even received it, let alone sold it. I phoned HMRC to enquire about options and was relieved to find that I could apply for a licence to carry on an excise trade which meant, provided I met certain conditions, that I received the wine without paying duty until I actually sold it. Phew! But it thus seems that not only do I need to be a pub but a bonded warehouse as well. At one point I asked about personal use of the wine, i.e. drinking it myself, or for friends and family. Surely I don't have to pay duty on that. I was told that I was entitled to an annual personal allowance.

"How much," I said.

"Five and a half hectolitres," I was told.

"What the hell is a hectolitre," I think and look up after I put the phone down. One hectolitre equals one hundred litres so five and a half hectolitres equals about seven hundred and thirty bottles.

"That should be enough," I think (though it is, of course, illegal to sell any wine you have declared for personal consumption). I apply for the licence and am a little taken aback that I have to provide not only a business plan, as previously mentioned, but also annual accounts, proof of funding, details of business assets, a list of suppliers, business bank accounts, plan of where it will be stored and more, seemingly way over the top. Thinking about it I realise that whilst I'm just the smallest of fishes, larger operators will be deferring payment of hundreds of thousands, perhaps millions, of pounds annually and HMRC wants to make sure that if they are going to make this concession to delay payment of duty they are going to get paid eventually. I provide all the required documentation and in due course receive a licence to carry on an excise trade and official approval to receive and hold alcohol.

In addition to the regulatory hoops I'm pointed in the direction of several organisations that exist to provide help and advice to small businesses, particularly those just starting up. It's a bit hit and miss. Business development is a devolved issue in Wales, so most of the funding originates in Cardiff. Wales, like most nations, understands the importance of a thriving business community and has several publicly funded bodies to promote this but, in my experience, unless the' 'help' offered is focused directly on what you need, if you're not careful you can be side tracked down an alley that is justifying the existence of the particular agency you're dealing with rather than it being of any substantive assistance to your own business. I can only report the following as my personal involvement, maybe sometimes I was just unlucky.

Business Wales were very helpful and provided some free, focused and very useful courses. Branding, marketing and in particular using social media in business. The last one included an in-depth analysis of my website, which by this time I had somehow cobbled together. Its cobbled nature was highlighted in the analysis and much valuable advice subsequently provided. I've mentioned that the Welsh government is also funding a Special Interest Group to promote vineyards in Wales and that is providing invaluable support to the wine industry here. Taking a long term view, the Senedd sees vineyards as an area of strategic growth, beneficial for both employment and tourism, and is trying to develop the sector through this special interest group. There is much promotion of the sector and at the very least I benefit through association. As my business grows, I feel that every mention of Red Wharf Bay Vineyard on Anglesey ("I didn't know there was a vineyard on Anglesey") helps.

Cywain supports food businesses in Wales and an initial meeting seemed promising. In particular, there is a grant of £750 available to help with branding. Branding is not something I'm planning to go overboard with but I can see I will need basic things like a logo, the wine bottles will have to have labels and these need to look the part (as well as containing the correct legal information), maybe also flyers, maybe improving the website. I've done my own branding in the past and it's always looked as amateurish as my current website but previously that didn't much matter if, for example, the only places you are putting your company logo is on your invoices (as an IT contractor) or your covering letter with your annual return to Companies House. I'm wary of involving professional designers or graphic artists though, bills soon rack up, so the idea of a grant and perhaps being pointed in the direction of somebody who is used to providing the small-scale service I need is obviously attractive. I apply but am rejected because, as the grapes were initially going be bought in from Halfpenny Green, outside Wales, my wine won't be Welsh enough. I point out that my vineyard is in Wales and I will be encouraging Welsh tourism but am told the grant is for food businesses, not tourist businesses.

Visit Wales, the body that promotes tourism in Wales, are also a waste of time. As I was getting ready to open I contacted them as the tourist agency for Wales and, after some misdirection, was persuaded to pay one hundred pounds to be on 'the main tourist website in Wales', the one everybody will look at. I do wonder why the government is at huge expense funding agencies to help businesses like mine get started and then wants me to pay the tourist board for promotion. Surely it should be free? Still, my hundred pounds is going to lead to lots of people visiting, isn't it? I fill in the forms and go through the procedures and eventually they tell me I'm live on the website. I open my laptop and try to pretend I'm a tourist coming to North Wales looking for something to do for the day, hoping that I'll find my vineyard is, if not prominent, at least an option. I look under Food and Drink, Things to do, Activities, Attractions and the vineyard doesn't appear anywhere.

The site is huge and incoherently ordered, many pages seem illogically organised and using the search facility generates a seemingly random selection of places or activities. I must be buried in there somewhere so I look specifically at things to do on Anglesey and still no mention, though a wine bar in Cardiff is third in the results. How is somebody visiting my local area looking for something to do on holiday ever going to be presented with the option of a tour of Red Wharf Bay Vineyard? I want to at least check my listing is in there somewhere so I narrow the criteria to 'vineyards on Anglesey', an unlikely search by a tourist looking for casual suggestions as to something to do one afternoon and probably unaware that there is a vineyard on Anglesey. I'm amazed to find I'm third in a list of three. There have been two other vineyards on Anglesey in the past but in 2017 both were closed, one for at least ten years. It's amazing that they are still paying their subscription every year. The only visit I get all year via Visit Wales is the 'incognito' inspector. I don't renew my subscription. The Anglesey Tourist Association is private but none profit making, their Discover Anglesey website is much better focused and they are much better value for money (especially as they cost less than £100 per annum). On their website every category you click eg. restaurants, places to visit, etc. brings up a map showing you where all the restaurants, places to visit etc. are; then you click on those you like the look of. How simple and straightforward, did nobody at Visit Wales think of doing something similar?

Shortly after finishing planting I attended my first Welsh Vineyards Association course, about Vineyard Floor Management, at White Castle Vineyard in Monmouthshire (you will remember, White Castle is run by Robb and Nicola Merchant and this was when I first met Robb, as chairman of the association). On the course I meet a representative of Farming Connect, who have sponsored the training day. She suggests that it would be beneficial to the development of my vineyard if I join them. Farming Connect is the body through which the Welsh Government channels help and support to farmers and the rural community. I know very little about the organisation but by reputation I believe it does an excellent job and the local representatives were great, really helpful. I just fall foul of the bureaucracy.

I contacted the local office and when the representative paid a visit, I have to admit that I felt a bit of a fraud. Farming is obviously a serious industry in Wales but there is no way I can think of myself as a farmer, I've just planted a few hundred vines in our small field. The normal threshold for joining Farming Connect is to be farming a minimum of three hectares and our field is about one acre, or about 0.5 of a hectare. However, I'm told that there is also a category for niche farmers and a small vineyard should qualify in that category. That sounds reasonable enough but I'm wondering what practical use it would be. When I make further enquiries the benefits turn out to be pretty impressive. The vineyard industry in Wales has advanced sufficiently that Farming Connect can now offer personal technical support of the type presented at the course I've just been on at Whitecastle. Also, one to one mentoring with an established Welsh vineyard owner or manager is possible. The rep then talks about knowledge exchange schemes with continental farmers and, if I'm importing grapes from Spain, maybe I should go on a factfinding trip to visit vineyards over there. That sounds promising! I've no trouble funding my own trips to Spain but to visit vineyards there with an introduction to the owners, that would be fascinating and useful. Maybe I could set up my own supply line of Spanish grapes for future years? I'm also becoming more mindful that at some point in the next few months or so I'm going to have tourists visiting my vineyard and I will have to have a story to entertain them when they do. Talking about a partner vineyard in Spain would be a nice angle. The rep even talked about the possibility of Farming Connect funding the planting of the rest of the field in return for being able to host a couple of events a year at the vineyard. Yes, of course I'm interested, who wouldn't be? There's a lot of money thrown into supporting business activity and to encourage small business start-ups. My experience has been that a lot of it is not well focused but this was focused technical and financial help, I couldn't have asked for anything better. I fill in the paperwork, including a business plan that has to be approved but that's fair enough, and wait.

All seems to be going well for a few weeks and then I get an email from somebody in Cardiff, 'Thanks for registering with Farming Connect, can you just fill in the attached spreadsheet, please?'. I open the spreadsheet, which turns out to be a generic form to record what type of farming I do. How many Pigs? None. How many Cows? None. Sheep? Turkeys? Guinea Fowl? Ostrich? Alpaca? Brontosaurus (the only one I'm joking about is the last one). Erm, none. There's a section for land and I divide mine between the vineyard and grassland sections and send the form back immediately. Forty two minutes later I receive another email, "Unfortunately, as you have fewer than 3ha of land you are unable to register as a Farming Business, and as your activity does not meet the standard labour hours requirement set by the Welsh Government you are unable to register as a Niche Farming System." The criterium for niche farming hours is that I have to work more than 550 hours a year on the farm/business, just over ten hours a week. I know I'm doing that easily but it seems the government's formula comes up with something different and, if I've only got one acre, says that I can't possibly be working so many hours (you come and bloody well try it mate, see how you get on). I phone straight away.

"Welsh Government, blah, blah; our hands are tied, blah, blah."

However, it transpires that all is not lost and other ways to join the organisation are suggested. I could apply as a New Entrant but that would mean I would have to meet the three hectare threshold within three years or pay back any support I receive. That's not going to happen, I know that I definitely won't be farming three hectares in three years time. There's a final category, niche farming looking to establish a new farming system (yes!) but employed less than 550 hours a year (well, no but they've told me that's the case) and with relevant agriculturally orientated experience or educational qualifications (Geography degree, yes! Three years researching agricultural systems in Nepal, yes! Morag, as company secretary has a PhD in forestry). I'm told it's judged on a case by case basis and would I please fill in a different form. I do so and it turns out this is fine, it's been long winded but I'm accepted! I gleefully resend my business plan and accompanying bumph and receive a reply within the hour. Sorry but in the category you have now registered in you are not entitled to all the help we offered you when we thought you would be registered in the more than 550 hours category. However, we will pay part of the fee for a few more courses, if you want. A complete waste of everybody's time really. I do eventually get some indirect help from Farming Connect via the vineyard association in the form of some courses, like the one at White Castle where this bit all started. They ask Robb what skills would be beneficial to members and organise and pay for day courses to provide the skills: vine nutrition, canopy management, pruning; etc. which you have to say is a wonderful initiative.

Finally, let's end on a positive note with another local business hero, Paul Gibson of Firecracker Design. I've mentioned my fear of the financial implications of involving professional designers and graphic artists to sort out branding but step forward Paul, a local lad who moved away and then came back to set up a graphic design and printing business in Benllech, two miles away. I hear about him when I'm on one of the Business Wales courses and somebody recommends him. I go to see him and we get on well. He starts off by designing a logo, we have a chat and he plays about with a few ideas and sends me some examples. He just charges me for the time he takes, and he gets on with stuff pretty quickly. Over the next few weeks we move on from the logo to the wine bottle labels, graphics for my website, a large weather proof banner to display at markets and design and printing of ten thousand flyers. It costs me around four hundred quid in total, including printing the flyers, which seems pretty good to me. Big problem solved and I've had lots of compliments about my branding ever since. Thanks Paul.

The Wider Picture X:
Micro Economics

My wine currently costs £18 per bottle – but I'm afraid it might be more expensive by the time you read this. I'm pleasantly surprised that most people find this a reasonable price for a small local business to charge for a bottle of wine. When I first started trading I feared that people would think it too expensive and if you compare it to the cost of most (all?) of the bottles you can buy in Tesco or the like that clearly is the case. Some people say this but I don't mind, they are obviously right, so it's a fair enough thing to say. When I first started selling bottles people would ask the price and I would be almost embarrassed to tell them, and at times they would be visibly taken aback. I learned that it's best to have a nice big sign with the price on, so that's it's obvious and I avoid that uncomfortable moment when I've been asked and I'm thinking, "It's probably a bit more expensive than you are expecting." I find that if the price can be seen up front and people have a few seconds to assimilate it then in general they seem to realise that it's a reasonable amount to pay for a speciality product. After they subsequently taste the wine (A vineyard in North Wales! Wow, that's nice wine! And it's red!) some even go on to say that I should charge more, and of course I'm always grateful for such comments. If people have the time to listen, I'm happy to explain why my wine and wine from most other small British producers tends towards the upper end of the price scale. There are three main factors that force up the price; HMRC, overheads and the climate.

It's not a very original thing to say that the only certainties in life are death and taxes but the latter is definitely true of wine. Let's try to be rational, the government needs to raise revenue to pay for hospitals, schools, infrastructure, social services, pensions and all the rest, and it seems to me that alcohol, being not essential and consumed voluntarily, is a reasonable product to tax – just maybe not at quite such a high rate, eh? I sell alcohol so HMRC want their whack and there's no point worrying about it. The law is the law, don't complain and send them a cheque every month (for the correct amount or woe betide) and you console yourself that the more tax you've paid, then the more wine I must have sold (remember that I'm licensed to receive the wine duty free, so I only pay duty as I sell it). However, I've recently become aware that to compensate for the disproportionately high overheads of smaller producers, small beer and cider makers get duty exemptions to make it easier to compete with larger, national and international companies and that historically this exception couldn't be extended to wine producers because of EU competition laws. Well, EU competition laws don't apply here anymore so this small vineyard (and my customers) would be grateful for similar treatment for the wine industry. I'm happy to pay tax on the product I sell but maybe it could be reduced a tad?

The second major factor pushing up the price of my wine is alluded to above, the problem of disproportionately high overheads in a small business. Overheads, as I'm sure you know, represent all the things I have to pay for that don't directly contribute to the cost of the wine in the bottle but have to be absorbed somehow. Things like the equipment I need to maintain the vines, petrol, insurance, replacing breakages, travel to Spain to buy things (ok, so that's part of the fun bit but I've still got to go), computers, regulatory fees and the endless list of similar things, small and some large. If I have overheads of £7000 a year (pretty modest) but I'm only producing a thousand bottles each year, that's £7 I have to add to the price of every bottle before I can think about making a profit. Somebody producing 100,000 bottles a year will undoubtable have much higher overheads in total but the overhead per bottle will be much lower, maybe £1 or less. It's a huge difference and there's not much I can do about it if I'm going to remain a small producer, which I am. I would like to expand a little, maybe to 2 or 3,000 bottles a year but I have no grandiose plans for world dominance. Maybe if the government cut alcohol duty for small producers of wine it would level up the playing field a little (have I said that already)?

The final major pricing factor is actually climate, even though it's getting more conducive to grape production. The UK is now firmly established as a wine producing region but the climate is still a bit marginal, especially when you get as far north as Anglesey. I've explained winter pruning and that I'm trying to get the balance right between maximising the number of grapes I get the following harvest and the worry of getting too greedy, leaving too many grapes on the vine and finding that, come the next October, the plant hasn't had the strength to ripen them. Vineyard owners around the world are making the same calculation but in different climates they can have greater expectations. As a very rough generalisation, vines grow in the same way in France as they do in Wales and a vineyard owner in France has to cope with much the same problems and issues as I do. But the climate in France will allow the vine in France to produce about twice as many grapes as my vine in Anglesey. So twice as much product for much the same input and expense (and less tax). In the south of France and Spain there might be three times as many grapes and there are places in the world, the Central Valley of California and certainly in Australia, where you can get four times as many grapes off each vine as I do in Wales. Obviously, if you are getting four times more product for much the same unit cost input, you can charge a much lower price.

Going back to wine in Tesco and the rest. In such supermarkets you can get, if not a great, then a perfectly drinkable bottle of wine that's been shipped all the way from Australia for about seven quid. Have you ever thought to break that figure down? The tax on wine in UK retail outlets is the same for everybody so getting on for half the seven pounds you are paying at Tesco is going to HMRC (roughly £2.20 per bottle duty and about £1.20 VAT). From the rest you have to pay for it to be transported it all the way from Australia, and the producer in Australia and Tesco themselves have to make a profit. You can see that it's not costing much to produce the wine in the first place, is it? And the main reason is that the climate is such that it's so cheap to produce the grapes (and the economies of scale of the huge production operations they have over there helps as well). These are not prices that I'm ever going to be able to compete with and so I'm very glad that most people are willing to cut small businesses like mine a bit of slack and appreciate it's a specialist product from a small producer. My wine is pretty good (something else I might have said before) but I know it's unlikely that people are going to buy several cases of the stuff, say to quaff every Friday and

Saturday night. My market is mostly people who have had a taste of the wine, like it and buy a bottle or two for a special occasion. Or as an unusual present (who expects decent wine from Anglesey?) or to remind them of their holiday. As such, I'm grateful that they are willing to pay a little extra so that I can cover my costs and carry on with the business. Mind you, maybe if the government cut alcohol duty for small producers of wine it would level up the playing field a little.

CHAPTER 13

Made in Spain

In parallel to making the business legal and proper I make several trips to Spain to find products to hopefully sell to people visiting the vineyard, and maybe also at craft fairs, markets and the like. I'm now completely committed to the idea that the vineyard will have a Spanish ethos and I've made considerable strides to implement this. I'm having grapes imported from Spain and made into my Red Wharf Bay Vineyard Spanish red wine and there's going to be another wine that is a blend of the Rondo and Spanish grapes. I'm going to be serving 'Anglesey Tapas', small snacks of local produce, and it's all going to be under the banner of 'Linking Anglesey and Andalucia'. To augment that I want to bring back merchandise from Spain, ideally with a bit of a story attached to make them more interesting. I come up with a list of four possibilities. Ceramics, the brightly painted plates, bowls and jugs etc. you see all over Spain (and many other Mediterranean countries); leather goods, very Spanish; Cowbells, I know, a bit left field but I bought one as a present for Morag years ago and I like it and think it evocative of the Spanish countryside; and Dave and Paqui's olive oil.

You will remember right at the start I mentioned that Dave and Paqui were working to get Paqui's family land back in shape. At that point they had recently managed the first olive harvest for many years and had their first batch of their own olive oil. And it's not just any old olive oil but cold pressed, extra virgin, prized olive oil from a unique variety of olives harvested from hundred year old trees (I gave up on the idea of putting a picture of Paqui on the label, at least for now). I confess to knowing very little about olive oil other than when you buy it in the supermarket extra virgin is best. I don't even know what 'extra' virgin means. Dave and Paqui's oil is a blend of the Hojiblanca olive, itself prized, and a unique type of the Manzanilla olive that only grows around Alora. And to add a bit of extra colour to the story, I helped with the harvest – and bloody hard work that was. On many olive estates, certainly the bigger ones, you spread nets out beneath the tree, attach a machine that then violently shakes the tree and all the olives fall off into the net. Easy! Dave doesn't do that because he thinks the machine can damage the tree, and he hasn't got a machine anyway. The alternative is to still spread the nets but then get a sort of stubby, wide toothed comb like device, like something you might find in a child's sandpit, and literally hand rake the olives off the trees. Once you get to the point you can't reach high enough you get a big stick and whack them off. It's only fun for about five minutes.

Nonetheless, the harvest was duly gathered and, lest you think that when I say they make their own olive oil that means they brew it in some mysterious manner with dubious hygiene in their own kitchen, then no. As in most Andalucian towns the olives were crated up and dispatched to the local community pressing plant from where the oil returns in sealed bottles with a certificate of provenance. I thought that if I took some back to the UK not only would it enhance my vineyard's Spanish links, fresh Anglesey bread dipped into Andalucian olive oil, but maybe local restaurants would be interested. However, if there are Food Standards and Wine Standards there are bound to be Olive Oil Standards and I didn't even know what I'd be allowed to write on the label and what evidence I would have to provide to back it up. I decide it would be best to take the first batch back in unlabelled bottles, see if people like it when I start the tours and also go to a few restaurants with the unlabelled bottles as samples to see if there might be any interest. Jumping forward, I've been serving it to people for a while now to know it's a premium product and generally it goes down well, better than that, most people love it. However, I couldn't get any of the restaurants I tried to contact to even answer an email and, thinking I'm trying to start a wine business not an olive oil business, I decide to drop the idea of supplying restaurants and just use it as part of my 'Anglesey Tapas'.

What could be more Spanish/Mediterranean than those brightly painted ceramics you see at markets and in shops almost everywhere in the country? You know, dishes, plates, jugs, plant pots, etc. etc. We've often bought them in garden centres there and the walls of the house in Alora are adorned with ornate plates (what else do you put on the wall of a house in Spain?). They were not cheap when you buy them in the garden centres (though not that expensive either) but the garden centres obviously weren't the producers. If I was going to buy them in wholesale quantities I needed to find a manufacturing source but they are so ubiquitous in Spain I thought it must follow that there will be loads of ceramic makers. But it takes me a while to find what I want.

It turned out that most ceramic manufactures produce floor and wall tiles, not the plates, bowls, jugs etc. that I was looking for so it took a bit of searching in the lower pages of Google (how did we do this sort of thing before we had Google?) to get to the kind of thing I was looking for. Eventually I came across a place called La Rambla and things suddenly became much easier. La Rambla, not to be confused with the famous street of Las Ramblas in Barcelona, is a large village about twenty miles south of Cordoba. They have made ceramics there – the kind of ceramics I want, not the tiles – since pre-Roman times and these days it has been granted special designation by the Andalucian government and is known as the 'Potter Village'. The whole village is centred on the ceramics industry and it seems to be just the ticket. Even better, it's only a two hour drive from Alora. I continue my trawl though Google and find the names of several manufacturers, all of which seem to have both showrooms and public retail outlets in the village. I select three at random and using my best Spanish (maybe also a bit of Google translate) I email them, explaining that I have a shop in Wales and I'm interested in buying about a hundred pieces from them to take back there. Can I come and visit and have a look at their products, please? Almost immediately I get an affirmative reply from Ceramica El Titi and in the ensuing email exchange I tell them that I'll be in Spain the following month, and we make an appointment for me to visit and have a look.

A few weeks later in October 2017, I'm driving north along the motorway from Malaga towards Cordoba. The 'village' is going to be easy enough to find, it's just four kilometres off the motorway on a direct road link. What's going to happen when I get there is anybody's guess and I haven't a clue how this will pan out. My first problem is going to be finding the ceramica. I don't have Sat Nav in this hire car nor, at that time, a phone that could perform that function for me, just the more traditional type of directions on paper. On the map the 'village' seems to be about twice the size of Alora and it wouldn't be the first time I've floundered round a Spanish town looking for a place that I eventually find (or not) hidden at the end of an obscure back alley. As I drive along I also wonder about how much the ceramics will cost, there being no indication on their website? In the couple of days I've been here this trip I've revisited a few garden centres and, as expected, the prices of ceramics from such outlets are too expensive to make taking them back to the UK a viable venture. However, naturally the prices in garden centres will include a retail mark up. Will prices direct from the manufacturer be low enough to allow me to ship them to the UK and still make a profit? I further worry is that when (if) I get to the ceramica any ensuing discussions are almost certainly going to have to be conducted in Spanish. Very little English is spoken in inland Andalucia and I'm not sure my language skills are up to the depth of conversation that might be needed to set up a business arrangement.

In the years since we bought the house in Alora I've made an effort with my Spanish despite having proved beyond doubt back in my schooldays that I had no affinity for foreign languages. In France, home of the only language the school had tried to force into my head, my attempts at conversing in the native language have been just embarrassing. In Spain, perhaps with more motivation than in my school days, I've made much better progress (and it's gratifying that the Spanish are a lot more tolerant of the mistakes of somebody 'having a go', definitely unlike the French) – but sometimes it's been a painful slog. When I talk to a native Spanish speaker I can usually make myself understood, if the listener will excuse my appalling grammar. I can write in Spanish, with slightly better grammar because I have time to think and correct some of the mistakes. I can read at the standard of a tabloid newspaper, so long as I have dictionary at hand to look up the words I don't understand. But I can't manage the more sophisticated broadsheets, which seem to delight in using very long words, many of which that aren't even in my dictionary. What I really struggle with is listening to people and understanding what they are saying, which makes conversation rather difficult. When I'm speaking I use the subset of the language I know. When Spanish people are speaking they cheat and use the whole language, so their talk is peppered with words I don't understand, or words that I recognise but have momentarily forgotten the meaning of, and I quickly flounder. If you then add to this the regional Andalusian accent, at its finest a rapid, guttural, bastardisation of words (imagine learning English in Surrey and then going to live in Liverpool or Newcastle), I soon struggle. I usually quickly chicken out with my stock phrase, "Lo siento soy Ingles, hablo Espanol solo un poco." "Sorry I'm English, I speak Spanish only a little," which clearly wasn't going to be appropriate here.

I arrive on the outskirts of the 'village' and the first building I see is reassuringly a small ceramics factory. As I get closer I thankfully see that it has a retail outlet. I drive a little further and almost at once there's another ceramics factory with another retail outlet. In fact, I soon realise that there's a retail outlet selling ceramics on virtually every corner. So a great start, I'm certainly in the right place and even if I can't find the ceramica I'm looking for there will be plenty of places for me to at least go and visit on spec. I continue down the road, my map says that I'm looking for a prominent left turn which soon comes into view, another few hundred yards and I come to a roundabout dominated by a large shop which proudly displays the sign 'Ceramics El Titi'. Bullseye, first shot. With relief I pull up in the parking bay outside the door. But now comes the hard bit.

The plan is not to buy anything this trip, I couldn't imagine getting that far on this exploratory tour. I just want to see if the concept of buying ceramics at a price at which I think I could make a profit is possible. And if it is, what arrangements I'll have to put in place to buy and store the goods and then to transport them back to the UK. I tentatively walk into the shop and I'm delighted to see that its overflowing with just the stuff I imagined buying. Plates, bowls and jugs of all sizes and an array of other products that I hadn't thought of, olive oil bottles, butter dishes, bells, butterflies pinned to the wall, candle holders, serving trays, light fittings. All beautifully finished and highly decorated in a rainbow of colours. There were a couple of other customers deep in conversation with the lady behind the counter, so I look around whilst they were dealt with. Most things are priced, albeit in a slightly odd format that includes what I took to be a stock code – I bit sophisticated for this small operation, I thought – but I'm relieved to find the prices are very reasonable. I'm doing quick calculations in my head now that I can see the actual products. If I buy that plate for six euros and pay to ship it back to the UK, how much do I think it could sell for there? Naturally there's a certain amount of guesswork as of course I have no experience of selling Spanish ceramics in the UK but from my quick initial calculations it seems viable at the prices I can see. I walk around for a bit longer and eventually the other people leave, so I introduce myself to Anna, who runs the shop.

After making the appointment a few weeks ago I've been finding excuses to keep emailing Anna in the hope that when I eventually arrive she would remember the correspondence and there would be sufficient basis of understanding to negate the need for me to explain everything from scratch. On the journey up I've also been practising saying in Spanish, "I am Kevin, from the shop in Wales, I've been emailing you about buying ceramics." I reel off my sentence and on the second take she thankfully understands and welcomes me with enthusiasm, showing me round all corners of the shop. She explains the odd pricing format. The number that I thought was a stock code was not that at all. The prices were clearly displayed, say €6.00 as on the plate I had looked at, but that was the price for tourists, the pottery traditions of La Rambla being sufficient to attract a steady stream of these to the town. The price to me buying in bulk was indicated by the 'stock code'. On the plate the code was 93904. I was to ignore the first and last number and the remaining three numbers told me the wholesale price. In this case, three euros ninety, not six euros. With this knowledge I look around and realise everything is going to be about a third cheaper than when I looked two minutes ago. Wow! This is getting better. She also tells me that they are all hand painted, which I take with a pinch of salt. The decoration is so elaborate that there can't possibly be that much hand painting on each piece, at that price. I think that it must be done with a stencil or something but I'm not quibbling. However, I find out on a subsequent visit, when I go to the workshop, that it's true. I watch an array of incredibly skilled women hand painting every stroke at a speed that is hard for the eye to follow.

I tell Anna that, "Yes" I would definitely like to buy her ceramics and that I would be back in a month or so to purchase maybe a hundred pieces. If I had known it would be so easy I could have bought them there and then but I never expected it to go so well. We talk a bit more and I say that I will confirm everything by email the next day and with that arranged I soon leave, the language barrier stalling any real attempt at small talk. As I drive away I realise I was only in the shop for fifteen minutes and that this surely must be one of the best business meetings I've ever had. I found the shop straight away. I saw exactly what I wanted at a decent price and then found that they were even cheaper and in only fifteen minutes I've got a new supplier and set the basis for a steady income stream for the business. If only everything went so well. The next month I returned as promised and chose and bought 116 pieces, quickly and efficiently packed for me to take back to Alora on the first leg of their trip back to the UK where, a few months later, I start selling them at Knutsford market. Every six months or so since I've enjoyed going back to Ceramica El Titi with bigger and bigger orders.

I wasn't quite so successful sourcing leather goods, though. The first steps went smoothly, thanks to Mike and Lynne, friends all the way back to schooldays, who are also frequent Spanish travellers with a place in Elviria, on the coast. We are talking one day and I told them of my plans to bring back goods from Spain. They suggest that if I want to buy leather goods I must visit the town of Ubrique and, indeed, they volunteer to take me there. They tell me that Ubrique is famous for its leather industry and that remarkably many of the world's famous fashion houses have their products made there. Intriguingly, Ubrique is also in the middle of nowhere, in the hinterland about a hundred kilometres south of Sevilla, fifty kilometres west of Ronda and eighty kilometres up from the coast. However, though it is in the middle of nowhere conveniently, as was the case with La Rambla, it's only two hours' drive from Alora. Buoyed up by my success with the ceramics, this sounds very promising. We agree a date for a visit when we are both in the country and eventually, bright and early one morning, set off. We have an uneventful drive to Ronda and find ourselves ten kilometres beyond that town easily enough. Then we turn off on a narrow winding country road through a valley. Like the journey to Competa this road just goes on and on and on. It's only another forty kilometres to Ubrique but it takes us well over an hour, mainly because of all the bends but also because we often have to pull off the road when something is coming the other way. The scenery is spectacular, forests, mountains, soaring limestone crags but as we are driving along I can't help feeling that this just doesn't add up. We are supposed to be going to a centre of the European fashion industry and it feels like we are headed to the remotest of mountain villages.

We eventually approach the town and see the spread of houses, factories and other buildings and I have to wonder how a community of this size came to be in this back end of beyond. We park and it has the usual familiarity of a small Spanish town, until we walk down the main street and I see that some of the shops wouldn't be out of place in Bond Street. I'm very optimistic, particularly after my success in La Rambla. The whole town is dedicated to the production and selling of leather, surely I can find something suitable here. We look round, have some lunch, go into a few shops and drive round some of the factory estates but in reality there's not much else to do that day. I wasn't sure what I would find here and just wanted to come for a look. If I'm going to find a supplier I think I need to set things up in advance the way I did at Ceramica El Titi and then come back with meetings pre-arranged.

When I get back to the UK I look for more information about the town. I find a fairly recent BBC article that says that the leather industry started there more than two hundred years ago and now it seems that more than half the town's residents work in the trade, "passing complex and elaborate skills down from father to son" (hopefully also mother to daughter). They must know what they are doing. Louis Vuitton, Gucci, Hermes, Chanel, Chloe, Loewe and Carolina Herrera are all reported as having products such as handbags, wallets and belts made here (though nobody admits to anything). Apparently first one of the fashions houses heard of the town, ran a few trials and started sourcing products there. Word spreads and another fashion house found out it, then another, then another. So today we have the unique situation of a small town in the middle of nowhere in southern Spain that is, indeed, a centre of the European fashion industry.

I try to make contact with producers by email but they are not as forthcoming as the ceramic producers in La Rambla. I found out eventually that because the major fashion houses are involved secrecy is paramount, so most are so uninterested in me that many emails go unanswered. I've also since found out that all the factories who work for the big fashion names have to sign secrecy agreements, not just the business itself but every individual employee, so that designs don't get leaked and pirated. But all the factories can't be contracted to the fashion houses, can they? Surely there are some producers who sell to the general retail trade and would deal with the likes of me? I eventually get a response from one factory owner and make an appointment to coincide with my next trip. At least I've got one appointment. I'll see how I get on and perhaps I could also try just going to the reception desk at other factories as a 'buyer from the UK' and I might get to talk to somebody.

Soon I'm back in Ubrique and my appointment is with Juan, not at his factory but at an office in town. I find the address I've been given and knock apprehensively. Even though, as on the ceramics trip, I've sent emails in advance I have the feeling that this isn't going to be as easy as in La Rambla, and so it proves. He meets me at the door, a pleasant middle-aged owner of a family business, but he doesn't speak any English at all. He shows me into his office and I'm in a face to face meeting with a Spanish businessman and I have to do it all in Spanish. Shit, this is not like being in the ceramica at all, when pointing at the various products and other gestures helped me through. This is a proper meeting in a stark, business like office with no convenient 'language props'. I stumble over my words, can't think of the right phrase, can't understand what he's saying and generally feel like an idiot. We get as far as him producing sample handbags and the quality, even I can tell, is stunningly good. The main thing I remember about them is the softness of the leather, the feel on my fingers, but I'm also struck by the depth in the colour of them all. I'm worried what the price is going to be for such quality and he gives me a sheet of figures (I'm on safer ground with numbers). The prices I can cope with if I could buy, say, ten handbags to see how things go but the minimum order is such that

I would have to spend at least two thousand five hundred euros, and that's just on one style of handbag. That's much too much for me and I'm out of my depth. I know as much about selling handbags as I do about selling ceramics but with the ceramics I'm risking a few hundred euros to see how it goes, here it would be several thousand. How much would I sell them for, it would have to be maybe £100 each? They would seem to me worth that but what do I know? And selling £100 handbags is a step up from asking fifteen quid for a ceramic plate. By pointing at the figures I can explain that the minimum order is too much for me and I can't think of anything else to say. He says nothing, does he think I'm trying to bluff him into lowering the figure? No, I just can't think of anything to say. As I think I understood it they seem to have production runs linked to individual orders I can't imagine an order of the size I can afford is feasible. I just want to get out. I come up with the idea to say that I am a man and want to ask the opinion of my wife and, I think he's had enough as well, and we decide to end the meeting. I'm back out on the street. Another fifteen minute meeting, I reflect and in contrast to Ceramica El Titi, maybe the worst business meeting I've ever been in. However, I would, one day, when the business is hopefully on a more confident footing, love to go back and buy some of his wonderful handbags and see what happens when I try to sell them.

The day doesn't get much better after that. I revert to Plan B, to go directly to the factories and see if they will entertain a visit from a buyer from the UK. Accordingly, I drive to an industrial estate where I've seen there are some likely places. I pull off the main road and start to drive round the estate, looking for anything that might be encouraging. As I drive round I think it's like the sort of normal small industrial estate you would see in any such town, except I suddenly realise that hardly any of the buildings have signs on them to indicate what type of industry might be conducted within. I'm hoping to find something that has piel (leather) in the company name or that leather manufacture is indicated in some other kind of way, maybe a picture or a sign. But there's nothing. I do see a furniture manufacturer that does have a sign and even a retail outlet. Similarly a bathroom fittings manufacturer but most buildings are just a blank facade. And, as for my plan to go to the reception area and ask if I could speak to somebody, they don't even seem to have reception areas.

Eventually, I see one building which is accessed through a single side door through which a steady trickle of people come and go. Nothing ventured, I park and approach, "No permiso, no permiso," I'm told firmly as I get closer. I see people approaching a second building and this time I get as far as the door but, "No, es no possible," I'm told just as firmly. I decide that I will try one more and, coming across another open door, I have a bit more luck and this time manage to engage with somebody long enough to say that I want to buy leather goods for my shop in Wales. He tells me it's not possible at that factory but I eventually comprehend that he's also saying that his friend has a business in the next street and I should go there. Okay, great, it seems I'm getting somewhere. He gives me thankfully very simple directions, next right, first building on the right, then picks up his phone and says his friend will be there in five minutes. I thank him and set off as directed, finding the building easily as there's no other on the street that it could be. But then I wait outside and half an hour later I'm trying to decide if they are having a joke or if something has just gone wrong. I go back to where I spoke to the guy but nobody is there and realising that I can't articulate what I want to say, "I met a man here half an hour ago and he told me that his friend would meet me…". Too many tenses and personal pronouns for me to put together anything in an order that would make sense to anyone. Feeling that perhaps they don't want people like me hanging around anyway, I give up and drive off.

I head back into town and when I get there shops are starting to reopen after the afternoon siesta. I decide to walk around and as I don't want it to be a completely wasted trip I wonder if I could buy something from the shops, albeit with the retail mark up added, and take those back to at least test the market back in Anglesey. I go into a couple of shops, looking round without much enthusiasm and leaving quickly. Everything is either very expensive, high quality handbags like I saw in my meeting that morning but with a whopping retail mark-up, or tourist tat with an obviously equally whopping mark-up. However, I then find a small shop on a side street that looks more interesting. It has a feel of something less than up market chic but more artisan than the tourist booths. I go in and talk to the proprietor, "I have a shop in Wales and want to buy ten or fifteen handbags to sell in my shop. Is a discount possible?" If by any chance, after I've been telling you how I happily wander up and talk to all these strangers in Spanish, you think I'm being modest about my linguistic prowess, I ask that you think of the hidden English airmen that keep popping up in a TV series you might remember called 'Ello, 'Ello. But as I've said, the Spanish are much more tolerant of you chewing up their language, which gives you more confidence to open your mouth in the first place.

My conversation with this particular shopkeeper was pretty painful but I was able to work out that he was independent of all the factories, he had his own workshop and everything in the shop was made by him and his family. The quality was nothing like that I'd seen and felt earlier in the day but at least the story would fit in my vineyard tours. Independent producer in this town famous for the quality of its leather goods etc. etc. I selected about three hundred euros worth of handbags, wallets and purses and bought them. Having finally made some progress and happy to retrieve something of the day, maybe I got a little carried away. The wallets, purses and a few of the handbags I bought were of good enough quality to jell with the story but with a lot of the handbags I was perhaps too influenced by the rich colours I'd seen earlier in the day and when I got back home they were dismissed by the three women in my life with derision, "Gaudy handbags bought by a man."

Cowbells: still in the pending tray. Maybe next year.

Having assembled a stash of various goods in the house in Alora, ceramics, olive oil and leather goods, my thoughts turn to the detail of how to get them back to Anglesey. It's one thing to know that it's possible to transport a tonne of black pudding from Bury to Malaga and similarly send goods back in the other direction, but how do I get hold of somebody who actually does the trip and what do I need to do about practicalities such as safe packing? A friend of Brian had once obtained an informal, phone quote for me of euro 235 to take a pallet of goods from Alora to my door in Pentraeth, the premium over the one fifty quid to transport the black puddings presumably being because Anglesey is a bit further off the beaten track. But I was worried about the ceramics. The leather and olive oil will take a bit of rough handling but certainly not the more delicate earthenware. Once I set them on their way they would be totally out of my control until they arrived. How benignly would they be treated? I had no feel for what constituted secure packing, how high could I stack them on the pallet (where do I get a pallet from?), would other things be put on top of them? This was a test run, I suppose I just had to see what happened but if half were broken when they arrived I would be back to square one. When the ceramica was packing up everything for me I had the idea to also buy some of their empty cardboard boxes, just in case, so I now also buy a large roll of bubble wrap and some parcel tape, unpack everything and re-pack them with half the amount and much more cushioning in each box. It made me feel a bit better but it took all afternoon and I now had twice as many boxes.

That evening I was walking past Margaret's estate agent office and popped in to say 'hello'. I've said that they also import antiques and bric a brac from Scotland. Obviously they had to go back to Scotland to pick up the stuff but I had assumed that was once in a blue moon. I asked on the off-chance if they had a trip planned in the coming months and she said that they always had a trip planned in the coming months. The antiques were so popular in Alora that she and her husband Alistair were now making the trip four or five times a year. Hope mounting I asked if they did the reverse trip empty and she said, "Yes, usually, more or less" and so I told her what I'd been quoted and asked if she would bring my stuff to Anglesey for the same 235 euros. I'm happy to pay that amount. If you think I'm shipping two hundred or so units at a time that's about a pound a unit and I would trust them to be looked after a lot better in the back of Margaret's van then on a pallet in a random lorry. She's happy because she's going to the UK anyway so effectively gets paid euro 235 for a three hour round trip diversion off the M6. We agreed on the spot and a month later that's what happened.

The Wider Picture XI:
Macro Economics

I've previously mentioned the increase in vineyard acreage and wine production in the UK over the last fifteen years or so. Since 2005 the number of vineyards has increased from about 350 to over 800, vine acreage has quadrupled and wine production quintupled. But the overall economic picture of the industry is not so straightforwardly onward and upward.

So you have this great idea, you're going to plant a vineyard in the UK. Lots of people have and it's becoming a much more viable proposition in this country. What a wonderful thought, to own your own vineyard, wouldn't that be brilliant! Then you follow up the idea and some, like me, will plant maybe just a few hundred vines, or a thousand or so, as a small business. Some will plant much the same as a glorified hobby, perhaps to sell a few bottles and turn up at dinner parties with 'Wine from the estate," to general appreciation and envy. To such people failure is a disappointment but not a catastrophe, it's not their livelihoods and they've not banked a lifestyle change on its success. Others are more ambitious, maybe planting five, ten, twenty thousand vines as a serious business enterprise. I've asked some of my peers why they planted and reported the variety of responses earlier, so you can perhaps understand the attraction and the motivation of such people. A new challenge, a move away from office work, a windfall provoking a change of lifestyle, relocating from city to the countryside, a farmer looking to diversify. The very best of luck to you all but at the scale of several thousand or more vines it's a substantial economic commitment that needs a lot of thought and planning.

The cost of setting up a vineyard from scratch varies depending on the circumstances but at the upper end of the scale it's not cheap. Costs can be split roughly into three main headings; firstly purchasing the land on which you are going to plant; secondly, buying and planting the vines and buying and then installing the trellising systems needed to support the vines; and finally the 'miscellany', any or all of land preparation, equipment, drainage systems, storage capacity, regulatory costs, etc., etc. I've seen ball park figures reported for the cost of setting up a vineyard as low as £5000 per acre and as high as £20,000 per acre. It depends......... in this case on the circumstances you find yourself in. Vines and trellising are fairly predictable costs, give or take; X thousand vines cost Y thousand pounds and you need Z length of trellising system to support them. But your overall outlay can vary enormously depending on the cost of the land and the amount of 'miscellany' you need to involve yourself in. If you are a farmer who is diversifying you already have the land. If your lifestyle change has already involved you in buying a small holding, then perhaps you have just acquired the land you need anyway. If like me you just 'happen' to have a field, again there is no capital cost to purchase the land. If you do have to buy land, if you are somewhere where agricultural land is less expensive then things will be better for you but if you are situated somewhere like Surrey, Warwickshire, Oxfordshire or similarly affluent parts of the UK, you either have to have pretty deep pockets or get on really well with your bank manager. The point I'm making is that to set up a vineyard on such a commercial scale involves quite a lot of money. Even if you are 'just' planning to start at the lower end of the scale with, say, a less substantial five acres or so, you have to come up with quite a lot of the readies.

Either you are lucky enough to have the kind of money needed to start up the enterprise or you have to find funding; either borrowing or taking on partners. But here's the rub. Once you have planted your vines that money is dead for four or five years, maybe longer. I've already explained that you won't get a grape harvest until the third year but that will be the smallest harvest you ever get (frost, general weather and pests not withstanding) and it might be the fourth year before you get a commercially viable crop. Then there is the small matter of making the wine, either buying a substantial amount of equipment to do it yourself or to pay somebody a substantial amount of money to make the wine for you. Then you have to wait nine months for the wine to be produced (assuming it's still wine), so it's probably going to be about five years from when you first ordered the vines (maybe six months before you planted) to when you sell your first bottle of wine. During that time you are servicing any capital you have borrowed by paying interest, or if you are lucky enough not to have needed to borrow in the first place you lose the use of your money for all those years and can't wisely invest it in something less complicated (like the Stock Market, BitCoin or a tech start-up company).

Not only that, the vines aren't going to look after themselves and at the scale you have planted you have to be paying people to look after them for you. So you invest a lot of money, work hard, worry about it all the time and continue investing more money for five years until (hopefully) you start to get a return. I've explained my path to market, which involved buying in wine to sell and then starting to do vineyard tours whilst the vines are still very immature and not producing grapes. So yes, you could do that. But buying in wine to sell to bring in the money needed to offset your vineyard investment on the scale I'm discussing here is effectively a separate business and involves expending even more capital to buy in somebody else's wine before you try to flog it for a profit. The money you originally invested in the vineyard is still dead and remains dead until you sell the first bottle of the wine made from your own grapes.

When I was on the course at Plumpton, as I've told you, we talked a little about business plans. Something else that came out of this was that almost everybody there had or was planning to plant grapes varieties for sparkling wine. The reason for this is obvious. I've explained that good British sparkling wines will sell at £25, £35 or more per bottle. I've also already highlighted, as a small producer, my problems with overheads and explained how my wine is always going to be relatively expensive. It stands to reason that if you can sell your wine at £25, £35 or more per bottle instead of £18 per bottle, you have more scope to absorb your costs and will have more likelihood of a margin of profit. However, there's a down side to sparkling wines when you are starting up. When you are making still wine it will be ready about nine months after the grapes were harvested. When you are producing sparkling wine it will normally be ready about two years after the grapes were harvested. That's another fifteen months that your money is taking a holiday from doing anything useful, like paying its way. So if you plan to produce sparkling wine you invest a lot of money, work hard, worry about it all the time and continue investing more money for six years or so until (hopefully) you start to get a return.

When you initially planted and you dutifully sent in your returns to Defra, not only do you tell them how many vines you have planted, you also have to tell them which varieties of vine you have trusted to thrive on your land. I've told you that in 2019 over three million new vines were planted in the UK. I didn't tell you that ninety percent of the vines planted that spring were varieties that will eventually produce sparkling wine. That is, more than 2,700,000 vines planted that will eventually produce sparkling wine. When they all eventually mature that will be enough sparkling wine to refloat The Titanic (I've no idea if that is true but I enjoyed writing it). But hang on, isn't there a bit of basic economic theory to consider here? If all these people are planting vines for sparkling wine, if all these people are investing a lot of money, working hard, worrying about it and continuing to invest more money for six years before they (hopefully) start to get a return. When that time comes isn't there going to be a wee bit of excess supply? Indeed, the pipeline is going to be bulging. And doesn't basic economic theory suggest that when a market is flooded (I'm refraining from saying 'literally') the price will drop. Surely there's only so much demand for premium priced UK sparkling wine and by the time you get to market, is there not a great danger that the price will have collapsed and you are more likely to be competing on the shelves with the likes of ten quid bottles of Cava and Prosecco? I'm glad I don't have half a million quid invested in my vineyard.

But there's another side to this story. I've told you that in ten- or fifteen-years time the climate of Champagne may no longer be conducive to producing Champagne. What if the reputation of British sparkling wine continues on its upward trajectory, as climate change makes the climate in British vineyards more conducive to producing sparkling wine (of course, we can't call it Champagne if it's not from the geographic area of Champagne) and the quality of the real Champagne continues to deteriorate? When we get to that time, five, ten, fifteen years into the future when English and Welsh sparkling wine has become recognised as being superior, when you are planning your big celebration; your daughter is getting married; a Christening; your Golden Wedding; a party for a big new contract for the company; even just Christmas. Are you going to splash your dosh on that French muck as the quality deteriorates by the year, or are you going to buy the real deal, British sparkling wine of proven and renown quality, as is denoted by the universal praise it receives and all the awards won? British will be Best! Our wines are already coming out on top in blind tastings throughout the world. In a few years maybe English and Welsh sparkling wines will dominate the premium sector of the market. As I write British sparkling wine producers have less than one percent of the sparkling wine market in the UK. When it becomes fashionable to drink fine British sparkling wines and that French muck has, well, lost its sparkle, it's not going to take much to push the market share of British producers skywards. An increase to just three percent of market share for home producers represents a tripling of their overall market by volume. Ten percent is an order of magnitude growth. Why not twenty percent, maybe thirty percent of market share once things really take off? When that happens all that excess supply will not be being used to refloat The Titanic, it will be whizzing off the shelves at £25, £35, £50 per bottle and all those producers who invested a lot of money, worked hard, worried about it and continued to invest more money for six years will be coining it in and be lauded as farsighted and shrewd. I don't know which way it will flop and I'm still glad I don't have half a million quid invested – but it sure is going to be an interesting decade or two.

CHAPTER 14

Market Trading

Well, my wine might be still brewing at Halfpenny, it's the middle of winter and the vineyard looks pretty bleak and all the 'legal and proper business' stuff it's yet to be properly in place but Margaret and Alistair have delivered a consignment of ceramics, leather and olive oil from Spain and I'm keen to get something started. I have previously had the thought that I will sell the ceramics and leather at markets and craft fairs as well as at the vineyard but so far it's an unstructured idea. I don't know of any local markets and I've no inkling as to how you get to trade in one, or what that entails. In the summer I've occasionally seen that there are fairs for tourists in North Wales and there's a big Christmas fair every year in Conwy, about twenty five miles away, but that's about the sum of my experience. Maybe winter isn't the best time to start trading but I have all these lovely products and I want to know how things will go. The opportunity presents itself when, talking to Mike and Lynne again, they tell me that there's a thriving market on the first Sunday of every month in Knutsford, just across the English border in Cheshire. Knutsford is a pretty affluent area, perhaps just the type of place where people will want to buy unusual and stylish ceramics and leather. It's eighty miles away but more or less on the way to Newton-le-Willows, where I grew up and my mum still lives, and Warrington, about whose environs my sister's family are scattered. I suggest to Morag and the girls an outing to see my family and to look at the market on the way, on the next market day, 4th February.

It's a cold, bright, sunny winter's day when we duly arrive at the market and Knutsford is buzzing. I had no idea that things like this happened on Sundays in the more sedate bits of leafy Cheshire. The market is squeezed into back streets behind the shopping centre and even though it's the middle of winter the streets are full of stalls and people. There's lots of delicious smelling street food and an eclectic mix of all kinds of stuff on sale, from upmarket antiques to pet supplies to water colour portraits to pots and pans. At the far end there's a large pub that's packed and lively with, despite the cool weather, lots of occupied tables spread over the open pavement. There's also a very jolly band set up in one corner happily belting out stuff from the sixties and seventies. Looking around, I think that they've judged the age group of the audience well. It seems pretty much perfect for what I think I want and I ask one stall holder who organises it all. I'm told it's a company called Market Makers and they run many such events throughout the North West. The next Knutsford Market, in a month's time, would seem to be the perfect place for Red Wharf Bay Vineyard to start trading, albeit selling ceramics and leather goods rather than wine.

Next day I look up Market Makers on line and send them an email. I tell them that never traded at markets before, what does it involve, would my ceramics and leather be appropriate and how much would the stall cost me? They reply that, 'yes' the produce would be appropriate but I would need to bring my own gazebo and table to display the stock, get public liability insurance and the pitch would cost me three fifty. Wow! there must be some money floating around these markets if all the stallholders are forking out three hundred and fifty quid for their pitch. I think about how much I would then have to sell to make a profit, probably about a third of everything I've brought back from Spain. It's good to know that there's such vibrant trading but if I take part and it works out at that scale, I'll sell everything even before I open the vineyard, which will negate much of the Spanish ethos of the operation. And, as is more likely, I don't sell anything near enough to make back the £350 cost, I'll just lose a lot of money. Neither are attractive so it seems this avenue is blocked off for now. Out of courtesy I email to say that sorry but £350 is a bit out of my league at the moment and get an immediate reply to say that it's not 350 but £35. 350 was a typo, if you miss the shift key when you're going to type '£' you get an extra '3'. I gratefully sign up, and now all I need is a market stall.

I look on eBay and there are lots of adverts for pop-up gazebos, anything from fifty to five hundred quid. But we have a gazebo at the back of the shed that's been there since we used it for the party the day after our wedding fifteen years earlier, surely that would do? I get this out and there's lots of poles to bolt together and some fiddly bits to keep the roof up. I'm pleased that I diligently packed it away safely all those years ago and all the pieces, particularly the nuts and bolts, are present and correct. But takes two hours to erect and I have to keep asking one of the children to hold the polls while I'm bolting them in. This isn't going to work when I'm trying to erect it quickly on my own at a market, so I give up and buy one of the cheaper pop-up gazebos on eBay. A few days later it arrives, resplendent with green roof and green and white striped columns at each corner. It does sort of 'pop-up' (with a bit of practice, anyway) but when up I'm a bit unsure. It's supposed to be a garden gazebo and that's what it looks like. I also buy three collapsible tables and bright white tablecloths on which to show my wears, and I go to B&Q and purchase some stripped oak board and fix in screws so that I can display the plates (which have wires fixed to the back). I put it all together on the lawn and get out the ceramics and leather and, even if I say so myself, maybe it doesn't look that bad.

I receive a set of instructions from Market Makers about joining, set up times, parking, insurance and gazebo weights, etc. Insurance is surprisingly easy to arrange and quite cheap, £57 for the year but I wonder if the weights are really necessary? I manage to improvise with a couple of very heavy old, rusty, cast-iron sun umbrella stands which have been lying around since God knows when, which doesn't improve the look but I want to limit my spending until I know this works (I do now know that the weights are vital, I've seen more than one unweighted gazebo go cartwheeling across the grass when the wind gets up a bit). I look at it all again and take a few photos. I try to regard it critically and decide that I'm as ready as I can be so let's get on with it. I pack it up and a week or so later at 6am on Sunday 4th March, with everything safely stowed in the back of the car, I set off down the A55 to begin my new career as a market trader.

I really like being a market trader. My mum, who as I write this is ninety three and still living independently, scolds me, "We gave you a good education and you had a good career and now all you do is sell things at a market." She also notes that she ran the family sweet and grocery shop on the High Street for years so, "It must be in my blood." I enjoy my days at market, working there is straightforward enough. I get on with it without having to worry about much and at the end of the day I have a glass of wine and think I've done a good day's work (if I've sold enough!). I don't have to worry about deadlines, meetings, office politics, constant reviews and all the other banes of normal working life, so I enjoy the lack of stress. Usually I get there quite early, set up, pass the time of day with the other traders, choose which street food to eat, chat to customers and sell stuff, pack up and go home. I've never met another trader that I disliked or worried about. Pleasant people trying to make a living, or at least supplement their income. Some are full time traders, for some it's an outlet for a more conventional business, others just have a side-line selling crafts and the like. What they all most definitely are doing is getting off their backsides and trying. Whether to the goal of working independently, running their own business or earning a little extra money they're working hard to do it. And I like meeting the customers as well. There's the odd drunk/druggie/idiot but so far they have never been more that mild irritants. Mostly there's just people, people from all walks of life who are usually lovely to talk to for a bit. They've stepped away from their houses to browse around, buy a present, find something different, to see what's what and are happy to be out for a few hours. The mood in very benign and I meet interesting people. To me it's a pleasant and friendly job – but then I don't go hungry and I'm not short of money if I go through a bad patch and I'm not selling much.

It didn't start well, though. Unlike at the February market, on that Sunday in March the streets of Knutsford were definitely not buzzing. Forty eight hours earlier, overnight Thursday to Friday, as The Guardian reported, "Beast from the East meets storm Emma, causing UK's worst weather in years: Snow chaos causes deaths, disrupts travel and closes schools and hospitals across the UK as Met Office issues red alert." By Sunday it's calmed down a bit but the aftermath is still being felt. All the traders have to pay for their pitch in advance but more than a few have decided it's not going to be worth it and just don't bother to turn up on that Sunday. This is my first time and I want to get going and test things out so, unless they had actually cancelled the market, I was going to be there. I'm very nervous though, I've never done anything like this and I don't know what 'the form' is. Will they welcome a newcomer or will I be thought of as muscling in on their patch? Despite all my preparations, have I forgotten something? Will I stand out as a 'rookie' who doesn't know what he's doing? Will they laugh at my garden gazebo and my makeshift weights? It shouldn't really matter but I don't want to be laughed at. These and other thoughts bounce around my head as I'm driving across the top of North Wales from Anglesey to Cheshire, thinking of more and more absurd things that could go wrong. Do I need a Market Traders Licence (no)? What if the admin has gone wrong and I've not even been allocated a pitch? Will I sell anything? Will it be cold, wet and miserable and I just give up? What will I do when I want a pee (would people nick everything when I wasn't there)? Etc., etc.

Not knowing what I'll find when I get there I made sure that I arrived an hour earlier that the official time to start setting up but it's already quite busy. I have a map showing me how to get to the street where my pitch should be but this route in to the market area is blocked by stalls that have already been erected. I stop and ask how I get in. I'm told to take the next left and turn left again after about a hundred yards, ignoring the 'No Entry' road sign. I don't like instructions like, "Ignore the No Entry sign" and this does nothing to ease my general anxiety. However, I drive past the sign and into another street with stalls already erected but with a channel left for vehicles to get down. The street where I'll find my pitch is a right turn off this one but just before the turning there's a van blocking the way as somebody is unloading. This seems a bit off (it was) as they could have pulled in ten yards past the stall to let others past but I'm not sure what I should do and maybe it's accepted to cut people some slack to unload and stuff (it is but don't take the piss). None of this is helping my nerves and I take a breath and think it best to just get out of the car and offer to help. I do so and I'm putting a couple of boxes down behind the man's stall when somebody pulls up behind my car and sounds their horn. Not a loud blast, more a, "Come on guys, what's going on?" Does he think it's me that's unloading and blocking the way? The guy who really is blocking the road flaps his arm dismissively at the newcomer and

I'm in the middle. Fortunately, his van is soon unloaded and the driver gets in and moves off to the parking area. I turn to the guy waiting and give my best, "What can you do?" shrug and start to move off as well.

Now definitely unnerved, with apprehension I turn into the street where my pitch will be, another narrow street with stalls already erected down one side. I now know that there are two types of pitch. All the stalls I've been passing so far are the main bit of the market, pre-erected cheek by jowl for the regulars and it's difficult to get one of those spaces. The other type is for people like myself who are willing to bring their own gazebo to erect around the periphery (I've actually come to prefer this as it gives me more space). I continue driving for another twenty yards or so and then the street opens out into two small car parks. This is where the 'own gazebos' will be grouped. A cheerful guy with a clipboard stops me, "Who are you mate?" I tell him and he looks down his list, "Ah yes, Red Dwarf (if I had a pound for every time…), you okay by the wall over there?" I'm delighted, he can't possibly know how delighted I am. He tells me to unload at the pitch and then drive down to the end of car park where it's free parking for the day. This I do and I get to work.

There are already a few, very professional looking, gazebos set up and I start on mine. It's freezing but thankfully there's no wind (I've come to realise that you can put up with the cold and wet but the wind's a right bugger). Pop-up gazebos do literally more or less just pop-up (with practice). You can do all this on your own but it's a bit of a dance, going round from corner to corner pulling each pole out another foot or two, then sliding down the collapsible legs. It looks like a wonky giant crab for a while and the stress points are in the wrong place until you can get all four legs up. I start the assembly dance and the guy in the next pitch immediately comes over and offers to help. He's a photographer and we get talking. I tell him this is the first time I've done a market and he suggest to me that it's not a great day to start! But he and a couple of others couldn't be more helpful. In particular, they see I'm on my own and say that if I need to leave the stall for a few minutes just let them know and they'll keep an eye on it for me. So that's the toilet break sorted! The one thing my fellow stall holders are concerned about is that I don't have weights (I have hidden my two cast iron stands out of the way on the back legs) and, as they are also familiar with gazebos cartwheeling down the street, they are worried that it could happen to me. I show them my makeshift kit and they are a bit dubious but thankfully the wind remains benign all day. I will get some weights asap, however. All in all, I'm beginning to feel a lot more comfortable. I finish setting up and go to view the result of my labours from the other side of the car park. It seems okay, not the most stylish or elaborate but certainly not out of place. I take some photos, get a cup of coffee (now I don't have to worry about the toilet break) and wait for people to arrive.

Activity slowly begins to develop. You wouldn't say there was a flood of people but there's a steady trickle. A few show interest in the ceramics and I tell them they are from 'The Potter Village' in Andalucia, that they're hand painted and made by a family that have has a business there for more than thirty years. Soon I have my first sale, a large bowl for £18. The guy offers me a twenty pound note and I'm taken aback. Surely everybody pays by card these days, naively I haven't bothered to bring any change. A worry had been that I wouldn't be able to accept debit and credit cards on the stall. Normal retail outlets obviously all have card readers but surely it's expensive for the retailer to set up and the cost would be prohibitive to a small trader like myself. Not so, I subsequently found that I was able to purchase a secure card reader that links to my phone for a one off price of only £23. I set up pictures of my wares on my phone, tap the image of whichever I'm selling, the price is transferred to the reader and the buyer puts in their card, inputs their pin and it all works without letting me see any of the card details, so the customer feels safe. Wonderful technology! The money actually goes to the company behind the card reader and they take a further 1.75p in the pound for every sale before sending it to me. Quite cheap I think for the service I can then offer. However, I had it in my head that everybody would pay by card but at markets that's not the case. Many people make the assumption that they should pay by cash and, indeed, many are surprised I can even take cards.

So the guy stands there offering me the readies and I flounder. I start to search through my pockets for any coins I may have, thinking I'm going to lose my first sale and he says, "It's all right mate, keep it" and walks off with the bowl. Wow! thank you. On the stall there's a few very small bowls, Anna actually gave me these four as extra as I was leaving the ceramica to say, "Thank you" for the order and I've put them out at four pounds each. A short while later a lady buys one of these, I'm grateful that she pays in cash with the right money, and I feel I'm up and running. Mike and Lynne turn up to offer moral support and I ask them for all their change. Thankfully Lynne has a purse full of it that she can let me have but I needn't have bothered, the small bowl was my last sale of the day. The trickle of people mostly dries up. It snowed twice but only lightly, but it's cold and people obviously aren't in the mood to loiter and look. We all start packing up early and the traders collectively agree this is the worst day they have ever known. My £24 of takings is not the lowest, a couple have sold nothing at all and they insist that I shouldn't go away thinking this is typical.

I drive home thinking of how much I've taken against how much I've paid out. £35 for the pitch, £40 for petrol, the cost price I've paid for the ceramics and let's add to that say a pound per piece for transport from Spain. When I worked at the university they had a concept called full economic costing when pricing out projects, to try to best reflect monetary reality. In this case it would mean costing the journey to and from Anglesey at 0.40p per mile instead of just petrol (thus another £64 to add to the total), and it would mean also costing in my hours. I get home at 6.30pm, so twelve and a half hours plus another for loading and unloading the car, what's that multiplied by the minimum wage? I happily think of all the different ways in which I can calculate how much I've lost that day. Plus there's all the expense of buying the gazebo and the rest which though, of course, if I'm going to do this regularly that's all stuff I need but has to be included in the costings somehow. I find that I'm not in the least bit despondent. I take the positive that the logistics worked, I set up the stall and had the feeling that in better circumstances the stuff would sell, and I looked like a proper, if inexperienced, market trader. Just need to sell a bit more (and get some weights).

I go back to Knutsford market several times and it gets better (it couldn't get much worse) but it never thrives. At Knutsford the 'own gazebos' are down the side streets, away from the main thoroughfare and many people don't even bother coming to look at that part of the market. Market Makers start a new market in Warrington a couple of months later, where both type of pitches are together and I find I do much better there (and it's close enough to Newton that I can visit my mum after the market). Full time traders get to know the characteristics of the various markets and I was told by one that the people of Knutsford like to go to the market to enjoy the ambience, in Warrington they go to the market because they want buy stuff. A very unscientific survey but it was my experience as well and after a few months I drop Knutsford and just do Warrington. There's an unexpected bonus though, as it gets towards time to open the vineyard for tours. When I'm at the markets I also hand out the leaflets that Paul printed for me.

"Would you take this about my vineyard on Anglesey, please?"

"I didn't know there was a vineyard on Anglesey" is most common response.

"Oh, that's interesting, we go to Anglesey a lot."

"Do you do tours? That would be a perfect birthday present for my Dad."

"Whereabouts are you? We're coming for a hen weekend in September." The responses are so upbeat that hope and a smattering of confidence grows that the main part of the venture, running the vineyard, will be a success. As it happens, I still get people on vineyard tours who say they picked up a leaflet at Knutsford market, even though I've not been there for more than a year.

The Wider Picture XII:
The Future

So what does the future hold for the UK wine industry, and in particular as far as I'm concerned, the Welsh wine industry? The UK as a whole is pretty much established as a wine region, albeit comparatively small compared to some others. I've reported that, at the time of writing, in the last fifteen years the number of vineyards in the country as a whole has more than doubled, vine acreage has quadrupled and wine production has quintupled. Also I've stated that the climate is getting warmer and suggested that nothing is going to stop that in the immediate future. In the short to medium term growing conditions are going to get more favourable here in the UK, it's likely that more and more people are going to be attracted by the idea of planting their own vineyard and that the industry will continue to expand apace. But the majority of this is in England. What about in Wales, where the climate is a little more marginal, especially in this northern outpost? Well, I think something special might happen here. I've said that I tell my children that I'm a visionary, that in a few decades time when the wines of Wales are famous throughout the world I'll be remembered as the far-sighted founder of the famous Red Wharf Bay Vineyard, the oldest vineyard in the Anglesey 'appellation'. People will come from all over the world to visit the wineries here on the island and especially to view the vine filled slopes of Red Wharf Bay at the centre of it all. I've also told you that they don't believe me and I have admitted that I don't say it with much conviction. But...

Let's try to imagine what the Welsh vineyard industry will look like in forty years' time. I pick this time frame not at random but for two specific reasons. Firstly, it's about that long ago, as mentioned in a previous chapter, that the modern commercial vineyard business started in Wales with the planting of vineyards such as Glyndwr and Parva Farm (I'm excluding Lord Bute's eccentric exploits at the end of the nineteenth century). Since then there has been steady and accelerating progress and looking at the same time frame in the future seems reasonable. The second reason is to draw a parallel with a country that in many ways can be compared to Wales, whose wine industry forty years ago to some extent resembled the circumstances we find in Wales today.

New Zealand has many similarities to Wales, and that's not just a love of rugby. Just like Wales, New Zealand is a small, mountainous country with world famous sheep and dairy industries. Forty years ago the population was about that of Wales today, though now it has increased. On the face of it the climate of New Zealand then was more favourable to wine production than the climate of Wales is now as latitudes there are the southern hemisphere equivalent of central and southern France, but this is tempered by its maritime nature and higher rainfall. I've said repeatedly that the climate is going to change here and become more conducive to viniculture. The climate here will thus almost certainly edge slowly closer to resembling the environment of New Zealand four decades ago. For both the above reasons picking a forty year period and a comparison with New Zealand seems a reasonable framework in which to consider the future of the wine industry here. So what will the wine industry be like here in Wales in forty years' time?

The wine industry of New Zealand around 1980 was more advanced than that of Wales today, as their total production was then considerably higher than at present in this country. About 5 million litres per year is the most accurate figure I can come up with, much more than is currently produced here. But looking at things in another way and New Zealand was then way behind where we are in Wales today. In his book 'Wine in New Zealand', published in the 1970's, Frank Thorpy cast a keen eye over the prevailing state of the wine industry there and asked, amongst other searching questions, "How good are our [New Zealand's] wines?" Dividing wine quality into four classes; great, fine, standard and ordinary, he states bluntly that at that time New Zealand had no great or fine wines and laments that whilst perhaps some could be classed as standard the majority were ordinary, which he defined as, "no pretensions to quality, with a definite alcoholic strength." I think I'm taking that to mean that it was good for getting pissed with your mates on a winter's night in the sheep station but not much else. You also have to say that in New Zealand forty years ago wine was probably thought of as a bit of a wussy drink. It was held in such low regard that it wasn't even stocked in most supermarkets. I read an account of a Welsh lady who emigrated to Wellington in the late sixties describing the barroom ethos as beer, beer, beer, beer and maybe a brandy. If you think of that as the drinking culture in New Zealand at that time and compare it to Wales today, we have some definite advantages in this country in that there's certainly no shortage of a market for wine here and in the rest of the UK these days (it just needs bending a little towards home production). And, as I've previously reported, there is a deserved recognition of the quality of current day Welsh wines, which wasn't the case in New Zealand forty years ago.

But things changed in New Zealand when at some point around 1980 the country decided to get its wine act together, as is happening now in Wales as the government looks to support the Welsh wine industry. The effects of this can be seen if we jump to around the time of the Millennium. In 2002 Michael Cooper published 'The Wine Atlas of New Zealand' and in this book reflects on the advancement the wine industry there in the last two decades of the twentieth century. He reports of a change in production methods galvanised on the one hand by several large vineyards consolidating and on the other by the growth of small artisan operations. And he details an export drive fashioned on the back of vineyards moving away from producing a cheap, everyday drinking commodity to creating quality wine suited to the burgeoning European and American markets.

Expansion over those two decades had been truly seismic and by the year 2000 acreage of cultivated vines had increased by more than twenty fold and production is at seventy eight million litres, an increase from only five million in just twenty years. Most importantly, the quality of the wine had come to be recognised throughout the world. All was not straightforward, for instance in some years there was over-production and dumping on the market at cheaper prices, which caused problems in both production and reputation. But on the whole it was a story of continued success and growing confidence, perhaps best illustrated by the formation of the famous Family of Twelve, a group of the most prestigious artisanal wineries who came together in 2005 and promoted themselves, "to nurture long term relationships both at home and in our key export markets [ ] and the promotion of New Zealand wine at its best." And the part of their philosophy that made me think immediately of Welsh vineyards, "We have contrasting personalities, different wine regions and styles make up our family and we celebrate these differences." By 2020 vine acreage in New Zealand had quadrupled again and production had mushroomed to three hundred and twenty nine million litres. Three hundred and twenty nine million litres! From a base of about five million litres only forty years ago to an industry worth over one billion pounds per year. If you had talked to producers in New Zealand forty years ago and put such figures in front of them as a projection for the future, they would have assumed you were drinking too much of the stuff with, "no pretensions to quality, with a definite alcoholic strength."

Could the same happen in Wales in the coming forty years? Wales's future is likely to be different in certain aspects. The current crop of vineyard owners are already committed to cultivating a high quality, premium market position and are gaining such a reputation, so we have a head start there. Welsh vineyards are also heavily focused on wine tourism as a primary source of income, which only happened latterly in New Zealand, so another advantage to Wales. The lack of wineries in Wales holds us back a little, but that should change as demand for such a service increases. The climate is still marginal, but it's warming and forty years is a long time. The future is likely to see a significant growth of independently-minded vineyard owners, encouraged by the country's wonderfully diverse range of microclimates to produce varied, quality wines. Can we expand to the extent that we match the growth in New Zealand over the past forty years? I don't know but I can promise you that by 2060 there will be a lot more vineyards in Wales, that many of those vineyards will not just be growing fantastic fruit but also be producing their own wine and that Welsh Vineyard owners creating their own wines on site will add a wonderful richness to the wine tourist's experience. Tourists will be arriving in droves to visit the vineyards and to taste and buy the wine. I tell my children that I'm a visionary, that by 2060 when the wines of Wales are famous throughout the world I'll be remembered as the far-sighted founder of the famous Red Wharf Bay Vineyard, the oldest vineyard in the Anglesey 'appellation'. People will come from all over the world to visit the wineries here on the island and especially to view the vine filled slopes of Red Wharf Bay at the centre of it all. They still don't believe me.

CHAPTER 15
Red Wharf Bay Vineyard

Then finally the whole project comes together. The last piece in the jigsaw is the arrival of the wine, which means that I'm more or less ready to open the vineyard. Martin brings the wine, driving it up from Halfpenny Green himself. Every couple of years he likes to visit all the vineyards that use Halfpenny to make their wine, to see what's going on and to offer help and advice if it's wanted. Exceptional and invaluable! The day before the wine is due to arrive Morag asks what I'll do if it tastes like vinegar. I know it won't, I've been going back to Halfpenny for regular tastings during the production. She strikes a chord though and I'm suddenly anxious again. I have risked the next twelve months on the wine turning out okay and what if was rather unpleasant? That would put me back to square one and I realise how grateful I should be for the expertise of Clive and Ben and their team. Obviously we taste it as soon as it arrives and of course it's not at all unpleasant, indeed the opposite. It's very good wine. I know that I've said that before (have I suggested you drop in to try it?) but this was the first time I'd tasted the finished product: Red Wharf Bay Vineyard wine from a bottle labelled Red Wharf Bay Vineyard, being drunk overlooking the vines at Red Wharf Bay Vineyard. Wow, it felt good! The Rondo is spot on, though very different to the heavy red wines that seem to prevail these days. It's light, fruity and mellow and very easy to drink. The Tempranillo tastes like a typical smoky Spanish Tempranillo, as it should, and the blend has worked well. Ben had said that the trouble with a blending two different grapes at random is that it can bring out the worst in both wines but this has combined the flavours of each and has certainly enhanced the smokiness of the Tempranillo.

I've said that I had decided that the two things I need in place before I can start inviting people in for tours round the vineyard are to have a vineyard that looks like a vineyard and to have some wine for people to taste. Well, the wine is now here and I'm looking round the vineyard and thinking it's starting to look the part as well. My second-year vines are thriving, lots of greenery sprouting healthily skywards, and the more mature vines on the bank are now better managed and certainly looking much improved from previous years, even having a decent splattering of grapes. It will be several years before the vineyard is fully mature and in the second year of growth I'm stripping any emerging grapes of the vines in the field, to encourage them to concentrate on strengthening their root systems. So I'm pleased that the mature vines on the bank will provide definite proof to visitors that it is possible to produce grapes outdoors in Anglesey.

I start to plan the tours in detail. According to my market research (as usual, guessing) my target audience should be tourists visiting Anglesey looking for something to do for an afternoon, and probably a few interested locals as well. I'd been to an Anglesey Tourist Association meeting a few months previously and during one of the presentations it was stated that the previous year there had been 1.7 million visitors to Anglesey, which is quite a lot of people. I never trust the way people present statistics and I wonder if these are visitor days, i.e. if a family of four stay for a two weeks holiday that counts as 4 x 14 = 56 visitor days, which in my experience is the manner in which less scrupulous marketeers will happily warp statistics. I ask the presenter at the end of the meeting and she says, "No." There were one point seven million individual visits to Anglesey the previous year. That is indeed a lot of people and if zero point one percent of those want to visit my vineyard over the coming summer I will be overwhelmed.

I decide on a marketing strategy based on telling nobody about the vineyard, for the most part anyway, and to have nothing that identifies the place as a vineyard to passers-by. I admit that this is perhaps an unusual way to launch a new tourist business but I do it this way partly because I don't want to be suddenly overwhelmed by an influx of people and partly because we live in an Area of Outstanding Natural Beauty and I'm very anxious to make sure that

I don't do anything that is out of keeping with the ambience here. The conservatory is licensed as a pub, the cabin is bonded premises, the kitchen is registered as fit to prepare food to sell to the public. I'm worried that the neighbours will think I'm setting up some huge operation here: coaches full of tourists, restaurant open all day, pub open 'til midnight, noise and rowdiness late at night. No, there are going to be a small number of cars in the drive for a couple of afternoons a month with a few people having a drink in the conservatory or on the lawn. The planning authorities are happy with that, the licensing authorities are happy with that, the police are happy with that, I'm happy with that and I think it's in keeping with where we live so I hope, once it gets underway and they see the small scale of things, I'm sure our neighbours will be happy with that.

This is never going to be a Halfpenny Green sized operation or anything remotely like it (I recognise that ideas of buying adjacent land to expand onto are pleasant whimsies, usually indulged late at night after a glass too many). And the vineyard is not even going to open to the general public, it's not feasible. To be open to the public there has to be somebody here during regular, advertised opening hours to service customers as they arrive and I can't do that on my own. I don't want people arriving and wandering around when the house is empty and I can't really expect the children, now easily old enough to be left home alone, to cope with passing strangers, curious to have a look round, when I'm not there. So there's not even going to be a sign to say we exist. No, the plan is for tours by appointment only, though I am very happy to sell wine to people who just want to drop in and have a quick look. Please just phone or email first. And the tours are going to be small and infrequent. A further problem is that I will always be constrained by lack of parking space. There's room for three cars on the drive, or maybe a minibus, and that's it. The configuration of the house plot is such that it's not possible to expand this (and I don't want to). Even if I reverted to the original layout we inherited from the builder (which there is no chance of) that would only makes it easier to turn a car round, there's no room for further parking – and the lane outside is also too narrow to leave cars in. The plan is for a very limited number of vineyard tours and for more revenue to be generated away from the vineyard than on the premises and so the marketing strategy is, at least initially, to mostly not tell people the vineyard is here.

However, I do realise that there has to be some conduit by which people know of the vineyard's existence and you will remember that I had, over the winter, cobbled together a website. Once I knew the date the wine would arrive, I advertised four tour dates for June and July online to see what would happen. I judge the market perfectly and get tour bookings for three, four, zero and six people respectively for the four dates advertised. Great, just the right size of groups to test everything out and get the show on the road. I'm happy for things to continue in this low-key manner for rest of the summer to see how it goes, then to take stock in the autumn. But before then I have groups of three, four, zero and six people arriving and when they do I'm going to have sort out something to entertain them for a couple of hours.

For a while I've been mindful that if I'm going to invite people to the vineyard, or more pertinently, if I'm going to ask people to pay to come and look round the vineyard, then I have to provide something to interest them. I can't just leave them to wander around the field for a bit and then offer them a couple of glasses of wine before packing them on their way. I need to find something a bit more attractive and appealing than that to entertain them. I think about what I would like if I was on holiday (or a curious local) looking for something to do of an afternoon and, well, it doesn't have to be a huge production, does it? Just something interesting and enjoyable. I already have several big advantages. It's a vineyard and people are interested in, even fascinated by, vineyards. It's a vineyard in North Wales and just as I was when I first saw Andrew's vines, people don't expect that and are surprised, "I didn't know there was a vineyard on Anglesey." Also, it's a vineyard in a stunning setting, in Area of Outstanding Natural Beauty overlooking Red Wharf Bay and a delightful place to come to sit and enjoy a glass of wine. And last but not at all least, I can be proud of the wine. The vineyard tour is going to end with people eating 'tapas' and drinking wine, sitting on a terrace enjoying a glorious panoramic outlook. You have to think that the basic structure is there. I just need to put together an interesting enough tour, to tell a story that's sufficiently entertaining. If I can put such a package together I don't see why it wouldn't work.

I set about getting the place looking like somewhere you can entertain paying guests and this turns out to be quite easy as our conservatory rather lends itself to the task. It already has a dining area at one end and a seating area at the other. I'll just put the food and wine on the table and they can help themselves, buffet style. The bathroom is next to the conservatory, so that sorts out the toilet issue and I think that's all I need as regards serving and seating guests. And there's also the patio and lawn area for further seating in the hopefully good weather. I look around with as critical an eye as I can manage and think, well, there's domestic clean and restaurant clean and I decide we don't come up to restaurant clean. There are lots of plants in pots on the window ledges and these collect dust and dead insects around them and Morag is pleased to see me scrupulously dusting and brushing. Less pleased when I take all the ornaments off the dresser so that I can display the ceramics and leather there. I finish my work and I'm pleased with the result. A regular repeat of the cleaning I've just done and a quick wipe with antiseptic spray before each tour, as per my food standards course, and I think it will now pass muster.

You will remember that I had decided to serve 'Anglesey Tapas' with the wine, small portions of Anglesey produce. So now I needed to get that sorted but Anglesey is famous for its local food and I don't expect it to be much of a problem, as indeed it wasn't. I go to local café/restaurant and farm shop Bryn Celin, about five miles away, and explain what I trying to do. Proprietors Ron and Margaret started by just selling pies over their garden gate but they became so popular that they decided to open a proper cafe. They've never looked back and we agree that they will supply me with pork pies (four varieties), homity pies (a traditional vegetable pie), fresh baked bread and local crisps for my tours. Nearby is Y Cwt Mwg Smokehouse and that's my next call. I have to say that the place feels slightly odd when you go there for the first time. The shop is just a small portacabin in a farmyard and often there's nobody there, please phone this number. I do and somebody quickly appears and shows me around. They smoke around thirty products, mostly local fish, meats and cheese. I decide that the fish and meat will cause too many food storage complications if I'm only doing infrequent tours but the cheese is perfect. They buy in several different varieties to smoke and they also make their own Anglesey goat's cheese, so I get not just cheese made on Anglesey but 'Anglesey' stilton, 'Anglesey' brie and 'Anglesey' camembert. They all taste delicious and it's all smoked on the island, so I think that fits the 'Anglesey Tapas' spec.

Paul, a colleague of Morag's, keeps bees on the north of the island so honey is added to the menu and I finish off with Angharad's pate. Angharad, by day a teacher, is a wonderful lady I met on one of the Business Wales courses I finished up going on. Her son decided to become vegan and she was worried that he would not get sufficient nutrients from such a diet so set about devising tasty and nutritious dishes suitable for his new dietary regime. These included her pates, which people tasted and suggested that they were so good she should go into business selling them. Deli de Bruin pates was born and I'm delighted to include them in my offerings. If you add in Dave and Paqui's olive oil and Anglesey bread to dip the oil in and accompany the rest of the food, I think that's enough and so it proves. Indeed, too much. At the start I over cater for every tour, I think I'm just afraid of people being disappointed and over compensate. After a few events the family are heartily sick of me palming off the spare pork pies on them. Cheese, honey and olive oil I can keep for the next time but pork pies have to be eaten within a day or so or thrown. I hate wasting them, "Go on, have another slice."

I love a pork pie but they are not the healthiest of food, are they? I tend to restrict my consumption to special events, picnics and the like. For me, pork pie event of the year is definitely the trip a group of us make to Old Trafford, where we go religiously for one day's cricket watching each summer. What better than sitting watching cricket, pint of beer in hand, pork pie on lap, ideally enjoying England putting Australia to the sword. Last year I went to get my food for the big day and looked at the pork pies in the delicatessen counter but I just couldn't face the idea of buying and eating another one. The next day was fair and warm and it was great to be on our annual outing but the overpriced hamburger I was eating was a poor substitute and I would definitely say that not enjoying a pork pie detracted from the perfection of the day; that and Steve Smith grinding out 200 odd to put The Ashes all but out of England's reach.

Finally came the day of the grand opening and the pending arrival of the group for the first vineyard tour, well the expected three people. They duly turned up and it all went remarkably smoothly. I spent the morning preparing the food, setting up the conservatory and fussing around in the garden looking for places people might trip or snag and roping them off, totally unnecessarily. It's sunny, the sky and sea are blue and vineyard is green. They arrived and we had a chat over coffee and then I took them out into the vineyard to show them how everything was going down there. Having the original vines on the bank was very useful when explaining things to people because I could contrast the bank vines to those in the main field and show them the mistakes you can make when you start, with examples! I'd written a script, well, a checklist of things I would cover and I did find that under the pressure of effectively speaking in public (even to only three people) that I forgot some of the points and muddled the story a bit – must practice more – but they seemed tolerant of me. We went back inside and the crunch moment came when people from outside the bias and sympathy of the family would become the first to taste the wine – and they were very impressed, and liked the food as well. I had been worried about telling people that the grapes that formed the wine were not yet from my field but that was accepted as part of the story. They left after two and a half hours, buying wine and three pieces of ceramics. I ask if they've enjoyed themselves but they obviously have, and so have I. I'm bouncing up and down (I did join in the wine tasting) and I take the dog for a sprint round the vineyard. It worked!!

The second tour was just as successful except that my delivery of the story was worse, the narrative wandering all over the place (a bit like this book really, what's Steve Smith got to do with this story?). One of the guests commented to that effect, in the interest of being helpful, as I had told them this was only the second time I'd conducted a tour. Definitely have to practice and improve. I didn't know at the time but the person who commented also wrote a wine blog and a few days later he send me a link to the review he had posted, which was very favourable and for which I was very grateful. Over the summer and autumn I did another six tours and they all went well – and my delivery got better. By the end of October I was feeling pretty satisfied that this was working. And come harvest I even got some grapes off the original vines on the bank (those newly planted were still a year away from providing a crop) to take to Halfpenny.

So far so good, the concept seems to be working but how to build on it if I want to develop the business away from the vineyard? I got the chance to do my first external event in July, that year. Ron and Margaret at Bryn Celin suggest that I bring my market stall and set it up one Sunday afternoon and bring the wine for people to taste as well. I'm not sure if it will work but the idea is to try things out, so this is an ideal opportunity. I am a bit worried that if I offer free wine tasting there might be a lot of tasting and not much buying, but let's see. The idea is not to do a talk, just to set up as I usually do at the markets but with wine tasting added which, as Bryn Celin is licensed, is not a problem. The agreed date arrives and it thankfully turns out to be nice and sunny. I set up near the parking area just outside the café and people start to arrive. Bryn Celin have quite a following on Facebook and they've advertised it there and it turns out to be a busy afternoon. I've brought my tasting glasses from the vineyard and I keep running out but they are quickly turned round by the kitchen when dirty. My fears about 'excess tasting' proved groundless and people buy both wine and ceramics. A bonus is that I meet a lot of local people a didn't know before, "We didn't know there was a vineyard on Anglesey," and even some of my old university work colleagues turned up, which I really appreciated. A pleasant and successful market day really. How things have moved on from the Beast from the East in Knutsford a few months before.

I wonder about trying to set up other tasting events away from the vineyard but don't really see how I can make it work other than in places like Bryn Celin, where I can get glasses washed and other support, being pitched outside a permanent trading establishment. I've seen other traders selling spirits, particularly gin, and liquors at markets by offering a tasting in a small plastic shot glass. Also I've seen beer and cider makers do the same with small paper cups, which hold more liquid than shot glasses but then beer and cider are much cheaper by volume than gin or wine. I think wine tasting would have to be in small glasses or at a push paper cups but I don't think plastic shot glasses would work. However, I don't have enough of my own tasting glasses to keep me going for a day at a market and I couldn't imagine taking them there if I did. There's no way that I can wash them as I go and I can imagine broken glass all over the place by the time I finish. I think paper cups would be okay but a wine tasting sample is going to look miniscule in the bottom of a cup and if I pour the same amount as the beer people I'll go through twenty bottles a day. Warrington market, where I might test this out, was having problems with its alcohol licence anyway and by the time I give it any real thought winter is approaching, so not much is going to happen. I park the idea for a bit.

I thought winter would be a pretty dead period for the business but surprisingly quite a few things happen. Out of the blue I get an email from a lady in Derbyshire, who is arranging an engagement party for her and her fiancé and all their friends here on Anglesey, where they have taken over a holiday complex for a weekend. She's seen my website and wonders if I can do a talk and wine tasting for about 30-35 people (it turned out to be forty five) on the Saturday afternoon, 1st December. Another challenge, I've never done a talk away from the vineyard, I usually just try to sell things from the stall. Despite my stuttering start, doing a talk about a vineyard with a vineyard as a backdrop is now going okay. Doing a talk about a vineyard without a vineyard as a backdrop is going to be another thing entirely. I think about it and I'm supposed to be testing whatever opportunity comes along so should give it a go. But I'm nervous because I don't want to mess up and spoil their afternoon. And if I do mess up and spoil their afternoon I would feel obliged not to accept whatever fee we agree and I don't want that either. In the end I gather enough confidence to decide it will work. I'll need to adapt the story a bit but I think there will still be enough of a tale and I'll make sure that there will be plenty of wine to taste. I say, "yes" and we meet to sort it out, agreeing that I provide the 'Anglesey Tapas' and sell the ceramics and leather as well. Thus, on 1st December I give my first talk away from the vineyard. They are a wonderful bunch, just a (large) group of friends looking to have a good time for the weekend. They seemed pretty engaged and to have enjoyed themselves but I ask the hostess afterwards if she thought it was okay, "Yes" she said, "I know this lot, if they'd been bored they would have just walked out."

So I can now earn money by giving talks away from the vineyard, even in winter. The next such event happens after I run across the manager of another holiday complex at one more Anglesey Tourist Association event (much better value than Visit Wales). I put on a few events at that venue, which also work well. This is great, I start to think, I don't even need a vineyard, just a few pictures and a few bottles of wine and I could go on tour!

Around this time I also have the idea of selling Gift Letters. Most vineyards will offer to sell vouchers for tours that people can give as presents but I think I can do this differently and make it more personal by providing the voucher in the form of a letter from me to the recipient of the largesse. I set up a system whereby I send the person giving the present a generic copy of the letter with blanks for them to fill in with the recipient's name and other details. They send it back to me and I print it off, sign it and post it back to them. At the appropriate time, they hand it to the recipient, who opens it to find a letter that starts, "Dear xxxx, My name is Kevin Mawdesley and I am the owner of Red Wharf Bay Vineyard on the Isle of Anglesey. I'm writing to you because your daughter xxxxxx has bought you your wife a personally conducted tour of my vineyard...". I think that's lovely, don't you? In the run up to Christmas I sell a good number of these, mostly at the various markets I attend.

Activity continues through the winter at the vineyard as well. I hadn't imagined that people would want to come on a tour at that time of year but there's a steady trickle of enquiries. I was dubious the first couple of times as to whether people would enjoy it as much as they had in the summer. The leaves have now shed from the vines and the field doesn't look that exciting, the bay still opens up below but the view is broodingly bleak (personally, I love it like that). I tell this to people but it doesn't put them off and I think, why not? The story is the same and the wine still tastes as good and my fears prove to be unfounded.

I get a call one Friday afternoon to as whether I can do a tour for four people the next day. It's a bit short notice but I say, "yes" anyway. My problem with last minute tours is not that I don't want to do them but that the local produce has to be bought in, particularly the stuff with short sell by dates like the savouries and the bread but also anything else I'm running out of, and I need time to do that. Out of curiosity I ask how they have heard of me and I find I've inadvertently started a second online marketing drive. I had put myself on Google Maps to help people find the vineyard. The people who had just called had been looking at the Google navigation app to find their accommodation and as they drove along they noticed the vineyard label on the map, so decided to call. For the two years I've now been open I found this is a regular occurrence. The main road round the east of the island passes through Pentraeth, only half a mile away and people looking for their accommodation on their phones can hardly miss noticing that there's a vineyard. Many are then curious enough to have a look at the website and subsequently phone to book a tour.

The unexpectedly eventful winter continues with a couple of hen parties. These are going to be afternoon tours, between their more serious hen activities of the evenings, and both turn out to be great fun. And the numbers were a bit higher than I'm used to, ten and fourteen respectively, so I'm getting used to dealing with larger groups (so long as they come in a minibus that's okay) and starting to gauge what I can comfortably cope with, which is helpful. A further source of clientele opens up when I get a call from 'Experience Day' organising company Into The Blue. They are looking for new events to enhance their portfolio and are interested in including my vineyard tours. It's a very slick operation, somebody wants to buy a present from their website, a voucher is issued and the recipient just gets in touch with me to book the tour. I iron out the details with Into The Blue over some emails and phone calls and my 'experience' is added to their website and subsequently bookings trickle in via this route.

All in all, considering my marketing strategy has been to tell nobody about the vineyard, it's been an active seven or eight months. As the anniversary of my first foray to Knutsford comes up I take stock and I'm quietly satisfied. I'm trading at markets, running successful vineyard tours for slowly increasing numbers, doing tastings and talks away from the vineyard and selling vouchers. Not bad bearing in mind the original plan was not to start trading until mid 2020, still fifteen months in the future. With the spring and the start of the new season approaching, confidence and optimism are growing.

I carry on taking stalls at markets over the following summer but this continues to be a bit hit and miss and I definitely feel that I'm missing an opportunity, that I should enhancing my offering by providing wine samples for people to taste from the stall, hoping that they will subsequently purchase a bottle. There have been enough other things going on to keep me busy but this eventually niggles enough for me to try to do something about it. But what? I know taking the tasting glasses won't work and I've convinced myself that I need those. I've never offered anybody wine in anything other than a glass. Morag thinks it will be okay to use plastic shot glasses and I pull my nose up. She said that she had tasted wine like that on markets and reminds me that she even bought me one bottle as a result. She reckons people will make allowances, so I order some plastic shot glasses online and decide to give it a go. I'd noticed that the gin sellers were back at Warrington Market, so I guess they had their licensing sorted out, which turned out to be the case. After making sure the market operators are happy with my new endeavour, I set out to the next market with my wine to see what happens.

I decide on a strategy of standing at the front of the stall handing out leaflets about the vineyard, "Can I give you this about my vineyard on Anglesey, please?" If anybody shows any interest ("I didn't know there was a vineyard on Anglesey"), I offer them a taste of the wine. Admittedly, this was received better at two thirty in the afternoon than ten thirty in the morning, which I suppose is a bit early. However, most people like the wine and the number of times people say something to the effect of, "That's really good," is gratifying (and, as ever, I forgive them for the surprise in their voice). Quite a few then buy a bottle, so it's working and I have a new way of earning money away from the vineyard. Nobody at all objects to sampling from a plastic shot glass. I come away from the market thinking that I've taken a big leap forward, glad I've resolved the sample glass issue but irritated with myself for not having done so six months earlier. Previously at the markets I sometimes did no better than break even, especially in places like Warrington when I have the expense of travelling a fair way. I was happy to continue doing these events because I wanted to see how things developed, and also the alternative was to not do them and just sit at home. I've now evolved four ways of making money at each of these events; selling the ceramics (I've lost confidence in the handbags bought by a man and don't take them to the markets anymore); wine tasting and hopefully consequently selling a bottle; selling the gift letters; and the tours booked from the leaflets I've handed out (though it's hard to keep tabs on how effective this is as it may only come to fruition months or even years later). Nevertheless, market trading is now another facet of the business that's working really well.

This success is amplified when I start doing Food Festivals which, to all intents and purposes, are themed markets. They have never been the type of excursion that attracted me as a person, "Can't we walk up a mountain, or go to a cricket match, instead please?" In my head I have the idea that they will be something of the scale and atmosphere of a village fete but I find this is a massive underestimation. Some of them are colossal events. I'm told about Beaumaris Food festival, which is held over two days in early September, and that's the first one I do. I think that at least going to market six miles down the road in Beaumaris is a lot more attractive than going to market a hundred miles away in Warrington, so I book my spot and turn up at the time instructed. I'm astounded by the scale of it. Several rugby pitches worth of space has been fenced off on the green near the sea front. There are three or four very big marquees and many smaller ones. It's fenced off because it's so popular that they can even charge for entry but once people are in there's enough to keep them entertained for hours. Every conceivable type of food and drink, every craft you can think of, buskers and street artists and all kept jolly by a succession of bands, all with the dramatic backdrop of Snowdonia across The Straits. If there was a down side it was that, because they have paid to get in, some people were going to make sure they had their fair share of samples. But who can blame them and I learn not to be too generous.

Two great days, I really enjoy the festival and do well, I want there to be one every week. And pretty soon it seems like that's the case. Once I start looking for them and as I'm willing to travel to more or less anywhere in North Wales, I tap into a series of local events. Most are not as quite grand as Beaumaris but usually worth the effort, people love the idea of a vineyard on Anglesey and buying from a local business. And then the food festivals morph into a series of Christmas fairs, which seem to be held in every town in the festive season. And if they are much the same as the Summer Food Festivals but colder and with fairy lights, they are no less popular or successful.

Vineyard tours have been steady all thorough the second summer and with the food festivals and the like, and especially now that I'm offering wine to taste and sell at the markets, and with everything else that's going on, the business really feels like it's taking off. I do get the feeling that more and more things are happening, more and more is working out and I'm beginning to understand what I need to do to make this business work properly. What I need to focus on to take this onwards successfully.

Things go so well in the last six months of 2019 that I even start paying myself a salary. £500 per month isn't exactly a fortune but it's the first money I've taken out of the business. Indeed, I find I've been inadvertently steadily dripping it in. The first company accounts for the period I've been trading are ready in January 2020. My accounting year ended the previous April but you get nine months leeway to send the accounts to Companies House and, of course, I do everything at the last minute. After the initial investment I promised Morag that this wouldn't become a money pit but when I see the accounts I'm initially shocked at how much more money has sort of just slipped in. The Director's loan account, the money the business owes me for things I've been paying out of my own pocket, stands well into five figures. How did that happen? I look through the pages of the accounts and pick up that just by driving around doing the things I need to do for the business, going to the markets, etc. I've clocked up over four thousand business miles in the year. I always just pay for petrol with my personal debit card, so at the 40p per mile I'm allowed to charge the business I've increased my 'investment' by £1,600. Often I buy things for the business but buy household things as well and pay with my personal card rather than the business card. When that happens I just ring the items on the receipt that are for the business and throw it in a box, where it stays until the dreaded day that the accounts have become so urgent that I have to get the box out and laboriously work my way through the year high pile. But this all adds up but nothing like to the extent that it goes into five figures. I ask my accountant if she can explain and she says something about depreciation and the way stock is valued but if I understood what she was saying I wouldn't have to bother having an accountant in the first place.

After the shock of realising the size of the 'loan' I wonder if the business is really doing as well as I thought. But I look through the accounts again and realise that the underlying figures are very sound. My accountant also tells me that the silver lining is that I can pay my 'salary' by repaying the Director's Loan, i.e. the business is paying me back for the money I've lent it. This is good as it means I don't have to pay tax, I'm just being paid what I'm owed. I again think back to the original 'plan', which was to plant the vines, wait a few years until they started producing grapes and then make wine to sell to local people, shops, pubs and restaurants, probably starting in mid-2020. The goal was to enjoy myself and if one day I was adding £5000 a year to my pension, that really would be a bonus. It's now early 2020 and, thanks to the idea of buying in grapes, I've already been trading for two years. I'm definitely enjoying myself and as I can now afford to pay myself £500 per month, i.e. £6000 a year, I've already smashed the original (okay, pretty unambitious) monetary aspiration. But I feel like I've only just started, with everything I have lined up for 2020 I will be very disappointed if I don't double my turnover, when I sit down and work through some spreadsheets, tripling turnover doesn't seem beyond reach. What figure should I pluck out of the air as the next target (I begin to wonder if it's possible to buy the adjacent field)?

I go through plans for the following year. I've already identified and mostly signed up for twenty odd days of festivals and the like. As well as the ones I did in 2019 I've found events like Abergele Food Festival, Denbigh Carnival; Old Colwyn Summer Fair; even a military recreation fair at a big National Trust house; and there's many more. If I can do about fifty days away from the vineyard that's a good balance between working, earning and the rest of life. I don't want to increase the number of vineyard tours but a couple a month with a few more people, the dozen or so that I've shown I can cope with rather than five or six, would also feel like a good balance. To this end I'm delighted when I'm approached by a company that runs tours for the cruise ships that dock in Holyhead, who are looking for places on the Island to entertain their customers. The plan is that once a month they bring a minibus full of people for the vineyard tours. Wonderful, (people coming from all over the world to visit Red Wharf Bay Vineyard!) and if that happens I'll have to start employing somebody, as least on 'match days', which I never foresaw.

Then of all things, BBC Countryfile puts me in their Top Ten Places to Visit in Anglesey on their website (I'm number 7). I'm picking up Elinor from friend Ela's house and Ela's mum Vicki says to me, "Congratulations Kevin, well done." I'm quite happy to be so feted but on the rare occasions it happens I usually have a clue what people are talking about. I look blankly and she says, "BBC Countryfile!" and she shows me on her computer. There it is, Red Wharf Bay Vineyard, No. 7 in the Top Ten Places on Anglesey. I'm guessing this is just lazy journalism, nobody from BBC Countryfile has been to the vineyard or even been in touch. They do quite a lot of features on Anglesey on the programme and maybe they thought they had better jazz up their website to back that up. I bet they just sat at their desk and Googled what to do on Anglesey. "Oh look, there's a vineyard. Make it number 7!" Whatever, I'm there and I'll milk it (they'll probably take it down if they read this but if they get shirty I'll send them an invoice for using my company name in their advertising without my permission).

But it's another success, everything is just going so well and it feels that 2020 is going to be the year the business really prospers. It's now the second anniversary of that first market day in Knutsford and another review seems appropriate, and it's even more satisfying than that of the previous year. I'm still doing everything I was doing a year ago but everything has just grown. Plus I'm now doing wine tasting, and selling wine, at the markets; I'm going to bigger and more appropriate festivals and other events and selling wine there as well; tourists from the cruise ships will be coming; and with everything else that's been going on I've not even started with online sales, which I know is an opportunity I'm neglecting. It feels like I'm now in charge of where the business goes, rather than running round trying anything and everything and hoping that some of it works. I can plan out the year, I have a good idea of income and expenditure (and profit) and be fairly confident that it will happen more or less as planned and that I'll enjoy it.

The final stage on the journey is to improve the grape yield from the vineyard and increase the number of grapes in each bottle that come from my field, rather than having been bought in. The vines, those planted in 2017, will continue to mature and steadily produce more grapes year on year. Once they get to maximum yield that should continue at that level for maybe twenty or thirty years (they are slow to get there but once they do they carry on giving for quite a while). The original vines on the bank are looking well with the improved management. I also feel confident enough to plan to plant the rest of the field and will do this in the next planting season, spring 2021. It will be a bigger outlay than when I planted 325 vines three years ago as there will probably be about another six hundred, plus attendant posts and trellising systems, and the fencing will need renewing to keep the neighbouring sheep out as well. I've decided to stick with Rondo and Solaris and produce just still wine, none of the complications of the fizzy stuff. Keep things simple and not have small parcels of different varieties all over the field. I've seen that the two still wines, plus the blend of Rondo and Spanish grapes for its novelty value, has worked well at tastings and feel that I don't need to be over elaborate at the scale I'm operating. I've also decided that I need a new building and I'm planning to have a decent storage unit built. The piles of ceramic boxes, wine boxes, tables, gazebo and all the rest are multiplying and encroaching and I need space to get things properly organised. All in all, it's going to be another fair chunk of capital but I think the time is right. I don't have to decide for definite until I have to order the vines in the autumn but I don't see any reason why I shouldn't go ahead. But, all in all, I've done it. I've set up a comfortable little business for me to enjoy and keep me busy for the next decade or more (assuming I stay healthy enough).

It's Friday evening in February 2020 and we're having a drink. Morag and I with a glass of wine (not my own, we can't afford it on a regular basis) and Elinor and Lili drinking cocktails with increasingly grownup sophistication. The sun is setting (I said at the start that this wasn't about us sitting basking in the success of our endeavours, drinking wine and watching glorious sunsets, but what the heck) and all is quite still and pretty. I've had another small breakthrough. For the first time I had a stall at the craft fair at a hotel in Beaumaris earlier in the week which went well. If they can get lots of people on a Monday in February, albeit half term, what's it going to be like in the summer? Definitely on the list. It's a lovely evening, eighteen years here and I still don't tire of the view, now enhanced by the rows of my vines in the foreground.

Maybe you have a picture of a vineyard in your head? Perhaps in France you would imagine it surrounding a chateau, or in Tuscany it would be next to an old farmhouse, or maybe it would be behind rambling Corjito in Rioja? There would be a large old stone built house bounded at the sides and back by tall, green pines. It would maybe be positioned at the head of a valley full of rolling fields, covered with vines as far as you can see, stretching out in perfect green lines. There's a cluster of old stone buildings with terracotta tiled rooves near the house. One is a tasting area for guests and you go inside and the walls are lined from floor to ceiling with racks crammed with bottles. "The estate was planted by the grandfather of my grandfather," you are told. "We produce 100,000 bottles of delicious wine every year and everything is perfect in this vinery paradise." Well, my vineyard is nothing like that. Red Wharf Bay Vineyard is a micro vineyard of currently four hundred vines. It's situated fifteen hundred miles from where it was originally planned to be in a fairly remote corner of the British Isles that, when I arrived in 2001, I hadn't seen for forty years and, even if I had ever thought about it, wouldn't have expected to see again. Where I still look around and gratefully think, "How did I get to call this place 'home'?" The vineyard is behind a house we obviously couldn't afford and in a field we didn't want. It was planted on a whim and totally mismanaged for many years. It feels like a series of random and arbitrary events have happened over the years and now there's a vineyard. It's doing alright, though.

Now what's this I hear about a virus coming out of China?

Milton Keynes UK
Ingram Content Group UK Ltd.
UKHW010825291123
433443UK00003B/71/J

9 781803 814704